Beyond Adolescence traces the lives of adolescents and youth from the late 1960s into the late 1970s and early 1980s. It is unusual for the length of time over which the study took place, as well as for the portion of the life-span it covers: early adulthood. The research extends and tests the theoretical framework that guided the study – Problem-Behavior Theory – and shows its usefulness for understanding young adult problem behavior and development from adolescence to young adulthood.

Beyond adolescence

Beyond adolescence

Problem behavior
and young adult development

Richard Jessor
John Edward Donovan
Frances Marie Costa
Institute of Behavioral Science, University of Colorado

CAMBRIDGE
UNIVERSITY PRESS

CAMBRIDGE UNIVERSITY PRESS
Cambridge, New York, Melbourne, Madrid, Cape Town, Singapore, São Paulo

Cambridge University Press
The Edinburgh Building, Cambridge CB2 2RU, UK

Published in the United States of America by Cambridge University Press, New York

www.cambridge.org
Information on this title: www.cambridge.org/9780521394178

First published 1991
First paperback edition 1994

A catalogue record for this publication is available from the British Library

ISBN-13 978-0-521-39417-8 hardback
ISBN-10 0-521-39417-1 hardback

ISBN-13 978-0-521-46758-2 paperback
ISBN-10 0-521-46758-6 paperback

Transferred to digital printing 2006

Contents

Tables and figures

Tables

Figures

Preface

It was over three decades ago, in 1959, that the psychosocial framework for this book was first elaborated. Over the past thirty years, we have continued to refine that framework, now called Problem-Behavior Theory, and have written and published numerous articles, chapters, and two previous books about it. The present book is the latest addition to the corpus of systematic research that has emerged from our endeavors. This ongoing exploration of a set of ideas has yielded, for us, a strong sense of cumulativeness, and that is one of its main satisfactions. It has also been gratifying to see that others have found those same ideas useful in the pursuit of their own inquiries.

Although the visible thread that winds through the larger fabric of our research is a continuing concern with problem behavior, we have used that concern to try to illuminate some of the fundamental issues in contemporary behavioral science: how to conceptualize the person, the environment, and their interaction in a way that is logically coherent; how to capture the texture of complex social behavior; how to formulate psychosocial development within the framework of a theory of action; and how to bridge the gap between description and explanation. This volume again deals with problem behavior, and again fundamental issues are explored, including the structure and organization of social behavior, the stability and continuity of personality, the description of development in the language of theory, the role of past experience in shaping subsequent growth and change, and others. The study of problem behavior, then, has provided us with a strategically placed window on some of the larger issues involved in understanding both human action and human development.

Quite obviously, no study of lives can be successful without the cooperation, indeed the collaboration, of the participants. Ours were selfless and unstinting in their willingness to reflect repeatedly upon their lives and to share their experiences with us. That nearly all of them would resume their participation in the follow-up study after such a long hiatus testifies to their involvement with and their commitment to the research. Without their profound contribution this book could not have been written. It is fitting that we dedicate it to all of them, and we hope that its publication will serve as partial compensation for their efforts.

To sustain systematic work over a long period of time requires confidence and support from many quarters. The research reported here was supported primarily by the National Institute on Alcohol Abuse and Alcoholism, Grant No. AA–03745. The willingness of that agency to contribute to research whose aims far transcended a narrow focus on alcohol use testifies to its breadth of vision, and that vision was implemented with unswerving conviction by our project officer, Dr. Tina Vanderveen. Additional support from the National Institute on Drug Abuse for some specific analyses is also gratefully acknowledged. A Faculty Fellowship award to the first author from the University of Colorado Council on Research and Creative Work provided the gift of release time for completing some of the writing for the book.

Beyond financial support, we have been fortunate to have the kind of support from others without which work such as this simply cannot get done. Our longest-term debt is to Dr. Lee Jessor, who was a full partner in the precursors to this research and an active collaborator in the early phase of the present study. Her contribution was essential to its initiation and, indeed, to its ultimate accomplishment, and we hope that what has been written here achieves the objectives she had for it. Locating all of our participants nearly a decade after our last contact with them, when they were spread across the nation and even the world, was a task carried out with extraordinary sedulousness by Averil Lerman. That heroic effort safeguarded the integrity of the follow-up cohorts. Our research assistants over the years, especially Ron Hays and Linda Schmid, and, more recently, Jill Van Den Bos, deserve our special gratitude. Support from the Social Science Data Analysis Center in our own Institute of Behavioral Science, especially the continuous and thoughtful assistance of Jani Little, was also essential to the completion of this work. Marilyn Sena kept the project on track throughout the decade of its existence, typed our endless reports, and also prepared most of the present manuscript. Her exceptional skills and her unfailing good nature sustained us from beginning to end. Debbie Ash and Greg Davis helped with the final drafts of these chapters, and we appreciate very much the care and the commitment in their work. Finally, we are deeply grateful to Dr. Charles M. Judd for his critical review of the entire manuscript and his very helpful suggestions and comments.

The book took longer to come to publication than we had wished. Some of the reasons are pedestrian – the usual things that deflect any deliberate course of action. Other reasons had to do with the pull of other research – new studies that had to be launched and that, happily, are currently under way. And still other reasons were simply personal. Nevertheless, the book's contribution to the social psychology of problem behavior and young adult development remains, we believe, an important one, and we are pleased that now, at long last, others can arrive at a judgment for themselves.

Richard Jessor
John E. Donovan
Frances M. Costa

Part I

The approach

1

Introduction

Young lives growing and changing and moving through time are among the most elusive and refractory of all objects of scientific inquiry. Yet, that is what this book is about. Of course, it is about other things as well, such as testing further the adequacy of a psychosocial theory, and reexamining the structure of problem behavior. But, at its core, it is about human development from adolescence and youth to well into young adulthood.

The difficulties of the longitudinal study of lives are well known, and the litany of its vicissitudes is all too familiar. One author takes note of the "widespread pessimism regarding the feasibility of such studies" and goes on to draw the analogy with efforts at international disarmament: "Too often, both sets of endeavors are undertaken by dreamers" (Vaillant, 1984, p. 61). Nevertheless, many investigators (that author included) continue to pursue that mode of inquiry, not out of foolhardiness but out of a keen sense of the unique vantage it provides on questions that cannot be addressed by other approaches. Understanding the integrity of the life course, tracing its continuity over large segments of time, distinguishing what is ephemeral from what is lasting, grasping the role that the past plays in shaping the future – all these, and more, are issues that yield only to research that is longitudinal or developmental in design. In short, given such interests and concerns, there is simply no alternative.

Despite much disappointment with the early longitudinal studies, there was – happily – something of a change in the zeitgeist about two decades ago. A new wave of longitudinal studies, more focused than before on the adolescent years and on behaviors of social concern, was initiated in the late 1960s and early 1970s. Much of that work has now come to fruition, and this book is one part of what is proving to be a rather plentiful harvest.

Several of the "new wave" longitudinal studies were galvanized by the societal concern with youth that emerged in the 1960s, especially concern with their use of illicit drugs (e.g., Bachman, Johnston, & O'Malley, 1981; Huba & Bentler, 1982; Kandel, 1975; Kandel, Kessler, & Margulies, 1978), but also with other problem behaviors such as delinquency (Elliott & Voss, 1974; Elliott, Huizinga, & Ageton, 1985; Kaplan, 1980). As these studies progressed in time, they expanded the domains with which they were concerned to encompass a broader range of behaviors, such as alcohol use and sexual activity; they sought to map the attainment of various statuses, and they began to assess a wider array of psychosocial determinants (e.g., Bachman, O'Malley, & Johnston, 1984; Elliott, Huizinga, & Menard, 1989; Kaplan, Martin, Johnson, & Robbins, 1986; Newcomb & Bentler, 1988). Other investigators began their work with a broader focus at the outset, concerned with understanding personality and social development and adaptation as a whole (e.g., Bachman, O'Malley, & Johnston, 1978; Block & Block, 1980; Magnusson, Duner, & Zetterblom, 1975; Silbereisen, Noack, & Eyfurth, 1986), and their studies, too, have been underway long enough to have reached maturity (Block, Block, & Keyes, 1988; Magnusson, 1988). With the exception of one or two, all of these longitudinal studies have followed their participants beyond adolescence, and they are now able to report on young adulthood. This body of research, much of it still ongoing, is compelling evidence that longitudinal studies – despite the well-known obstacles and impediments that must be supervened – are eminently doable.

The Young Adult Follow-Up Study

Our own longitudinal study began some 20 years ago, near the end of the 1960s. Its conceptual origins trace back before that, however. The conceptual framework for the research had been formulated a decade earlier as part of a large community study of societal and personality factors in nonnormative behavior among three ethnic groups in a small southwestern Colorado town (see Jessor, Graves, Hanson, & Jessor, 1968). Although that study was successful in illuminating person–environment interaction and in accounting for variation in social behavior, it nevertheless left us somewhat dissatisfied. Because it was cross-sectional research, the study was unable to reveal how things had gotten to be the way they were or to suggest where they might be going, and it could tell us very little about the dynamics and the directions of life change in the community.

That experience engendered an acute awareness that lives are inescapably foreshortened in cross-sectional research, and it led us to initiate a new study of young people in 1969 that was longitudinal in design. The guiding framework for the new study was, again, Problem-Behavior Theory, but now the theory was elaborated to account not only for action but also for development and change, the latter relying on a new concept called "transition proneness." In the first phase of the research, four waves of data were collected annually, from 1969 through 1972, on boys and girls who were in grades 7, 8, and 9 in the initial year; four waves of data were also collected annually, from 1970 through 1973, on young men and young women who were college freshmen in their initial year. These were, then, two parallel, independent, longitudinal studies carried along in tandem, one of adolescents and one of youth; both included males and females, and both were drawn from the normal population. Data from the first phase of these two studies were the basis for a comprehensive report dealing with problem behavior and psychosocial development in adolescence and youth (Jessor & Jessor, 1977).

The second phase of the research has followed those same cohorts as they have made the transition out of adolescence and youth and have moved through the third decade of life. Two additional waves of data were collected in this second phase, one in 1979 and one in 1981. By 1981, the younger cohorts, those who began the study in junior high school, had reached the ages of 25, 26, and 27; the older cohort, those who began the study as college freshmen, had by then reached the age of 30. There are, thus, six waves of data on the participants, with the last two of those waves collected when they all had become young adults. Those latter two data waves enable us to explore the life stage of young adulthood in the same systematic way that adolescence and youth were explored in the preceding volume. Their availability also opens up new possibilities for the pursuit of developmental linkages between the earlier stage of adolescence/

youth and the later stage of young adulthood. These are the main concerns of the present book.

The life stage of young adulthood

There is a remarkable lacuna in knowledge about young adulthood in comparison with other segments of the life-span, especially infancy and early childhood, even adolescence, and certainly old age. That young adulthood should have been ignored for so long is puzzling since it is a time in which critical and reverberating life choices are usually made, choices about the pursuit of advanced education, about entering the labor force and beginning a career, about establishing longer-term relationships of partnering or marriage, and about assuming the role of parent and the tasks of childrearing. The confrontation of these options, if not their resolution, marks the transition from adolescence/youth to young adulthood, and the decisions that are made about them often result in major changes – sometimes radical in nature – in the context of daily life, in the demands that it poses, in the social relationships it encompasses, and in the opportunities it presents for gratification and success or for frustration and failure. In short, young adulthood, largely unexplored though it is, can be seen as a pervasively influential time for shaping the remainder of the life course. It was a major objective of this research, therefore, to try to extend knowledge about young adulthood as an important segment of the life trajectory.

Because young adulthood has received so little attention and because it is relatively new as a focus of developmental inquiry, even descriptive knowledge about it is sparse. Beyond consensus on the tasks that ordinarily are engaged in this period, such as work initiation and family formation, there is not a great deal that is firm about what actually happens beyond adolescence/youth. The content and organization of young adult life and even its developmental structure are uncertain; with respect to the latter, for example, is it useful – as it clearly is for adolescence – to distinguish an early stage from a later one?

Unlike entry into adolescence, where there are clear biological and anthropometric demarcations, becoming a young adult is determined largely by processes of social and personal definition related to roles and responsibilities and status attainments. How the latter are organized, which are central and key as markers, how much synchrony is expected, how extended the transition process is in time – all these are only beginning to be examined. Even less is known about *being* a young adult, especially when issues are dealt with that go beyond description of the role responsibilities related to work and family. In regard to young adult personality, what happens to the content, the structure, and the organization of personality in young adulthood? Do values and beliefs and attitudes and self-definitions characterize this life stage in a way that is different from other stages? And in regard to behavior, is its structure different from what it was in adolescence/youth?

The lacuna in knowledge about young adulthood noted earlier is, it would seem, pervasive, extending across all three domains that are encompassed by a behavioral science perspective – environment, person, and behavior – as well as their interactions and change. Our aim was, ideally, to contribute information about each of those domains, although the limitations of our study imposed severe constraints on the descriptive contribution we could hope to make. The small sample sizes of our two parallel, longitudinal studies as well as their selectivity with respect to representativeness preclude inferences about young adulthood in general. Nor is it possible with our samples to establish the role played in young adulthood by important parameters of social structure such as ethnic and racial membership. More important as a limitation, perhaps, is that our study is tied to a particular time in history, and there is no way of disentangling potentially important cohort effects from the observations of young adulthood that were made in the research.

Nevertheless, our samples retain great interest as a source of knowledge about young adulthood. Despite their relatively small size, they were drawn from the normal population rather than from the clinic, they include both men and women, and they reflect very different origins, one sample from a local setting and one from a more regional and even national setting. In addition, and especially important, they are samples with an unusual amount of information available on their previous stage of life. And finally, they are cohorts from an intrinsically interesting time in history – "baby boomers" born in the first half of the 1950s, adolescents during the Vietnam era and the time of widespread youth protest, and young adults in the complacency and inertia of the Reagan years. It was young people like these who galvanized societal attention and concern and whose activities as adolescents generated the gloomiest and most exasperated forecasts about how they would turn out and how their futures had been irreparably damaged by their recourse to drugs and their repudiation of conventional striving. What did indeed happen to them, and how did they in fact turn out? Surely something valuable can be learned about young adulthood from the lives of these young people. And, of course, there is the opportunity here – an exceedingly important one in any study of lives – to examine individual differences in the course and the content of young adulthood, despite the small size of the samples and despite their tie to a single, albeit extraordinary, period in history. Providing descriptive information about young adulthood was, therefore, a guiding objective in the conduct of this research.

Problem-Behavior Theory and young adulthood

Also guiding this research was a concern with theory. In our two earlier books (Jessor, Graves, Hanson, & Jessor, 1968; Jessor & Jessor, 1977), we elaborated the role of theory in field research, showed how theory provides a source of systematic measurement, and espoused theory testing as a compelling way of reducing ambiguity of inference and advancing knowledge. Our concern with theory derives most fundamentally from its contribution to the ultimate aim of scientific work – namely, *understanding*. Neither description nor prediction can provide the explanatory grasp that is achieved when observations and phenomena are embedded in a network of logically related concepts.

The theory relied upon in this study, Problem-Behavior Theory, has been revised, elaborated, and extended over the past three decades as a working framework for understanding a particular domain of human behavior, behavior that involves the transgression of personal and social norms. In restricting its focus in this way, Problem-Behavior Theory would seem to qualify as what Merton referred to as a "theory of the middle range," an example of "special theories applicable to limited ranges of data" (1957, p. 9). Applied to various populations in various contexts, the theory has helped to illuminate a broad array of problem behaviors engaged in by adolescents and youth. A key aim of the present research was to test the usefulness of Problem-Behavior Theory in accounting for variation in problem behavior *in young adulthood*. Would the concepts and theoretical structures already shown to be apposite to problem-behavior variation in adolescence/youth retain their explanatory relevance for the very same participants as young adults and in the new social context of young adulthood?

The content of Problem-Behavior Theory reflects the perspective of behavioral science in its preoccupation with three domains of variation: the environment, the person, and action or behavior. In later chapters it will become clear how these domains are defined and elaborated, so only a few comments need be made here. All three of the domains are treated as problematic rather than as given. Thus, the environment lends itself to both objective or structural and subjective or perceptual specification; the person is considered a bundle of relatively enduring rather than ephemeral attributes reflecting social experience; and behavior is treated as purposive and meaningful action. The impoverishment of the environment in so much of psychological research is well known, as is the long period in which the very idea of personality was denied scientific respectability. And in sociological research, inattention to individual differences has been typical. Fortunately, the work of recent years has begun to overcome this legacy and to adopt the more fruitful approach inherent in a general behavioral science perspective. Under the rubric of "interactionism" (Magnusson, 1981), psychologists have returned to accounting for social behavior by invoking both person and situation attributes and by examining their joint contribution. Our own efforts are strongly identified with that trend, and Problem-Behavior Theory should be seen as an interactionist theory.

A final point is worth noting here about theory. Since each of the three domains included in the behavioral science perspective is enormously complex, it is unlikely that their structure and differentiation can be represented adequately by only one or two concepts or measures. Research that is driven by interest in a particular variable or a single measure – for example, socioeconomic status in the environment, or self-esteem in the person, or risk taking in behavior – has little likelihood of capturing the complexity of human action and the richness of individual and contextual variation. The conceptual elaboration of environment, person, and behavior in Problem-Behavior Theory constitutes a different approach, one in which a relatively large number of variables are specified and systematically articulated within each domain. Such a theory-driven approach, in providing a more comprehensive mapping of the three domains, has a better chance of yielding the textured understanding that behavioral science is seeking.

Development from adolescence to young adulthood

The third major focus of this research, beyond description and theory-testing in young adulthood, was on development, on the course and direction of psychosocial growth and change, and on the linkages that connect the earlier life stage of adolescence/youth with the one that succeeds it. For such purposes, of course, longitudinal design becomes uniquely valuable. The availability of successive waves of data on the same young people, data waves that represent both adolescence/youth and young adulthood, makes it possible to pursue fundamental issues in developmental change across life stages. These include the direction of change, the amount of change, the coherence of change, individual differences in change, and the antecedents and consequents of change. In one way or another, all of these issues are at least addressed in this research.

Charting the course of development

As we have shown in earlier work (Jessor, 1983; Jessor & Jessor, 1977), it is possible to represent psychosocial and behavioral development by graphic plotting of comparable measurements over time. These "growth curves" provide an immediate sense of both direction and amount of change; through examination of such curves for multiple attributes, it is also possible to determine whether there is coherence or systematic consonance among the disparate changes or whether they are, instead, essentially unrelated.

In relation to Problem-Behavior Theory, a key concern is to establish whether growth and change from adolescence/youth into young adulthood involve an enhancement or a diminution in problem-behavior proneness – that is, in the disposition and likelihood of normative transgression. In terms of growth curves, the question for each theoretical attribute plotted is whether the direction of development is problem- or conformity-prone for the samples as a whole or for component subgroups. Thus far, our findings suggest that development beyond adolescence is, on the whole, toward greater conventionality and, therefore, toward less likelihood of involvement with problem behavior. Increasing conventionality may constitute a major direction of psychosocial development toward adulthood. Whether that is indeed the case is one of the issues that will be addressed, and the examination of an array of growth curves will be central to that task.

At the individual level, it is of special interest to explore whether development involves continuity or discontinuity, at least in regard to the theoretical variables assessed over time in our study. Clearly, a great deal of developmental change must be expected to occur across two such different stages of life, but whether that change arbitrarily redistributes the sample on a particular attribute, or whether, instead, it conserves their initial position, is an exceedingly important issue in the charting of development beyond adolescence.

Predicting young adult problem behavior

A rather different issue in development from adolescence/youth to young adulthood concerns the predictability of young adult problem behavior. Can the profile of adolescent theoretical attributes forecast later-life behavior, especially when the time interval is lengthy and when an entirely different life stage is implicated? From an applied point of view, this is an issue of large significance. Not only would the demonstration of predictability of problem behavior across the life course provide the rationale for early intervention, but the key predictors would then become logical risk factors for intervention targeting. But predictability across the life course has even larger significance for the *understanding* of development. It constitutes the precondition for searching out the structures and pathways, in both person and context, that mediate the demonstrated linkage across time. Is it the stability of personality that underlies predictability? The constancy of the life context?

The chronicity of problem behavior? Some complex arrangement of all three domains?

In earlier work, Problem-Behavior Theory was relied upon to predict the occurrence of a particular kind of subsequent behavior, what we have called "transition behavior," namely the onset of drinking, of marijuana use, and of first sexual intercourse (see, e.g., Jessor, Costa, Jessor, & Donovan, 1983). Young adulthood does not lend itself as well to such singular, behavioral transition markers, and we have focused instead on a measure of intensity of involvement with problem behavior as the young adult behavioral criterion to predict. As we shall show, young adult involvement in problem behavior can indeed be predicted from the Problem-Behavior Theory measures that were collected in adolescence. Modeling the structure that may underlie that predictability should add a further increment to the understanding of young adult development.

The impact of adolescent problem behavior on young adulthood

Yet another developmental question about the linkage between adolescence/youth and young adulthood warrants exploration. The insistence with which the question has been asked since the late 1960s testifies to the importance of its answer to society. Most simply stated, does involvement in problem behavior in adolescence – alcohol abuse, illicit drug use, precocious sexuality, delinquent behavior – determine a different outcome in young adulthood? Do those experiences foreclose options, for example, for educational or occupational attainment, for family formation, for friendship ties? Is the life course irretrievably deflected, or are those experiences assimilated and homogenized in the ordinary course of development into young adulthood? Put otherwise, to what extent does involvement in adolescent problem behavior mortgage future development? Several of the longitudinal studies mentioned earlier will soon be able to provide a response, and at least two of them have already done so (Kandel, Davies, Karus, & Yamaguchi, 1986; Kandel, Simcha-Fagan, & Davies, 1986; Newcomb & Bentler, 1988; Yamaguchi & Kandel, 1984). Since our own data are also germane, we have examined that same question ourselves, within the limitations of our samples. What we found, and our own answer, are part of the presentation in this report.

Overall, then, it should be evident that young adult development has been a central preoccupation in this second phase of our longitudinal study. It should also be evident that we have tried to use theory and a continuing concern with problem behavior as our major sources of illumination.

The plan of the book

In the chapter that follows, there is a presentation of Problem-Behavior Theory as it was revised and extended to apply to young adulthood. Reference to those changes is made in the presentation, especially to the effort to accommodate in the framework the key young adult life areas of family, work, sex, and friendship, and the stresses and satisfactions that characterize them. The systematic role that the theory plays in development is also elaborated. Finally, attention is given to the concept of stress as reflected both in life areas and in the experience of negative life events, and this new aspect of the theory is proposed for preliminary exploration as an alternative account of proneness to problem behavior. Testing of the theory can then be framed somewhat more felicitously as an appraisal of alternatives.

The longitudinal design, the samples, the measures, and the young adult data collection are all elaborated in Chapter 3. Nearly all of the measures, except for the ones that are new, are identical to those used in the earlier adolescent phase of the research or only slightly modified to be more appropriate for young adults. Also, the procedures that resulted in retention of 90 percent of the participants from the first phase are detailed.

Part II of the book focuses exclusively on the life stage of young adulthood. Chapter 4 is devoted to a purely descriptive, qualitative account of young adult life for the samples of men and women in each of the two parallel longitudinal studies. Family life and child-rearing, work and leisure time, sexuality, politics and religion, health, and friendship, among other topics, are touched upon briefly. The aim is to provide a very general characterization of what young adulthood entails for our participants so that the analytic and quantitative materials that follow will be as fully situated and grounded as is possible with our dataset. In Chapter 5, we address an issue that has interested us from the beginning of our research on problem behaviors – the structure of their interrelations – and we use latent-variable methods to examine whether there is support for a "syndrome" of problem behavior in young adulthood as there clearly was in adolescence. That examination provides the basis for constructing a summary problem-behavior index that is used later on as the key criterion measure in both cross-sectional and longitudinal tests of Problem-Behavior Theory.

The testing of Problem-Behavior Theory in young adulthood is the focus of Chapter 6. Cross-sectional explanatory accounts based on personality attributes, on environmental attributes, on other behavioral attributes, and on their combination are presented for the summary index of problem behavior as well as for five component problem behaviors – problem drinking, marijuana use, other illicit drug use, general deviant behavior, and cigarette smoking. The magnitude of the explanatory account in young adulthood is compared with that reported earlier for adolescence/youth.

In Part III, we turn to a variety of developmental issues. Chapter 7 is, again, largely descriptive. It deals first with the stability of the psychosocial attributes in the theory over the time interval between adolescence/youth and young adulthood. Major attention is then given to the psychosocial growth curves and to the direction and magnitude of change they portray. Finally, there is an exploration of interindividual differences in developmental change. Chapter 8 addresses the predictability of young adult problem behavior from problem-behavior proneness in adolescence/youth and, using LISREL, explores the structural model that underlies that relationship. Chapter 9 examines another kind of linkage between life stages: whether or not involvement in problem behavior in adolescence constrains later development and has a damping effect on achievement and fulfillment in young adulthood. The closing chapter, Chapter 10, presents a review of findings, an appraisal of the utility of the theory, and conclusions about the nature and course of young adult development.

With the issues discussed in this chapter as prolegomenon, it is appropriate to turn to the presentation of the conceptual framework for the research.

References

Bachman, J. G., Johnston, L. D., & O'Malley, P. M. (1981). Smoking, drinking, and drug use among American high school students: Correlates and trends, 1975–1979. *American Journal of Public Health, 71*, 59–69.

Bachman, J. G., O'Malley, P. M., & Johnston, J. (1978). *Adolescence to adulthood: Change and stability in the lives of young men.* Ann Arbor, MI: Institute for Social Research.

Bachman, J. G., O'Malley, P. M., & Johnston, L. D. (1984). Drug use among young adults: The impacts of role status and social environment. *Journal of Personality and Social Psychology, 47*, 629–645.

Block, J. H., & Block, J. (1980). The role of ego-control and ego-resiliency in the organization of behavior. In W. A. Collins (Ed.), *Minnesota Symposia on Child Development* (Vol. 13). Hillsdale, NJ: Erlbaum.

Block, J., Block, J. H., & Keyes, S. (1988). Longitudinally foretelling drug usage in adolescence: Early childhood and environmental precursors. *Child Development, 59*, 336–355.

Elliott, D. S., Huizinga, D., & Ageton, S. S. (1985). *Explaining delinquency and drug use.* Newbury Park, CA: Sage.

Elliott, D. S., Huizinga, D., & Menard, S. (1989). *Multiple problem youth: Delinquency, substance use, and mental health.* New York: Springer-Verlag.

Elliott, D. S., & Voss, H. L. (1974). *Delinquency and dropout.* Lexington, MA: D.C. Heath.

Huba, G. J., & Bentler, P. M. (1982). A developmental theory of drug use: Derivation and assessment of a causal modeling approach. In P. B. Baltes & O. G. Brim, Jr. (Eds.), *Life-span development and behavior* (Vol. 4, pp. 147–203). New York: Academic Press.

Jessor, R. (1983). The stability of change: Psychosocial development from adolescence to young adulthood. In D. Magnusson & V. Allen (Eds.), *Human development: An interactional perspective* (pp. 321–341). New York: Academic Press.

Jessor, R., Costa, F. M., Jessor, L., & Donovan, J. E. (1983). Time of first intercourse: A prospective study. *Journal of Personality and Social Psychology, 44*, 608–626.

Jessor, R., Graves, T. D., Hanson, R. C., & Jessor, S. L. (1968). *Society, personality, and deviant behavior: A study of a tri-ethnic community.* New York: Holt, Rinehart and Winston.

Jessor, R., & Jessor, S. L. (1977). *Problem behavior and psychosocial development: A longitudinal study of youth.* New York: Academic Press.

Kandel, D. B. (1975). Stages in adolescent involvement in drug use. *Science, 190,* 912–914.

Kandel, D. B., Davies, M., Karus, D., & Yamaguchi, K. (1986). The consequences in young adulthood of adolescent drug involvement. *Archives of General Psychiatry, 43,* 746–754.

Kandel, D. B., Kessler, R. C., & Margulies, R. Z. (1978). Antecedents of adolescent initiation into stages of drug use: A developmental analysis. In D. B. Kandel (Ed.), *Longitudinal research on drug abuse: Empirical findings and methodological issues* (pp. 73–99). Washington, DC: Hemisphere-Wiley.

Kandel, D. B., Simcha-Fagan, O., & Davies, M. (1986). Risk factors for delinquency and illicit drug use from adolescence to young adulthood. *The Journal of Drug Issues, 16,* 67–90.

Kaplan, H. B. (1980). *Deviant behavior in defense of self.* New York: Academic Press.

Kaplan, H. B., Martin, S. S., Johnson, R. J., & Robbins, C. A. (1986). Escalation of marijuana use: Application of a general theory of deviant behavior. *Journal of Health and Social Behavior, 27,* 44–61.

Magnusson, D. (Ed.). (1981). *Toward a psychology of situations: An interactional perspective.* Hillsdale, NJ: Erlbaum.

Magnusson, D. (1988). *Individual development from an interactional perspective: A longitudinal study.* Hillsdale, NJ: Erlbaum.

Magnusson, D., Duner, A., & Zetterblom, G. (1975). *Adjustment: A longitudinal study.* New York: Wiley.

Merton, R. K. (1957). *Social theory and social structure* (rev. ed.). New York: Free Press.

Newcomb, M. D., & Bentler, P. M. (1988). *Consequences of adolescent drug use: Impact on the lives of young adults.* Newbury Park, CA: Sage.

Silbereisen, R. K., Noack, P., & Eyfurth, K. (1986). Place for development: Adolescents, leisure settings, and developmental tasks. In R. K. Silbereisen, K. Eyfurth, & G. Rudinger (Eds.), *Development as action in context* (pp. 87–107). New York: Springer-Verlag.

Vaillant, G. E. (1984). The longitudinal study of behavior disorders. *American Journal of Psychiatry, 141,* 61–62.

Yamaguchi, K., & Kandel, D. B. (1984). Patterns of drug use from adolescence to young adulthood: III. Predicators of progression. *American Journal of Public Health, 74,* 673–681.

2

Problem-Behavior Theory and young adulthood

For more than a quarter of a century, our research has been guided by a social-psychological framework we refer to as Problem-Behavior Theory. Derived initially from the basic concepts of value and expectation in Rotter's (1954, 1982) social learning theory and from Merton's (1957) concept of anomie, the framework was first applied in a comprehensive study of alcohol abuse and other problem behaviors in a small, tri-ethnic community in southwestern Colorado (Jessor, Graves, Hanson, & Jessor, 1968). Subsequently, the framework was revised to accommodate a major, longitudinal study of problem behavior and psychosocial development in cohorts of junior high school adolescents and college youth (Jessor & Jessor, 1977). It also provided the theoretical basis for two large-scale, national surveys of junior–senior high school youth, with a special focus on the psychosocial correlates of alcohol and drug use (Donovan & Jessor, 1978, 1983; Jessor, Chase, & Donovan, 1980; Jessor, Donovan, & Widmer, 1980).

More recently, Problem-Behavior Theory, again revised and extended, has been guiding the follow-up study of the earlier longitudinal cohorts of adolescents and youth as they have traversed through young adulthood; that is the study reported in this volume. Finally, the theory has been elaborated further to guide our most recent research involving the larger domain of health-compromising and health-enhancing behavior in youth (Costa, Jessor, & Donovan, 1989; Donovan, Jessor, & Costa, 1991; Jessor, 1984).

By now, the concepts and measures of Problem-Behavior Theory have also been used by others in a large number of studies in the United States and elsewhere, and they have been applied to a broad variety of adolescent problem behaviors (e.g., Beirness & Simpson, 1988; Chassin et al., 1981; Chassin, Presson, & Sherman, 1984; DiTecco & Schlegel, 1982; Gerber & Newman, 1989; Hays, Stacy, & DiMatteo, 1987; Robinson et al., 1987; Rooney & Wright, 1982; Sadava, 1985; Sadava & Forsyth, 1977; Smith, Canter, & Robin, 1989; Vulcano, Barnes, & Langstaff, 1990; Wilson & Jonah, 1988). As it has evolved and been adapted to different social contexts, different age groups, different problem behaviors, different historical periods, and now to health-related behavior, Problem-Behavior Theory has conserved its psychosocial orientation, its basic explanatory structure, and its overriding concern to link person and environment with significant social behavior. In this chapter, we describe the theory as it was elaborated to encompass the developmental stage of young adulthood.

The conceptual structure of Problem-Behavior Theory

The primary concern of Problem-Behavior Theory is with the relationships that obtain within and between three major systems of psychosocial variables: the Personality System, the Perceived Environment System, and the Behavior System. As causal or explanatory systems, these three are presumed to be most directly influential on and proximal to the occurrence/nonoccurrence of any particular behavior. Within each system, the variables represent either *instigations* or *controls* that, together, generate a theoretical resultant, a dynamic state called *proneness*, that indicates the likelihood of occurrence of problem behavior. Since proneness to engage in problem behavior is a system-level property, it is theoretically meaningful to speak of personality proneness, environmental proneness, and behavioral proneness. When proneness in all three systems is taken together, their combination is summarized by the sovereign concept of *overall psychosocial proneness*. The latter is the key concept in Problem-Behavior Theory for the prediction and explanation of variation in problem behavior.

As a dispositional concept, psychosocial proneness represents the strength of the tendency to engage in a particular problem behavior and, therefore, its likelihood or probability of occurrence. It is a resultant or outcome of the balance of instigations toward and controls against engaging in problem behavior. Such instigations and controls have parallels or analogues in the epidemiological notions of risk and protective factors. The interaction or balance of the latter is often summarized simply as psychosocial risk. The concept of psychosocial proneness is essentially synonymous with that latter concept of psychosocial risk, and the theoretical variables in the three systems of Problem-Behavior Theory can just as well be characterized as *psychosocial risk (and protective) factors* for problem behavior. We shall be using "psychosocial proneness" and "psychosocial risk" interchangeably in this volume.

Although the primary emphasis of Problem-Behavior Theory is on the three systems of variables that are most proximal in the causal chain to the occurrence of a problem behavior – personality, perceived environment, and behavior – there has been from the beginning a concern with more distal systems of influence as well, most notably the social-structural and sociocultural environment. Indeed, in the Tri-Ethnic Study (Jessor et al., 1968), major attention was given to conceptualizing the distal social environment as constituted of a structure of opportunity, a structure of norms, and a structure of social controls, and to developing relatively "objective" measures of the variables encompassed by those structures. That effort represented a serious attempt to get beyond the usual reliance on a few readily obtained demographic indicators and to differentiate social space in a theoretically meaningful way, that is, in a way that had logical implications for behavior when mediated by the more proximal systems.

Subsequently, in the earlier phase of the present longitudinal study, we chose to focus more intensively on the more proximal *perceived* environment and we gave much less attention to the distal or socalled objective social environment (Jessor & Jessor, 1973). This decision was partly influenced by the logic of causality and partly by the relative homogeneity of social background of our in-school, relatively middle-class population of youth. We continued, however, to assess background demographic variables – education, occupation, religious membership, family structure – and also made an effort to map the sociocultural content of norms and values evident in the socialization practices of the family of orientation and in the peer group. In the present phase of the longitudinal study, we have made yet another foray into the social environment, this time seeking to articulate important *contexts* of young adult life – family, work, and friends – and measuring several key properties of those contexts, such as the stresses and satisfactions they are perceived to generate.

The conceptual structure of Problem-Behavior Theory as employed in the Young Adult Follow-Up Study is schematized in Figure 2.1. The main similarities and differences between this figure and the one that guided the earlier adolescent/youth phase of the longitudinal research will be addressed, but a direct comparison can be made as well by referring to our earlier book (Jessor & Jessor, 1977, p. 38).

Several general characteristics of the framework are worth noting. First, it includes a fairly large number of variables and reflects an attempt to achieve rather comprehensive representation in each of the explanatory systems. Second, within each system certain variables represent instigations to engage in problem behavior and others represent controls against problem behavior; as mentioned above, it is the balance between instigations and controls that constitutes the level of proneness – or risk – that characterizes that system. Third, some of the variables (e.g., Friends Models for Problem Behavior, or Attitudinal Intolerance of Deviance) implicate problem behavior directly, while others are linked to problem behavior only indirectly and by way of theory (e.g., Self-Esteem, or Parent–Friends Compatibility). The former are considered more proximal to and the latter more distal from problem behavior. Because of the obviousness of their connection with behavior, proximal variables generally yield stronger empirical relationships, but distal variables, being less obvious, are often of greater theoretical interest. In the Perceived Environment System in Figure 2.1, the variables are classified into distal and proximal structures; that very same distinction could also be made among the variables in the Personality System, but we have chosen instead to employ a different organization there, one that classifies them according to the instigation/control distinction.

Fourth, the figure illustrates the fundamental premise on which our work has been built, namely, that *all behavior is the result of person–environment interaction.* The logic of explanation of human behavior requires simultaneous mapping of both of those explanatory systems,

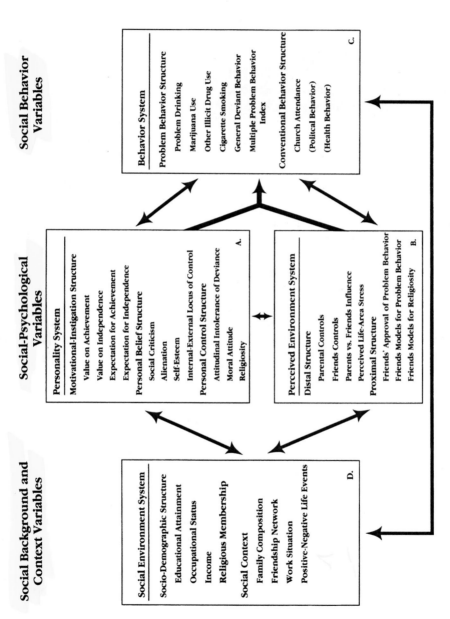

Social Background and Context Variables

Social-Psychological Variables

Social Behavior Variables

Personality System

Motivational-Instigation Structure
  Value on Achievement
  Value on Independence
  Expectation for Achievement
  Expectation for Independence
Personal Belief Structure
  Social Criticism
  Alienation
  Self-Esteem
  Internal-External Locus of Control
Personal Control Structure
  Attitudinal Intolerance of Deviance
  Moral Attitude
  Religiosity   A.

Perceived Environment System

Distal Structure
  Parental Controls
  Friends Controls
  Parents vs. Friends Influence
  Perceived Life-Area Stress
Proximal Structure
  Friends' Approval of Problem Behavior
  Friends Models for Problem Behavior
  Friends Models for Religiosity   B.

Behavior System

Problem Behavior Structure
  Problem Drinking
  Marijuana Use
  Other Illicit Drug Use
  Cigarette Smoking
  General Deviant Behavior
  Multiple Problem Behavior
    Index
Conventional Behavior Structure
  Church Attendance
  (Political Behavior)
  (Health Behavior)   C.

Social Environment System

Socio-Demographic Structure
  Educational Attainment
  Occupational Status
  Income
  Religious Membership
Social Context
  Family Composition
  Friendship Network
  Work Situation
  Positive-Negative Life Events   D.

Figure 2.1.   The conceptual structure of Problem-Behavior Theory used in the Young Adult Follow-Up Study.

and causal priority cannot be allocated to either one alone. This premise is represented by the heavier, unidirectional arrow showing the joint influence of the Personality System and the Perceived Environment System on the Behavior System. Among the classical interactionists, it was Kurt Lewin (1951) who, perhaps more than anyone else, gave salience to this orientation; he termed it the "field theory" perspective in social science. The revitalization of that perspective, after decades of neglect, has been led by David Magnusson (Magnusson, 1981; Magnusson & Allen, 1983; Magnusson & Endler, 1977), and it is currently referred to as "interactionism." (It is important to emphasize that this perspective is not equivalent to the statistical notion of interaction.)

Fifth, as alluded to earlier, the environment has been partitioned into the perceived environment and the social environment, the former now including representation of key life-area characteristics, and the latter indexed largely by background and contextual attributes. That conceptualizing the environment is a problematic endeavor has been argued elsewhere (Jessor, 1981; Jessor & Jessor, 1973), and distinctions among various kinds and levels of environments have been drawn. The position we have taken consistently is that behavior is most invariant with the *perceived* environment – the environment of meaning, definition, and significance. This is not at all to suggest that the more remote, objective social environment is unimportant, but only that the perceived environment – in the logic of explanation – is causally closer to behavior. That is precisely what is illustrated in the figure.

Finally, it needs to be emphasized that the figure is schematic in at least two important senses. First, it does not include many other variables that were measured in the research to be reported here. Some of those were employed for descriptive purposes, or to provide contextual illumination, or because they seemed to be of intrinsic interest. While some of them will be alluded to from time to time, they have been omitted from Figure 2.1 because they are not considered *systematic* components of Problem-Behavior Theory. Second, the variables that are shown in the figure are, for the most part, general or summary, multicomponent variables each of which may subsume several more specific variables. Thus, Friends Models for Problem Behavior incorporates as its components the more specific variables of Friends Models for Marijuana Use, Friends Models for Other Illicit Drugs, Friends Models for Drinking, and Friends Models for Smoking. Perceived Life-Area Stress, as another example, is constituted of more specific, multi-item component variables referring to stress in each of the four life areas of family, work, friendship, and sex. If these more specific variables were all to be represented in the figure, it would, of course, be more accurate and more informative, but it would also be more cumbersome to trace out and more cluttered. We have chosen to remain schematic in order to elucidate more clearly the fundamental content and the main dynamics of the overall framework.

The conceptual framework of Problem-Behavior Theory employed in the Young Adult Follow-Up Study is generally consistent, in both structure and content, with the framework that guided the earlier phase of the longitudinal study (Jessor & Jessor, 1977). Because of that degree of continuity, and because the basic rationale for the components in the framework was spelled out in detail in the earlier volume, the description presented here will be limited and relatively brief. Special attention will be given to the main changes – both additions and deletions – that have been instituted.

The Behavior System

As can be seen in Figure 2.1, we have continued a differentiated interest in the domain of problem behavior, but now as it pertains to the developmental stage of young adulthood. Five separate areas of young adult problem behavior are specified: problem drinking, marijuana use, the use of other illicit drugs, cigarette smoking, and general deviant behavior (such as lying, stealing, and physical aggression). In addition, there is an index that summarizes the degree of multiple involvement across those five behaviors. With the exception of cigarette smoking, all the other behaviors were used as criteria for testing the adequacy of Problem-Behavior Theory in the earlier adolescent/youth phase of this longitudinal study. And all meet the working definition of problem behavior: behavior that is socially defined as a problem, as a source of concern, or as undesirable by the social and/or legal norms of conventional society and its institutions of authority; it is behavior that usually elicits some form of social control response, whether minimal, such as a statement of disapproval, or extreme, such as confinement in prison.

Although cigarette smoking was not included in the earlier phase of this longitudinal study, there seemed good reason to deal with it as a problem behavior at this time. First, cigarette smoking, while licit, is essentially another facet of drug use. On that ground alone, its omission from the earlier phase was regrettable and unfortunate, and its inclusion now is appropriate. Second, our subsequent cross-sectional research with two national samples did include cigarette smoking, and we were able to show in those data that tobacco use was not only associated with other problem behaviors but was as well accounted for by Problem-Behavior Theory as those others (Jessor, Donovan, & Widmer, 1980). Third, the social climate in regard to smoking has changed substantially in the United States in recent years with increasing constraints, both legal and social, being implemented against its occurrence. These events have suggested to some sociologists that smoking is, indeed, in the process of being defined as a new social problem (cf. Markle & Troyer, 1979).

Included in the earlier phase as a problem behavior, but now omitted, is the behavior of sexual intercourse. This change nicely reflects the fact that certain problem behaviors are defined relative to age and are only considered problematic for those below a certain age or stage in life. Such age-graded problem behaviors – drinking per se is yet another example – lose their problem definition with accession to a later stage of life or with passing a legally established age standard. While precocious sexual intercourse, especially in early adolescence, can be considered a proscribed problem behavior, sexual intercourse in young adulthood is not only permitted but, in some situations – for example, marriage – actually prescribed. Thus, with development from adolescence to young adulthood, the very same behavior – sexual intercourse – shifts from problem to normative behavior.

The final variable in the Problem Behavior Structure of the Behavior System is a composite index devised to capture the degree of interrelatedness that exists among the various problem behavior involvements. Our earlier research has provided evidence that there is considerable intra-individual covariation in involvement in problem behavior among adolescents, and that it is useful to speak of a *syndrome* of problem behavior (Donovan & Jessor, 1985; Donovan, Jessor, & Costa, 1988; Jessor, 1984; Jessor & Jessor, 1977). The notion of "syndrome" is fully compatible with the interrelations presumed to obtain among elements within any system, in this case, the Behavior System. The Multiple Problem Behavior Index constitutes the sixth problem behavior criterion against which the overall social-psychological framework will be evaluated. Taken together, the six different behavioral criterion measures enable a relatively comprehensive assessment of the explanatory utility of Problem-Behavior Theory in young adulthood.

An even more exhaustive appraisal of the effectiveness of the theory entails a demonstration that the variables in the framework can also account for variation in the occurrence of *non*problem, that is, *conventional* behavior. To that end, three areas of conventional behavior have been constituted for inclusion in the Conventional Behavior Structure of the Behavior System. Church Attendance, a variable reflecting involvement with a major conventional institution of society, is perhaps the clearest exemplification of conventional behavior, and it has served as the key variable in this structure throughout our previous work. Two other areas of nonproblem or conventional behavior in young adulthood are shown in Figure 2.1: Political Behavior and Health Behavior. Although both could serve as additional criterion variables, there is some ambiguity about their implication of conventionality. We intend, therefore, to employ them primarily for descriptive purposes in relation to the nature of young adult life and to concentrate on Church Attendance as the conventional behavior criterion for testing the usefulness of Problem-Behavior Theory.

Proneness to problem behavior in the Behavior System, as with the other systems, consists of the balance between instigations and controls. When any specific problem behavior – say marijuana use – is the criterion behavior to be explained, behavior system proneness will reflect the instigation to marijuana use that derives from engagement in other problem behaviors and the control against marijuana use that derives from engagement in conventional behavior. *Proneness in the Behavior System*, therefore, refers to high involvement in *other* problem behaviors (e.g., problem drinking and general deviant behavior) and low involvement in conventional behaviors (e.g., church attendance).

The Personality System

As represented in Problem-Behavior Theory, personality refers to a patterned and interrelated set of relatively enduring, sociocognitive variables – values, expectations, beliefs, attitudes, and orientations toward self and society – that reflect social learning and developmental experience. The 11 variables in the Personality System in Figure 2.1 are organized into three structures depending upon whether they constitute instigations to problem behavior or controls against it, and depending upon whether, as controls, they are relatively proximal to or distal from problem behavior.

The Motivational-Instigation Structure is concerned with the directional orientation of action determined by the goals toward which a person strives. According to Rotter's social learning theory (1954, 1982), variation both in value placed on goals and in expectations for attaining those goals will influence the directional orientation of behavior. We have retained our interest in two goals – achievement and independence – that were the primary focus of this structure in the earlier phase of the research. They have, of course, been modified to reflect young adult life instead of adolescence/youth; that means that, for the goal of achievement, the content is no longer restricted to academic or school achievement and, for the goal of independence, the content is no longer relative only to parents.

In relation to problem behavior, the formulation about these two goals remains the same as it was in the earlier phase: A high value on independence theoretically indicates problem-behavior proneness, and a high value on achievement theoretically indicates conventional-behavior proneness according to the value-instigation hypothesis elaborated in the previous volume (Jessor & Jessor, 1977, chap. 2). The formulation about expectancy-instigation also remains as it was before: A low expectation of attaining either or both of these goals theoretically indicates problem-behavior proneness. Low expectations for goal attainment can instigate alternative, sometimes nonconforming behaviors to attain valued goals or to cope with the anticipation of failure or frustration.

Obviously, goals other than achievement and independence animate young adult life, and we have, in fact, assessed three other goals – affection, dependency, and altruism – for their intrinsic interest at this life stage. The systematic implications of these goals for problem behavior are unclear, however, and for that reason they have been omitted from the framework and its representation in Figure 2.1. This ought not to convey that there are no other goals the values of and expectations for which would contribute instigation to engage in problem behavior. Nor should it imply that values and expectations are the only sources of personality motivation and instigation. We have focused on value- and expectancy-instigation because of their continuity with our earlier work, and on the goals of achievement and independence because of their centrality in young adult life, their amenability to measurement, and their relatively unambiguous role in relation to problem behavior.

Whatever the source of motivation and instigation to problem behavior, whether the latter actually occurs depends not only on the strength of the instigation but also on the existence of controls against engaging in problem behavior. Both of the other two structures in the Personality System function as control structures, one encompassing more distal controls and the other controls that are more proximal. The variables in the Personal Belief Structure represent the more distal controls, and all of them – Social Criticism, Alienation, Self-Esteem, and Internal–External Locus of Control – are variables that were represented in the earlier phase of the research. The acceptance of societal norms, values, and practices implied by low social criticism, and the sense of purpose and meaning in daily roles and of connectedness with others implied by low alienation, both suggest the regulatory influence of belief-controls against problem behavior. With regard to the Self-Esteem variable and the Internal–External Control variable: High self-esteem suggests the presence of a personal stake that could be jeopardized by engaging in problem behavior – that is, there is much to lose; and an internal control orientation accepts the instrumental ideology of conventional society and rejects the view that whatever happens is a matter of luck, fate, or chance. The description of these four variables has stressed the direction of high control against engaging in problem behavior.

The variables in the Personal Control Structure are more proximal and more obvious in their control implications. Two of them, Religiosity and Attitudinal Intolerance of Deviance, were key personal control variables in the previous phase of the study. The latter is an attitudinal variable reflecting the unacceptability (in terms of "wrongness") of a variety of normative and legal transgressions. High *intolerance of wrongdoing* would serve as a direct control against engaging in such behavior. Religiosity is another obvious control; involvement with religion implicates moral concern with transgression and internalization of the perspective of a major conventional institution in society. The third variable in this structure, Moral Attitude, is new to the Young Adult Study. Like the Attitudinal Intolerance of Deviance variable, this one also has to do with the degree of wrongness assigned to various behaviors, but the behaviors included under this concept are ones that often elicit moralistic reactions – for example, getting divorced, having sexual relations outside of marriage, being a heavy drinker, having an abortion, and so forth. A highly moralistic attitude ought to sustain conventional morality and therefore restrain engagement in problem behavior.

Although we have assessed a number of other personality variables to enlarge our understanding of young adulthood and of the correlates of young adult behavior, it is only the 11 variables just described that constitute the systematic representation of personality in Problem-Behavior Theory. These variables, with only one exception, had all been included in the adolescence/youth phase of the study. Their retention in the present phase permits an appraisal of the relative usefulness of the Personality System in accounting for variation in problem behavior in these two important, yet very different, stages of life. The set of variables is large enough to yield a fairly comprehensive mapping of the person, and it is diverse enough to provide a textured sense of significant and enduring values, beliefs, and attitudes.

Organized into instigation and control structures, the variables generate a pattern that, taken together, constitutes *personality system proneness to problem behavior.* That pattern consists, theoretically, of low value on achievement, high value on independence, low expectations for both achievement and independence, high social criticism, high alienation, low self-esteem, high external control, low attitudinal intolerance of deviance, low moral attitude, and low religiosity. The more strongly this pattern of instigations and controls obtains, the greater the likelihood of engaging in problem behavior.

The Perceived Environment System

As indicated earlier, a logical analysis of the nature of environmental influence on behavior makes clear that it is the perceived, or meaningful, or phenomenal environment with which behavior is most invariant (Jessor, 1981; Jessor & Jessor, 1973). The variables in the Perceived Environment System in Figure 2.1 are all, therefore, aspects of the environment as constituted out of experience with it, and they reflect its socially organized dimensions of potential meaning or significance. A focus on the perceived environment, salutary as that decision may be for explanation and prediction, does not, however, automatically yield the differentiation of the environment that is required for the development of variables and measures. The latter task falls to theory. Reliance on Problem-Behavior Theory for the differentiation of the perceived environment resulted in a set of variables, some distal and some proximal, that refer primarily to perceived controls and instigations from significant others in the life space, particularly parents and friends.

The variables that are in the Distal Structure, although they may refer to transgression in general terms, do not *directly* implicate any of the criterion behaviors shown in the Behavior System. Three of the distal variables – Parental Controls, Friends Controls, and Parent vs. Friends Influence – had also been included in the earlier phase of the study. Parental Controls and Friends Controls refer to the perception that these social agents would actively interpose themselves to prevent and to show disapproval of transgression by the actor; a perception of strong parent and friends controls in the social environment would serve to lessen the likelihood of engaging in problem behavior. (Other sources of social control were measured, in addition, including co-worker controls and spouse/partner controls, but they are not included in the framework in order to maintain greater continuity with the earlier study.) The Parent vs. Friends Influence variable also implicates control, in that parental influence can be expected to be more conventional than that of friends. Acknowledgment of greater relative influence of parents in relation to important life decisions would suggest greater control over problem behavior.

A new variable has been added to the Distal Structure of the Perceived Environment System for the current phase of the longitudinal study, the variable of Perceived Life-Area Stress. It represents an effort to capture the degree to which stress is seen to characterize significant arenas of social interaction – family, work, friendships, and sex. In trying to discern the topography of young adult life, we decided that these four domains should be of central significance and that their characterization on a variety of dimensions, including perceived satisfactions as well as perceived stress, could have important bearing on behavior. The selection of perceived stress for systematic incorporation into Problem-Behavior Theory reflects an interpretation of environmental stress as an instigation to problem behavior. The perception of stress in important contexts of living should instigate various kinds of coping behavior including, for example, recourse to alcohol and other drugs, as well as to other problem behaviors. The rationale for this variable in the Perceived Environment System, therefore, is closely allied to that for low expectations for goal attainment in the Personality System; both should instigate alternative behaviors that, not infrequently, might include one or another of the various problem behaviors.

Finally, it should be noted that Parental Support and Friends' Support, two variables included in this structure in the earlier phase, have been omitted. The reasons for this decision were lack of clarity about their conceptual linkage to problem behavior and lack of empirical support for them in the earlier findings.

The three variables in the Proximal Structure of the Perceived Environment System are all more directly linked to problem behavior, with two of them – Friends' Approval of Problem Behavior and Friends Models for Problem Behavior – explicitly referring to the behaviors themselves. Because they are so proximal, these variables should be the two most strongly associated with problem-behavior variation of any of the variables in the personality or perceived environment systems. Little needs to be said about them; they refer to the perception of approval–disapproval among friends for engaging in the various problem behaviors, and the perception that friends themselves are actually engaging in those problem behaviors. The components of these summary measures are perceived approval and perceived models for drinking, for marijuana use, for cigarette smoking, and for use of other illicit drugs (friends models only). Both at the component level and at the composite summary variable level, high perceived approval and high perceived models for problem behavior should result in greater actual involvement in problem behavior. On the other hand, Friends Models for Religiosity should have the opposite effect; the more the perceived involvement of one's friends in religion, the greater the degree of control there should be against problem behavior from the perceived environment.

As in the other major systems of influence, *proneness in the Perceived Environment System* depends upon the balance between instigations and controls within both the distal and the proximal structures. The pattern of perceived environment variables that is most problem-behavior prone in the Distal Structure would consist of low parental controls, low friends controls, greater friends than parent influence, and greater life-area stress; in the Proximal Structure it would entail greater friends' approval and models for problem behavior, and fewer models for religiosity. The more this cluster of perceived environment variables obtains, the more likely the occurrence of problem behavior.

The Social Environment System

The social environment, as distinct from the perceived environment, is constituted of variables that locate individuals in the larger social structure and that characterize the more objective aspects of the context of social interaction and experience in daily life. As with the other systems, the Social Environment System has been differentiated into interrelated structures. The variables in the Socio-Demographic Structure are of particular interest since they include the traditional ones – occupation, education, and income – used to establish socioeconomic status. Insofar as lower socioeconomic status represents a location in the structure of opportunity for societal rewards that is limited or obstructed, it may conduce to greater recourse to problem behavior. With regard to the other variable, Religious Membership, it locates an individual with respect to an institution that can vary from conservative-fundamentalist, on the one hand, to liberal-atheist, on the other. This variation reflects variation in exposure to conventional social control, and it should have clear implications, therefore, for variation in problem behavior.

The variables referring to the Social Context are used primarily for descriptive purposes; they were not formulated in relation to their possible implications for problem behavior. Hypotheses could, of course, be drawn about various aspects of these contexts that might well be of interest to pursue (e.g., occupying a supervisory/executive position at work versus a nonsupervisory one, or marriage versus cohabitation in the family situation, or isolation in the friendship network), but we have not done this systematically. The same is true for Positive–Negative Life Events, occurrences that may well be of importance in shaping life chances and perceptions of self and others. They include both positive and negative life events such as receiving special recognition at work or school, death of a close friend, having a religious conversion, traveling abroad, a major improvement in financial status, moving to a new place to live, and so forth. Here again, our main interest lay in being able to describe the topography of young adult experience and the objective event-context within which life scenarios are played out. Nevertheless, negative life events do constitute a source of stress in the objective social environment and hence they might well instigate coping responses that could include recourse to problem behavior.

Although linkages can be specified among socioeconomic status, religious group membership, and negative life events, on the one hand, and problem behavior, on the other, those linkages are to a large extent dependent upon the meaning or significance those locations or those experiences have for the actor. This is another way of saying that their impact is considered to be mediated, for the most part, by the more proximal systems.

The Social Environment System is conceptually too distal from behavior to play a role equivalent in importance to that of the other explanatory systems, and it clearly occupies a secondary status in Problem-Behavior Theory. The role that it does play is shown schematically in Figure 2.1. It can be seen that the Social Environment System is linked both directly and indirectly to the Behavior System. Inclusion of a direct linkage reflects the possibility that certain aspects of the distal social environment may condition variation in the opportunity to engage in problem behavior; such aspects include the availability of funds to purchase drugs, the prevalence of public drinking contexts, the presence of older sibling models for problem behavior, and so forth. Overall, however, the variables in this system are of interest as much for their descriptive contribution as for their explanatory contribution. The characterization they permit of the social status of the young adult participants in the study and of the context of their lives can be most illuminating. In addition, variables reflecting socioeconomic status are important as analytic controls when hypotheses about other sources of influence are being examined.

Each of the four systems having been discussed, it is now possible to see the entire web of interrelationships posited by Problem-Behavior Theory. Each of the systems is connected to all other systems in a reciprocal fashion, and all of the arrows (but the heavier one) in Figure 2.1 are drawn to be bidirectional. This is even true of the arrows coming from the Social Environment System, unlike the way they were represented in the earlier volume. The reason for this difference is that the social environment in the present phase of the research refers to that of our participants whereas, in the earlier phase, it referred to that of their parents; it was, in that earlier phase, temporally antecedent and remote from the possibility of reciprocal influence or change. By contrast, all of the variables now shown in this system in Figure 2.1 can conceivably be influenced or modified by changes in the other systems.

Despite this characterization of the overall conceptual framework as a nondirectional "web," and despite the use of bidirectional arrows, there is nevertheless an "explanatory directionality" that is implied in the framework. That directionality derives from the fact that our primary interest is in accounting for variation in the Behavior System. It is that interest that structures the causal flow in Figure 2.1 from left to right and from distal to proximal. That interest also is the reason for representing the heavier arrow that links the Personality System and the Perceived Environment System jointly to the Behavior System as a *unidirectional* arrow. The latter expresses our commitment to a field theory account of the occurrence/nonoccurrence of behavior at a given point in time. Such an account relies upon a consideration of the personality and perceived environment variables as psychosocial predictors of, or risk factors for, variation in behavior. That such behavioral variation can influence, in turn, the variables or risk factors in all of the other systems is in no sense precluded; it merely requires the introduction of a time dimension into the conceptual framework, and a shift in explanatory focus. In this report, our emphasis will be largely restricted to exploring the impact of *psychosocial proneness* –

that is, of personality, perceived environment, and behavioral proneness, on variation in problem behavior.

Problem-Behavior Theory and psychosocial development

The discussion thus far has sought to elaborate the logic of Problem-Behavior Theory as a cross-sectional explanatory framework in young adulthood. But because the research we report here is longitudinal in nature, there remains the task of delineating the role of Problem-Behavior Theory in relation to psychosocial *development* from adolescence/youth to young adulthood. That role has a number of different facets some of which have been illustrated in the earlier volume and some of which are unique to the present phase of the research.

Of major significance, but a contribution that is generally downplayed in contemporary research, is simply the *descriptive* information about development that is provided by the successive waves of data on the concepts in the theory. Since the concepts are theoretically important in accounting for significant social behavior, knowledge about developmental change on the measures of those concepts constitutes an important addition to the psychology of development.

Beyond providing a theory-derived description of development, there is another developmental role that Problem-Behavior Theory plays, namely a predictive one. Reliance on the theoretical variables measured in adolescence/youth to predict later outcomes in young adulthood reveals whether the theory is relevant to an understanding of developmental growth and change during this period of life. If the antecedent theoretical variables can be shown to be successful in predicting later life outcomes, it follows that they must be influential in determining the course of development that has resulted in those outcomes.

A third facet of the developmental role played by Problem-Behavior Theory is its capability for specifying a state of "readiness" for transition. Transitions may refer to changes in behavioral statuses (e.g., virginity to nonvirginity), changes in role statuses (e.g., student to employee), or changes in marital status (e.g., partner to spouse). The degree to which the patterning of its theoretical variables at a given point in time is predictive of developmental transitions provides the basis for claiming further developmental relevance for Problem-Behavior Theory. Indeed, the concept of *transition proneness* is used in Problem-Behavior Theory to characterize that very theoretical pattern.

A final facet of the developmental relevance of Problem-Behavior Theory has to do with the possibility of characterizing the life stage of young adulthood as different from the life stage of adolescence. In our earlier work (Jessor & Jessor, 1977), it became empirically apparent that adolescence was a life stage of *increasing problem-behavior proneness*. However, postadolescent development is generally expected to entail the assumption of greater responsibility; entry into the conventionalizing roles of marriage, work, and childrearing; and a "maturing out" of adolescent problem behavior. Because Problem-Behavior Theory is focused directly on this issue, it will be possible to demonstrate whether, in actual fact, development into young adulthood is in the direction of decreasing problem-behavior proneness, and whether young adulthood can indeed be seen as a life stage of *increasing conventionality*.

In sum, our interest in this research was predicated on its potential contribution to an understanding of psychosocial development as well as to an understanding of cross-sectional behavioral variation. If the theory can provide variables for the description of significant developmental change, if it can predict outcomes in young adulthood from variables measured in adolescence, and if it can specify variation in readiness for transition, it will have demonstrated relevance for the study of psychosocial development into young adulthood. In later chapters, an examination of these several facets will be presented.

Conclusion

In concluding this presentation of Problem-Behavior Theory, it is useful to return to a consideration of the major explanatory concept in the framework – namely, *overall psychosocial proneness for problem behavior*. It will be recalled that this concept is made up of the components of personality system, perceived environment system, and behavior system proneness. Within each of these systems, proneness is the outcome of the balance of instigations and controls. In testing the explanatory adequacy of the concept of psychosocial proneness, we have relied upon an additive combination of all of the instigations and controls in the various systems operating in the theoretically prescribed direction. This model, essentially a systematic, multivariate one, is the one that was examined for its appropriateness to adolescence in the earlier volume. It is the one that will be examined here for its appropriateness to young adulthood.

In addition to testing the concept of psychosocial proneness, however, we intend to explore the relevance of another explanatory formulation, namely the concept of life stress. The concept of stress is a notion widely invoked in attempts to account for problem behavior, and that has led us to add it to the Distal Structure of the Perceived Environment System in our conceptual framework. Measures of stress, although limited, will be employed to enable a separate appraisal of its explanatory utility relative to that of psychosocial proneness as a whole. The present test of Problem-Behavior Theory will entail, therefore, two different explanatory concepts: psychosocial proneness and life stress. Such a theory-testing strategy may be a more satisfying approach than one that examines the usefulness of a single theoretical explanation alone.

References

Beirness, D. J., & Simpson, H. M. (1988). Lifestyle correlates of risky driving and accident involvement among youth. *Alcohol, Drugs and Driving, 4*(3–4), 193–204.

Chassin, L., Presson, C. C., Bensenberg, M., Corty, E., Olshavsky, R. W., & Sherman, S. J. (1981). Predicting adolescents' intentions to smoke cigarettes. *Journal of Health and Social Behavior, 22*, 445–455.

Chassin, L., Presson, C. C., & Sherman, S. J. (1984). Cigarette smoking and adolescent psychosocial development. *Basic and Applied Social Psychology, 5*, 295–315.

Costa, F., Jessor, R., & Donovan, J. E. (1989). Value on health and adolescent conventionality: A construct validation of a new measure in problem-behavior theory. *Journal of Applied Social Psychology, 19*(10), 841–861.

DiTecco, D., & Schlegel, R. P. (1982). Alcohol use among young adult males: An application of problem behavior theory. In J. R. Eiser (Ed.), *Social psychology and behavioral medicine* (pp. 199–233). New York: Wiley.

Donovan, J. E., & Jessor, R. (1978). Adolescent problem drinking: Psychosocial correlates in a national sample study. *Journal of Studies on Alcohol, 39,* 1506–1524.

Donovan, J. E., & Jessor, R. (1983). Problem drinking and the dimension of involvement with drugs: A Guttman scalogram analysis of adolescent drug use. *American Journal of Public Health, 73,* 543–552.

Donovan, J. E., & Jessor, R. (1985). Structure of problem behavior in adolescence and young adulthood. *Journal of Consulting and Clinical Psychology, 53,* 890–904.

Donovan, J. E., Jessor, R., & Costa, F. (1988). The syndrome of problem behavior in adolescence: A replication. *Journal of Consulting and Clinical Psychology, 56,* 762–765.

Donovan, J. E., Jessor, R., & Costa, F. (1991). Adolescent health behavior and conventionality–unconventionality: An extension of Problem-Behavior Theory. *Health Psychology, 10,* 52–61.

Gerber, R. W., & Newman, I. M. (1989). Predicting future smoking of adolescent experimental smokers. *Journal of Youth and Adolescence, 18,* 191–201.

Hays, R. D., Stacy, A. W., & DiMatteo, M. R. (1987). Problem behavior theory and adolescent alcohol use. *Addictive Behaviors, 12,* 189–193.

Jessor, R. (1981). The perceived environment in psychological theory and research. In D. Magnusson (Ed.), *Toward a psychology of situations: An interactional perspective* (pp. 297–317). Hillsdale, NJ: Erlbaum.

Jessor R. (1984). Adolescent development and behavioral health. In J. D. Matarazzo, S. M. Weiss, J. A. Herd, N. E. Miller, & S. M. Weiss (Eds.), *Behavioral health: A handbook of health enhancement and disease prevention* (pp. 69–90). New York: Wiley.

Jessor, R., Chase, J. A., & Donovan, J. E. (1980). Psychosocial correlates of marijuana use and problem drinking in a national sample of adolescents. *American Journal of Public Health, 70,* 604–613.

Jessor, R., Donovan, J. E., & Widmer, K. (1980). *Psychosocial factors in adolescent alcohol and drug use: The 1978 national sample study and the 1974–78 panel study* (pp. 1–167). Boulder: Institute of Behavioral Science, University of Colorado.

Jessor, R., Graves, T. D., Hanson, R. C., & Jessor, S. L. (1968). *Society, personality, and deviant behavior: A study of a tri-ethnic community.* New York: Holt, Rinehart, & Winston. (Reprinted by Kreiger Publishing Company, Melbourne, FL.)

Jessor, R., & Jessor, S. L. (1973). The perceived environment in behavioral science: Some conceptual issues and some illustrative data. *American Behavioral Scientist, 16,* 801–828.

Jessor, R., & Jessor, S. L. (1977). *Problem behavior and psychosocial development: A longitudinal study of youth.* New York: Academic Press.

Lewin, K. (1951). *Field theory in social science: Selected theoretical papers.* New York: Harper & Row.

Magnusson, D. (Ed.). (1981). *Toward a psychology of situations: An interactional perspective.* Hillsdale, NJ: Erlbaum.

Magnusson, D., & Allen, V. L. (Eds.). (1983). *Human development: An interactional perspective.* New York: Academic Press.

Magnusson, D., & Endler, N. S. (Eds.). (1977). *Personality at the crossroads: Current issues in interactional psychology.* Hillsdale, NJ: Erlbaum.

Markle, G. E., & Troyer, R. J. (1979). Smoke gets in your eyes: Cigarette smoking as deviant behavior. *Social Problems, 26,* 611–625.

Merton, R. K. (1957). *Social theory and social structure* (rev. ed.). New York: Free Press.

Robinson, T. H., Killen, J. D., Taylor, C. B., Telch, M. J., Bryson, S. W., Saylor, K. E., Maron, D. J., Maccoby, N., & Farquhar, J. W. (1987). Perspectives on adolescent substance use: A defined population study. *Journal of the American Medical Association, 258,* 2072–2076.

Rooney, J. F., & Wright, T. L. (1982). An extension of Jessor and Jessor's Problem-Behavior Theory from marijuana to cigarette use. *The International Journal of the Addictions, 17,* 1273–1287.

Rotter, J. B. (1954). *Social learning and clinical psychology.* New York: Prentice-Hall.

Rotter, J. B. (1982). *The development and application of social learning theory: Selected papers.* New York: Praeger.

Sadava, S. W. (1985). Problem-Behavior Theory and consumption and consequences of alcohol use. *Journal of Studies on Alcohol, 46,* 392–397.

Sadava, S. W., & Forsyth, R. (1977). Person–environment interaction and college student drug use: A multivariate longitudinal study. *Genetic Psychology Monographs, 96,* 211–245.

Smith, M. B., Canter, W. A., & Robin, A. L. (1989). A path analysis of an adolescent drinking behavior model derived from Problem-Behavior Theory. *Journal of Studies on Alcohol, 50,* 128–142.

Vulcano, B. A., Barnes, G. E., & Langstaff, P. (1990). Predicting marijuana use among adolescents. *The International Journal of the Addictions, 25*(5), 531–544.

Wilson, R. J., & Jonah, B. A. (1988). The application of Problem-Behavior Theory to the understanding of risky driving. *Alcohol, Drugs and Driving, 4*(3–4), 173–191.

3

Following up lives

This book reports the second phase of an ongoing, long-term, prospective longitudinal study that followed the lives of two samples – one of junior high school students, and the other of college freshmen – over an extended period of time, from the late 1960s and early 1970s into the early 1980s. During that time, repeated assessments were made of personality, social, and behavioral aspects of development from adolescence/youth into young adulthood.

For both samples, data were collected at six different times over an 11- or 12-year period. The first four data collections were carried out on an annual basis *within* the life stage of adolescence or youth; results from that initial phase of the overall longitudinal study were reported in Jessor and Jessor (1977). The fifth and sixth data collections were carried out in the later phase of the longitudinal study which took place *within* the life stage of young adulthood.

In this chapter, we describe the design of the overall study, the samples involved in the second phase of the study, and the comprehensive questionnaire that was developed for use with participants who had become young adults.

Overall design of the study

The design of the two, parallel, six-wave longitudinal studies of the High School and College samples is shown in Figure 3.1 and 3.2, respectively. As may be seen, the High School Study is based on a cohort-sequential longitudinal design, whereas the College Study is based on a simple longitudinal design. Since detailed information on the adolescent/youth phase of the research has been presented else-

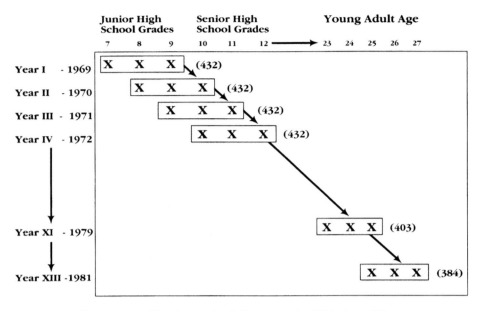

Figure 3.1.   The longitudinal design for the High School Study.

where (Jessor & Jessor, 1977, 1984), the present description will be brief.

The High School Study was initiated in 1969. A random sample of students, stratified by grade and gender, was drawn from the enrollment lists of three junior high schools in a single school district that served a small city (population around 70,000) and several surrounding communities located in a central Rocky Mountain state. A total of 1,126 students in grades 7, 8, and 9 were selected. Letters were sent to the parents of these students describing the research and asking permission for their children to participate in a study of adolescent development. Of the 1,126 parents contacted, 668 (59% of the designated sample) provided permission. Of the 668 students who received parental permission, 589 (52% of the original sample, and 88% of those with parental consent) completed self-administered questionnaires, after school hours, in the spring of 1969, Year I of the study. Each spring for the subsequent three years, these cohorts of students were recontacted to take part in the annual data collection

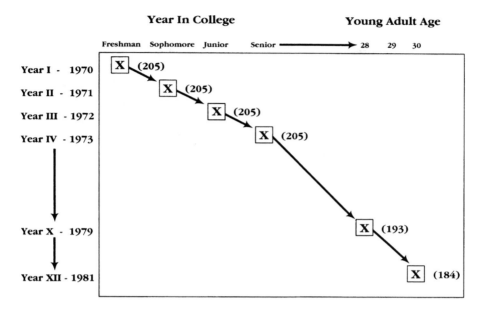

Figure 3.2. The longitudinal design for the College Study.

sessions. In Years II through IV, it was possible to carry out the testing during school hours. By 1972, Year IV of the High School Study, 483 students were still in the study, representing a retention rate of 82 percent across the study period. Of these, 432 students had completed questionnaires at all four data collections between 1969, when they were all junior high school students (grades 7 through 9), and 1972, when they were all in senior high school (grades 10 through 12). These 432 adolescents (188 boys and 244 girls) were designated as the core developmental sample, and the results reported in Jessor and Jessor (1977) were based on them. These same 432 former core participants were recontacted in 1979 and asked to take part in the young adult phase of the continuing longitudinal research.

The first phase of the College Study was initiated in 1970, a year later than the High School Study. A random sample of 497 freshman students was drawn from the enrollment list of the College of Arts and Sciences at a major university located in the same Rocky Mountain city. When contacted by letter and asked to participate in the research over the next four years, 462 of the students were still enrolled in school. A total of 276 of them (60%) participated in the Year I data collection which was carried out in small group sessions on campus in the spring of 1970. By the end of the Year IV testing in 1973, 226 students (representing a retention rate of 82%) were still in the study; at that time, almost all participants were seniors at the university, although a few had graduated or enrolled at other colleges, and some had dropped out of school entirely. Of these 226, 205 had taken part in all four of the annual testing sessions between 1970 and 1973. These 92 men and 113 women were designated as the core developmental sample in the College Study (see Jessor & Jessor, 1977). This same core sample of 205 participants was recontacted in 1979 to participate in the young adult phase of the research.

Relocating earlier participants for the Young Adult Follow-Up

The goal of the second or young adult phase of the research was to recontact the 637 former participants from the first phase of the study – 432 high school students, 205 college students – and to collect two further waves of longitudinal data on them as young adults. One wave of data was collected in 1979; the second wave was collected two years later in 1981. At the time of the 1979 testing, the former participants in the High School Study were between 23 and 25 years old, and the former participants in the College Study were about 28 years old.

The process of locating the 637 former participants in the High School Study and the College Study began in the fall of 1978 and was unusually successful, with all but one person located or accounted for after several months of intensive effort.

The High School Study location process

The general strategy employed with the High School Study sample was to concentrate first on obtaining current addresses for their parents, and then to contact the parents for the current addresses of the former participants. This approach assumed that participants' parents would have been less mobile over the intervening seven-year period and therefore would be easier to locate than the participants themselves.

The first step in the location process, a search that involved local telephone directories as well as the use of long-distance directory assistance, yielded addresses for 310 (or 72%) of the parents of the 432 High School Study participants.

Various methods were used to locate the remaining 122 former High School Study participants or their families. The most productive of these involved the use of privately compiled city directories (such as the Polk City Directory) which provided either addresses or clues that enabled us to locate an additional 43 of the former participants or their parents. Searches of publicly available county records, such as marriage license records, voter registration records, and motor vehicle registration lists, accounted for the location of another 33 former participants or their parents. Locating the remaining former participants required a good deal of "detective" work: telephone calls to parents' former employers, co-workers, and neighbors; to local people with the same surname; to churches; to real estate agents; and to former classmates of the participants. Leads were also provided by such sources as the clippings library of a local newspaper, high school records, college alumni files, the Armed Forces World-Wide Locator Service, and out-of-town post offices, city halls, utility companies, and libraries.

In May of 1979, letters were mailed to parents reminding them of their son's or daughter's earlier participation in our longitudinal study and of their child's agreement, in 1972, to be recontacted "even ten years from now." The letters asked parents to provide us with a current address for their son or daughter, and a self-addressed, business-reply postcard was enclosed to facilitate their reply. Where parents could not be reached, other sources, as detailed above, were used to discover a direct address for former participants. Within a relatively short time, addresses were available for 430 of the 432 former participants in the first phase of the High School Study. (Two of the 432 former participants, one man and one woman, both from the original 7th-grade cohort, had died in the seven-year interval between the 1972 data collection and the 1979 data collection.)

The College Study location process

The search process in the College sample also began in the fall of 1978. It focused on the former participants themselves rather than on their parents, and relied initially upon records available in the university's alumni office. Of the 205 former participants in the College Study, current addresses were available there for 117 (or 57%) of them. Use of local telephone directories and of long-distance directory assistance resulted in the location of addresses for another 61 former participants or their parents. After using just these two methods, addresses were in hand for 178 (or 87%) of the College Study sample or their parents.

Locating the remaining 13 percent of the sample was rather more difficult, however. The location process for these former college participants involved a search of the records available through the university's transcript records office, as well as the use of many of the same procedures relied upon in locating the High School Study sample.

As in the High School Study, letters were mailed in early May of 1979 to the parents of all those former participants for whom we had no direct address. Telephone calls and certified letters to the parents were also used to elicit addresses for the former participants. All but one of the 205 young adults who had participated in the initial phase of the College Study were eventually located by these procedures, and addresses were available for 203 of them. (One young woman had died in the interim between the 1973 testing and the resumption of the study in 1979.)

Contacting and testing the young adult participants

All of the former participants were recontacted by letter and reminded of the earlier phase of the study and of their expressed willingness at that time to be recontacted later on. The letter described the focus of the young adult phase of the research and asked them to resume the study with us. A self-addressed, business-reply postcard was included so they could indicate consent and provide us an address for mailing them the Young Adult Follow-Up Study Questionnaire.

Consent postcards were eventually returned by all but 12 (7 men,

5 women) of the 430 former participants in the High School Study (a return rate of 97%), and by all but 2 of the 203 young adults who had participated in the initial phase of the College Study (99%).

Questionnaire packets were mailed to each potential participant as we received the consent postcards. Each packet contained a Young Adult Follow-Up Study Questionnaire, a $10 bill as a token payment, a business-reply return envelope, and a consent form. The consent form was to be signed and returned in a separate envelope from the one used to return the completed questionnaire. Since questionnaires were identified only by special identification numbers, this procedure ensured that no one could discover who had filled in the questionnaire.

Follow-up letters, persistent local and long-distance telephoning, and even personal visits to the homes of participants living in the local area, yielded a high level of renewed participation in the Young Adult Follow-Up Study. Of the 634 participants from the initial phase of the research who were available in 1979 (3 having died), 596 resumed participation. The overall rate of retention was, therefore, 94 percent. Usable questionnaires were received from all but one of these 596 participants.

Table 3.1 presents information on participation broken down by gender, by gender within sample, and, within the High School Study sample, by grade cohort. With regard to the 1979 testing, 93 percent of the male former participants and 95 percent of the female former participants completed questionnaires. Overall, 403 (94%) of the 430 former High School Study participants, and 192 (94%) of the 204 former College Study participants took part in the 1979 testing. In the High School Study sample, 92 percent of the men and 95 percent of the women completed questionnaires in 1979. In the College Study sample, 95 percent of the men and 94 percent of the women participated in 1979.

The 1981 testing

In February of 1981, letters were sent to all 595 young adults who had completed usable questionnaires for the 1979 testing. This letter served to reestablish contact, to let participants know how many of them had taken part in the previous testing, to provide some descriptive informational feedback from the 1979 testing, and to alert them

Table 3.1. *Participation in Wave V (1979) and Wave VI (1981) of the Young Adult Follow-Up Study, by gender and sample (and by grade cohort in High School sample)*

	1979 testing		1981 testing		6-Wave sample	
	N available in 1979[a]	N(%) tested in 1979	N available in 1981[b]	N(%) tested in 1981	N available in both 1979 and 1981[c]	N(%) tested in both 1979 and 1981
High School sample						
Men						
7th-grade cohort	74	66 (89)	66	60 (92)	73	60 (82)
8th-grade cohort	60	54 (90)	54	53 (98)	60	53 (88)
9th-grade cohort	53	52 (98)	52	49 (94)	53	49 (92)
Total	187	172 (92)	171	162 (95)	186	162 (87)
Women						
7th-grade cohort	95	87 (92)	87	81 (93)	95	81 (85)
8th-grade cohort	82	80 (98)	80	77 (96)	82	77 (94)
9th-grade cohort	66	64 (97)	64	64 (100)	66	64 (97)
Total	243	231 (95)	231	222 (96)	243	222 (91)
Combined Total	430	403 (94)	402	384 (96)	429	384 (90)

College sample						
Men	92	87 (95)	86	84 (98)	91	84 (92)
Women	112	105 (94)	105	100 (95)	112	100 (89)
Combined	204	192 (94)	191	184 (96)	203	184 (91)
Combined samples						
Men	279	259 (93)	257	246 (96)	277	246 (89)
Women	355	336 (95)	336	322 (96)	355	322 (91)
Total	634	595 (94)	593	568 (96)	632	568 (90)

[a]Three former participants had died between 1972/73 and 1979: one 7th-grade cohort woman, one 7th-grade cohort man, and one College sample woman.

[b]Only 1979 participants were contacted again in 1981. One 7th-grade cohort man and one College sample man tested in 1979 died before the 1981 testing.

[c]These *N*s exclude only the 5 former participants whom we know to have died between 1972/73 and 1981. Some of the 38 former participants not tested in 1979, and hence not followed up, might also have died between 1979 and 1981.

to the imminent mailing of the 1981 version of the Young Adult Follow-Up Study Questionnaire. Some further detective work was required to locate some of these young adults, but this was minimal owing to the availability of participant and parent addresses that were less than two years old. Questionnaire packets were again mailed all over the world, including Germany, France, Italy, Japan, and Australia.

Through the use of several reminder letters and through an extensive series of long-distance telephone calls, we were able ultimately to elicit returned questionnaires from 568 of the 593 young adults who had taken part in the 1979 data collection and were still available (two more had died between 1979 and 1981). This represents a retention rate of 96 percent *within* the young adult phase of the research (see the middle set of columns in Table 3.1), and this same retention rate was achieved for both the High School Study (384 of 402) and for the College Study (184 of 191). It is this group of 568 young adults, tested four times as high school or college students and twice as young adults, upon whom the analyses reported in succeeding chapters of this book are based.

In summary, the present data are from two parallel six-wave, longitudinal studies, one that followed 384 junior high school students into their middle and late twenties and one that followed 184 college freshman students to the age of thirty. With these data, it becomes possible to examine the personality, social, and behavioral correlates of problem behavior within young adulthood, to describe change and development on these personality, social, and behavior variables, both within young adulthood and between adolescence and young adulthood, and to examine the young adult outcomes of adolescent involvement in problem behavior.

Description of the two six-wave longitudinal samples of young adults

The 568 young adults who had participated in all six data collection waves over the eleven or twelve years of the study from 1969/70 to 1981 represent 90 percent of the adolescents/youth who had taken part in the four annual testing sessions in the earlier phase of the study. As may be seen in the third set of columns in Table 3.1, the

384 members of the six-wave panel in the High School Study comprise 90 percent of those who could have participated all six years, whereas the 184 members of the six-wave panel in the College Study comprise 91 percent of those who could have participated all six years.

Within the six-wave High School Study sample, the 162 men and 222 women represent 87 percent of the men and 91 percent of the women who were contacted to participate in the follow-up study of young adults. Within the six-wave College Study sample, the 84 men and 100 women represent 92 percent and 89 percent, respectively, of those contacted to take part in the young adult phase of the continuing longitudinal project. These four gender-by-study groups constitute the core developmental samples for the young adult analyses.

At the time of the second young adult data collection in 1981, the average age of the High School Study sample men was 26.1 years old, which was also the average age of the High School Study sample women; within the gender-by-grade cohorts, the mean ages were 25.3 and 25.2 years old for the original 7th-grade males and females, respectively, 26.0 and 26.2 years old for the original 8th-grade males and females, respectively, and 27.2 and 27.1 years of age, respectively, for the original 9th-grade males and females. The average age of the College Study sample men in 1981 was 30.2 years old, and the average age of the College Study sample women was 30.1 years old.

With respect to the ethnic distribution of the six-wave samples, all four gender-by-study groups were predominantly white or Anglo. In the High School Study sample, 91 percent of the men and 89 percent of the women were Anglo, 3 percent of the men and 4 percent of the women were Hispanic, and 3 percent of both groups were Native American. Approximately 3 percent of each gender failed to specify ethnic background. In the College Study sample, 98 percent of the men and 95 percent of the women were Anglo, 1 percent of the men and 3 percent of the women were Hispanic, 1 percent of the men were Asian American, and, in the female sample, 1 percent were black and 1 percent were Native American.

Both the High School Study sample and the College Study sample came from mainly middle-class socioeconomic backgrounds. According to family background information supplied in the first year of the study (1969/1970), 59 percent of the High School Study sample men and 55 percent of the High School Study sample women had fathers who had graduated from college or who had had some post-graduate education; 26 percent of the High School Study sample men and 25 percent of the High School Study sample women reported that their fathers had only a high school education or less. The educational attainment level of parents of the young adults in the College Study sample was similar: Fifty-one percent of the College Study sample men and 61 percent of the College Study sample women reported that their fathers had graduated from college or had had some postgraduate education; and 24 percent of the College Study sample men and 15 percent of the College Study sample women reported that their fathers had only a high school education or less. With respect to the occupational status of jobs held by their parents, the majority of the fathers of the young adults in both samples had positions that could be classified as managerial or professional–executive positions (on Hollingshead's Index of Social Position). Within the High School Study sample, this was true of the fathers of 69 percent of the men and 63 percent of the women; within the College Study sample, this was true of the fathers of 77 percent of the men and 85 percent of the women in the six-wave samples.

Whereas the six-wave samples were composed largely of Anglo young adults from middle-class backgrounds, it should be mentioned that the character of the High School Study sample reflects the community from which it was drawn. The local school district serves a community that is the site of a major university with a national reputation for its research, as well as the site of a number of government and private industry laboratories and high-technology businesses. Similarly, the make-up of the College Study sample is consonant with other samples drawn from college student populations in the Rocky Mountain west.

Attrition and bias in the Young Adult Follow-Up Study samples

To establish whether the participants who continued in the study over time differed in any systematic manner from participants whose involvement was less consistent, we undertook several analyses. Given the focus of the research on problem behavior, it was especially important to determine whether the respondents who dropped out of the study were less conventional than the respondents who continued in the research.

In the earlier book on the adolescent phase of the research (Jessor & Jessor, 1977, pp. 46–47, 51), we examined the extent to which attrition across the four years of that phase of the study could have resulted in the retention of a core four-year sample of participants that was biased because of the loss of the adolescents who had dropped out of the study. In both the High School Study and the College Study, members of the core four-year sample were compared with two other groups – those who had taken part in the study for three of the four years, and those who had participated for only one or two years – on about two dozen measures of demographic, personality, social, and behavior variables that had been assessed in the first year of each study (1969 for the High School Study, 1970 for the College Study). Relatively few differences among these groups emerged in either study.

The effect of attrition over the time period between the adolescent phase of the research and the present young adult phase was also examined. Each gender-by-study group within the six-wave sample was compared on Year IV (1972/1973) data with those who chose not to participate as young adults. There were few significant differences overall, fewer than expected by chance. Only 8 of 124 comparisons of means showed differences large enough to reach statistical significance at the .05 probability level. (Six of these eight significant differences occurred in just one of the gender-by-study subsamples, the High School Study sample women.) Even when mean differences that were nonsignificant were considered, few additional comparisons, perhaps 15 or so, indicated any sizable differences between the two groups. Where the two groups did differ, however, the six-wave samples had scores that were consistent in indicating somewhat greater conventionality. The mean differences were small, however, in comparison to the variances on the measures. In no case did the group differences account for more than just 3 percent of the variance on the measures (as determined by calculating correlation ratios).

These analyses suggest that, overall, the six-wave longitudinal samples were not significantly more conventional – as a result of attrition since the first phase of the research, that is, after 1972/73 – than they might have been had the attrition not occurred.

Generality of earlier findings

Since neither of our longitudinal samples is large or representative of the population from which it was originally drawn, the generality of our earlier findings – their robustness as a basis for inference – had to be established by replication. A major source of confidence in the generality of the earlier findings derives from two national sample survey studies carried out by the Research Triangle Institute in 1974 and 1978 (Rachal et al., 1975, 1980). Both nationwide surveys used Problem-Behavior Theory as part of their conceptual background, and both included abridged versions of a large number of our theoretically derived measures in their questionnaires. The 1974 National Study of Adolescent Drinking surveyed 13,122 adolescents in grades 7 through 12 across the 48 contiguous states and the District of Columbia; the 1978 National Study surveyed 4,918 adolescents in grades 10 through 12 across the country. Both studies employed multistage, stratified random sampling techniques in order to include adolescents from all areas of the country, from areas with lesser and greater density of population, and from different racial and ethnic backgrounds. Also included in the 1978 study was a longitudinal panel of 839 11th- and 12th-grade students who had participated in the earlier 1974 National Study when they were in the 7th or 8th grade.

Analyses of the data from these two, independent national samples of adolescents have provided strong replications of our earlier findings based on the core four-year High School Study sample (see Donovan & Jessor, 1978, 1985; Jessor, Chase, & Donovan, 1980; Jessor, Donovan, & Widmer, 1980). Despite the far greater socioeconomic and racial/ethnic heterogeneity of the 1974 and 1978 national samples, findings were very similar to those based on our local community sample.

Not only were the same psychosocial variables correlated with the measures of problem behavior in our High School sample data and in both national samples, but also there was similarity in the actual values of the correlation coefficients in these different data sets. To cite just a few examples of this consonance at the bivariate level, intolerance of deviance correlated with involvement with marijuana $-.41$ for the High School Study males in 1972, $-.38$ for the 1974 National Study males, and $-.39$ for the 1978 National Study males;

analogous correlations of − .40, − .41, and − .43 were obtained for the females in these three samples, respectively. Expectations for academic achievement correlated with frequency of self-reported deviant behavior − .28 for the High School Study males in 1972, − .24 for the 1974 National Study males, and − .27 for the 1978 National Study males, while the analogous correlations for the three female samples were − .29, − .21, and − .28, respectively.

Results based on the core High School Study sample were also replicated at the multivariate level in the two national samples. Multiple correlation coefficients from regression analyses predicting variation in involvement in the different problem behaviors were very similar in magnitude across these different samples of adolescents.

Analyses based on the 1974–78 longitudinal panel subsample in the national sample data similarly replicated findings based on panel data from the core four-year High School Study sample. In both studies, similar results were obtained in predicting the time of onset of drinking from antecedent variation on personality and social variables, and in describing developmental change over time in personality and social environment attributes (see Jessor, Donovan, & Widmer, 1980, chap. 4).

Increased confidence in generality and robustness derives also from the findings of a number of other independent investigators who have replicated some of our earlier research findings. In a series of national surveys of high school seniors carried out between 1975 and 1979, Bachman, Johnston, and O'Malley (1981) found correlations among the behaviors of alcohol use, cigarette use, marijuana use, and other illicit drug use similar to ours, and also found, as we had, that religious commitment and liberal political attitudes (analogous to our measures of religiosity and social criticism) were important predictors of involvement with each of these categories of drugs. McLaughlin, Baer, Burnside, and Pokorny (1985) found attitudinal intolerance of deviance to be a major predictor of adolescent alcohol use, as we did, in two independent samples of adolescents. Brook, Lukoff, and Whiteman (1977) used our scales of intolerance of deviance, expectations for affection (they called it "friend expectations"), and parent–peer influence, and found correlations with adolescent drug use similar to ours. DiTecco and Schlegel (1982) found the social environment measures of Problem-Behavior Theory to distinguish between non-drinkers and moderate drinkers, and the personality measures to distinguish between moderate drinkers and excessive drinkers. Chassin, Presson, Sherman, Corty, and Olshavsky (1984) found that 17 of our (abridged) measures of personality and the perceived environment (all distal from cigarette smoking) provided a significant account of the transitions from never smoker to trier and from trier to regular smoker in their own longitudinal study.

In summary, there is considerable evidence that the findings from the first phase of the present research are similar to results found in other research based on samples with much greater sociodemographic heterogeneity and representativeness. Such robustness of results provides increased confidence that inferences based on analyses of these young adult data should have a similar degree of generality despite the initial unrepresentativeness of our longitudinal samples.

The design of the Young Adult Follow-Up Study Questionnaire

In both the 1979 and the 1981 data collections, a self-administered questionnaire was mailed to all of the participating young adults. The 1979 Young Adult Questionnaire was 65 pages long. The 1981 Young Adult Questionnaire, 49 pages long, was printed so that it could be optically scanned and scored by computer. In both years, the questionnaire required an average of approximately two and a half hours to complete.

As had been the case in each of the four previous data collections, the questionnaire consisted of a number of psychometrically developed measures designed to assess the Personality, Perceived Environment, and Behavior System variables of Problem-Behavior Theory. The majority of the measures included were highly comparable to the measures used in the earlier phase of the study. The multiple-item measures were either identical to the adolescent versions or revised slightly to be more appropriate for use with young adults.

Questions were organized in the booklet into sections having to do with several different life areas of importance in young adulthood – family, work, friendships, leisure, and sexual relations – and sections having to do with behavioral areas of interest – alcohol use, cigarette smoking, marijuana use, other illicit drug use, general deviant behavior, religious behavior, political activity, and health-related behavior. Interspersed between these larger topical sections were measures assessing a variety of psychosocial variables, life events, and sociodemographic characteristics. Sections were arranged within the questionnaire in a way that was designed to facilitate the development of rapport with the participants. Questions asking about sensitive behavioral areas, such as alcohol use, drug use, and sexual relationships, were placed toward the end of the questionnaire, whereas questions inquiring about less sensitive topics, such as political behavior, sex-role attitudes, and friendship, were placed early in the questionnaire. The questionnaire was further organized internally by the fact that a core set of variables was assessed in each of the different life areas. Within each life area, questions were asked about current satisfactions and stresses, perceived emotional supports, perceived social approval–disapproval for norm or legal violations, and perceived freedom of movement toward long-term goals. Additional questions specifically tailored to each life area were also asked.

Similarly, sections dealing with the various behavior areas – for example, alcohol use, drug use, or cigarette smoking – also shared a common architecture; a core set of measures describing variation in involvement, contexts of use, perceived functions, negative consequences, self-definitions, and social supports were used for each behavior.

Since almost all of the measures included in the 1979 and the 1981 Young Adult Questionnaires were identical, the present description of the measures will focus on the 1981 version of each measure. Information on the psychometric properties of the measures is shown in Table 3.2, in the following section.

Measures of Personality System variables

Eleven different measures of variables from the Personality System were included in the 1981 questionnaire.

Four measures were from the Motivational-Instigation Structure: Value on Achievement, Value on Independence, Expectation for Achievement, and Expectation for Independence. Each of these measures consisted of three items. *Value on Achievement* was assessed by questions asking, "How important is it to you" – "To know that other people respect you for how well you accomplish things?" "To know that people you respect also have a high opinion of you?" and "To be seen as a success in whatever kind of work you do?" Response categories ranged from "not important at all" to "very important." Higher scores indicate a higher value on recognition for achievement. *Value on Independence* was assessed by items asking about the personal importance placed on "saying what you think, even if other people may not agree with you," on "working out your own solution to a problem rather than turning to someone else for help," and on "deciding for yourself how to run your own life." Higher scores reflect a greater personal value on independence. *Expectation for Achievement* was measured by ratings of the subjective probability of attaining the goal of being recognized for achievement. It was assessed by use of the same three referents as were used in measuring value on achievement, but the expectation questions had to do with "how sure" the respondent was that each of the referent goals would occur (e.g., "that you will be seen as a success in whatever kind of work you do"). Response options ranged from "not sure at all" to "very sure." Higher scores indicate greater certainty of being recognized for achievement. *Expectation for Independence* was assessed in a similar manner, using the same three referents that were used to measure value on independence (e.g., "How sure are you that you will be able to come up with your own solution to problems without having to turn to others?"). Higher scores indicate greater subjective certainty of attaining the goal of independence.

Four variables were assessed within the Personal Belief Structure. These were Social Criticism, Alienation, Self-Esteem, and Internal–External Locus of Control. *Social Criticism* was a seven-item scale assessing level of agreement (from strongly agree to strongly disagree) with a series of statements either supportive or critical of American institutions and policies (e.g., "So much money is being spent on defense that a lot of important social programs are being neglected," and "We're all paying too heavy a cost because of the emphasis on success and getting ahead in our society"). Responses were scored so that higher scores reflect a more critical attitude toward American society. *Alienation* was an eight-item Likert scale assessing the extent to which respondents felt socially isolated from others, uncertain about themselves, and uninvolved in meaningful social roles. Illustrative items include the following: "I sometimes feel uncertain about who I really am"; "I often find it difficult to feel involved in the things I'm doing"; and "I often feel left out of things that others are doing." Higher scores indicate greater alienation. *Self-Esteem* was a nine-item composite measure assessing the degree to which respondents rated themselves highly on a variety of self-attributes (getting along well with others, ability to handle disappointments, interestingness to others, common sense, self-reliance, ability to handle important decisions, and ease of establishing relationships with others) that they also ranked as being important to their overall self-esteem. *Internal– External Locus of Control* was an eight-item Likert-type scale measuring the extent to which respondents saw themselves as responsible for the things – both good and bad – that happened to them versus the extent to which they saw luck or fate as determining those outcomes. Selected questions included the following: "Most of the problems I face are due to things that are beyond my control"; "Most of the time what happens to me is my own doing rather than fate or chance"; and "If you look at most people who have made a success of their lives, it's because of some lucky break rather than their own hard work." Higher scores indicate a greater belief in internal control of reinforcement.

Three measures were employed in assessment of the Personal Control Structure: Attitudinal Intolerance of Deviance, Moral Attitude, and Religiosity. *Attitudinal Intolerance of Deviance* was a 12-item scale assessing the rated "wrongness" of a variety of socially disapproved or delinquent behaviors, including damaging public or private property, shoplifting, lying on applications, starting a fight, and writing bad checks on purpose. Each behavior was rated from "not wrong" to "very wrong" on a nine-point scale. Higher scores reflect greater *in*tolerance of these socially disapproved behaviors. *Moral Attitude*, a seven-item scale, assessed how wrong it is to drive under the influence of alcohol, to engage in extramarital sexual relations, to have an abortion, or to engage in other, similar behaviors. Higher scores reflect stronger moral judgment against involvement in these behaviors. Finally, *Religiosity*, a nine-item scale, measured the importance placed on religious beliefs, teachings, and counsel for the direction of daily life. Selected items include: "How important is it to you to be able to turn to prayer when you're facing a personal problem?" "How important is it to you to believe in God?" and "How important is it to you to rely on your religious beliefs as a guide for day-to-day living?" Higher scores reflect greater religiosity.

Each of these summative, multiple-item measures of Personality System variables was evaluated for its psychometric adequacy by calculating two different indexes: Cronbach's (1951) *alpha*, an estimate of reliability based on the interitem consistency of responses; and Scott's (1960, 1968) *Homogeneity Ratio* (HR), a measure of the weighted-average interitem correlation among the components of each scale. These scale properties are presented in Table 3.2 for each of the Personality System measures and for each of the four 6-wave gender-by-study subsamples.

As may be seen, the scale properties of all but one of these measures are satisfactory. Within the Motivational-Instigation Structure, the measure of Value on Independence demonstrated less than satisfactory levels of interitem consistency in three of the four subsamples. The measure was retained, however, in order to maintain the theoretical symmetry within the structure of values and expectations for the two goals of achievement and independence.

Measures of Perceived Environment System variables

Seven different measures of variables from the Perceived Environment System were included in the 1981 questionnaire.

Four variables were from the Distal Structure of the Perceived Environment System: Parental Controls, Friends Controls, Parent vs. Friends Influence, and Perceived Life-Area Stress. *Parental Controls* consisted of a single question that asked respondents whether their parents would try to influence their behavior if the respondent "were going to do something illegal or that most people would think of as wrong." Response options ranged from "definitely would not" to "definitely would." Higher scores reflect a greater perceived likelihood of parental attempts to exert control. *Friends Controls* was a two-item scale that was concerned not only with the likelihood that friends would try to influence them if they were going to do something illegal, but also with the level of approval or disapproval friends showed if the respondent actually did something most people would think

Table 3.2. *Scale properties for the multiple-item measures of the Personality System and Perceived Environment System variables, based on 1981 young adult data*

1981 measures	Number of items	Scale range	High School Study				College Study			
			Men (N = 162)		Women (N = 222)		Men (N = 84)		Women (N = 100)	
			Alpha[a]	HR[b]	Alpha	HR	Alpha	HR	Alpha	HR
Personality System measures										
Motivational-Instigation Structure										
Value on Achievement	3	3–12	.79	.56	.66	.40	.80	.58	.71	.45
Value on Independence	3	3–12	.39	.18	.48	.23	.65	.38	.48	.24
Expectation for Achievement	3	3–12	.78	.55	.82	.62	.83	.62	.71	.46
Expectation for Independence	3	3–12	.58	.32	.63	.36	.62	.35	.64	.37
Personal Belief Structure										
Social Criticism	7	7–28	.70	.26	.77	.33	.80	.37	.77	.32
Alienation	8	8–32	.81	.34	.80	.33	.80	.34	.80	.34
Self-Esteem	9	−54 to 81	.75	.25	.78	.28	.85	.39	.78	.29
Internal–External Locus of Control	8	8–32	.64	.18	.61	.17	.71	.24	.57	.15
Personal Control Structure										
Attitudinal Intolerance of Deviance	12	0–63	.85	.35	.86	.37	.86	.37	.87	.40
Moral Attitude	7	7–28	.79	.37	.77	.36	.77	.33	.76	.33
Religiosity	9	9–36	.94	.65	.95	.68	.93	.62	.95	.67

(continued on next page)

Table 3.2 (*cont.*)

1981 measures	Number of items	Scale range	High School Study Men (N = 162) Alpha[a]	HR[b]	High School Study Women (N = 222) Alpha	HR	College Study Men (N = 84) Alpha	HR	College Study Women (N = 100) Alpha	HR
Perceived Environment System measures										
Distal Structure										
Parental Controls	1	1–4	—	—	—	—	—	—	—	—
Friends Controls	2	2–8	.74	.61	.63	.49	.73	.59	.68	.53
Parent vs. Friends Influence	2	2–6	.79	.65	.67	.51	.76	.61	.65	.48
Perceived Life-Area Stress	5	0–5	.67	.29	.62	.25	.58	.22	.56	.20
Proximal Structure										
Friends' Approval of Problem Behavior	3	−9 to +9	.45	.21	.57	.30	.26	.11	.43	.20
Friends Models for Problem Behavior	3	−9 to +9	.69	.42	.67	.41	.52	.27	.53	.28
Friends Models for Religiosity	1	1–3	—	—	—	—	—	—	—	—

[a] Cronbach's (1951) alpha estimate of reliability, a measure of interitem consistency.
[b] Scott's (1960) Homogeneity Ratio, a measure of the weighted average correlation among the items comprising a scale. Values around .33 are generally considered optimal; higher values reflect redundancy among the scale components.

wrong. Higher scores indicate greater perceived disapproval by friends for socially disapproved behavior. *Parent vs. Friends Influence*, a two-item scale, was concerned with whether respondents valued their parents' or their friends' opinions more when they had "a serious personal or career decision to make," and with the extent to which respondents perceived their parents or their friends as having had greater impact on their present outlook on life. Higher scores reflect a greater orientation toward friends than toward parents, whereas lower scores reflect the opposite.

Perceived Life-Area Stress was a composite measure of the extent to which respondents perceived the different areas of their lives as being stressful. The components of the index included the following: Total Family Life Stress, itself a composite of scores on three different four-item measures of the frequency of stressful events – one with regard to relationship with spouse or partner, one in regard to relations with their children, and one with reference to relations with their own parents; Total Work Stress, a six-item scale assessing the chronicity of stressful conditions at work; Total Friendship Stress, a seven-item scale of the frequency of stressful situations in relationships with friends; Sexual Stress, a nine-item scale of the frequency with which stressful situations arose in sexual relationships; and General Stress Across Life Areas, another composite measure of the overall amount of stress or pressure respondents felt they were under in each of the four life areas above (from "none at all" to "a great deal"). Each of the above components was itself dichotomized and scored 0 or 1, and these scores were added across the five components. Higher scores on the composite reflect more pervasive perceptions of stress across the different areas of life.

Three variables were assessed within the Proximal Structure of the Perceived Environment System: Friends' Approval of Problem Behavior, Friends Models for Problem Behavior, and Friends Models for Religiosity. *Friends' Approval of Problem Behavior* was a three-item composite scale assessing the frequency with which respondents had been encouraged, influenced, or pressured by friends to engage in general deviant behavior, drinking, or marijuana use. Each of these components was z-scored within each gender-by-study subsample, truncated at plus or minus 3.0, and added together. Higher scores thus reflect higher than average degrees of friends' approval for involvement in problem behavior. *Friends Models for Problem Behavior* was also a composite measure, encompassing perceptions of friends' behavior with regard to drinking, marijuana use, and the use of seven other categories of illicit drugs. Scores on these three measures were z-scored within gender-by-study subsamples and combined as above, so that higher scores indicate greater than average levels of exposure to friends' involvement with these substances. *Friends Models for Religiosity* was a single item asking whether their friends thought of religion as an important part of their own lives. Higher scores reflect the response that "most of them do."

Scale properties for the five multiple-item measures of the Perceived Environment System variables are also presented in Table 3.2. As may be seen, the scale properties of the measures of the Distal Structure are satisfactory for the most part. The composite measure of perceived stress, however, demonstrates less consistency across the different life areas in the College Study subsamples than it does in the High School Study subsamples.

With respect to the composite measures in the Proximal Structure of the Perceived Environment System, the measure of friends models for problem behavior has satisfactory properties in the High School Study, but exhibits lower levels of reliability or consistency across behaviors for the College Study subsamples. The composite measure of friends' approval of problem behavior exhibits relatively low levels of consistency across all four of the subsamples. The relatively low levels of consistency for these two composite measures may be due to the fact that both composites encompass a variety of different behavioral areas (e.g., licit drug use as well as illicit drug use).

Measures of Social Environment System variables

The main focus in the Social Environment System was on describing important aspects of the immediate social context. For the most part, these descriptions did not involve multiple-item scales.

The Socio-Demographic Structure of the Social Environment System included measures of four variables: Educational Attainment, Occupational Status, Income, and Religious Membership. *Educational Attainment* was assessed by a series of questions asking if the respondents had pursued any formal education since the previous questionnaire, what type of school was attended (e.g., vocational–technical school, junior college, graduate school, or professional school), and, if they had completed a course of study, what kind of diploma, certificate, or degree was earned. These data were categorized in relation to an index of educational attainment (some high school; high school graduate; some vocational–technical school; graduate of a vo–tech program, or some college education; college graduate; some postgraduate education; master's degree; doctorate or professional degree). *Occupational Status* was assessed by asking two fairly standard questions, one having to do with the kind of work the respondent does, and one concerning what they actually do at work and their responsibilities on the job. Responses were coded into the seven categories of Hollingshead's Two-Factor Index of Social Position (unemployed; unskilled; semiskilled; skilled; clerical–technical; managerial; professional–executive). *Income* was measured by a single question asking respondents to report personal income for 1980; eight categories were provided, from "less than $5,000" to "$26,000 or more." *Religious Membership* was a measure referring to the fundamentalism of the religious denomination to which the respondent belonged; five categories varied from most fundamentalist (e.g., Southern Baptist, Seventh Day Adventist, Pentecostal, Jehovah's Witnesses) to least fundamental (Quaker, Unitarian, Buddhist) to most liberal (none, atheist, agnostic).

Social Context variables assessed included family composition, friendship network, work situation, and positive–negative life events. In relation to *Family Composition*, a number of questions were asked that concerned current marital status, if they were living with someone, if they had any children, and the ages and genders of their children. With respect to *Friendship Network*, questions were asked about how many close friends they had, how many they saw on a regular basis, and how many other friends they had. Questions related to respondents' *Work Situation* had to do with whether they were self-employed, how many people they supervised or were responsible for at work, and how many friends they had at work. In regard to *Positive–Negative Life Events*, respondents were asked in 1981 whether each of 16 events had occurred since taking the questionnaire in 1979, and whether each occurred "in the past year" or "more than a year ago." They were also asked to rate each event that had happened,

using a five-point scale to express the impact it had on their life, from
"very negative" to "very positive." Events asked about included the
following: received a special recognition or award at work or school;
the death of a close family member; a serious illness, accident, or
injury to someone very close to you; a major improvement in financial
status; the death of a close friend; a severe financial or property loss;
got a special job or acceptance into a special school or program; did
poorly in school or flunked out; parents separated or divorced; bought
your own home; spouse or partner was fired or laid off; and so forth.

Measures of the variables of the *Behavior System* will be described
in detail in Chapter 5 since its focus is on problem behavior in young
adulthood. A variety of additional variables not described here or
mentioned in the overall theoretical framework were also assessed in
the 1979 and 1981 Young Adult Questionnaires. Where these are of
interest, or where they illuminate specific analytic issues, they will be
introduced and described in the following chapters.

Summary

This book is about a longitudinal follow-up into young adulthood of
two samples that had been studied annually for four years beginning
when they were either junior high school students or college freshmen.
Two additional waves of data were collected by mail questionnaire
in the young adult phase of the research. The six-wave longitudinal
sample consists of 568 adults who had taken all six questionnaires
over the 11 or 12 years of the larger, two-phase study.

Although the sample is mainly middle-class and Anglo in origin
and although it experienced substantial sampling loss at the outset in
1969/70, earlier research findings based on this sample have been
replicated in a variety of other studies including several based on
representative, nationwide samples of adolescents. Attrition between
the first, adolescence/youth phase and the present, young adult phase
was very modest and does not constitute a source of further bias.

The questionnaires that were administered in both waves of the
Young Adult Follow-Up Study consisted of a variety of psychometric
measures developed to assess the personality, social environment, and
behavior system variables of Problem-Behavior Theory. The young
adult measures were designed to be maximally comparable to the

measures that were used in the earlier, adolescent phase of the research. Almost all of the measures were shown to have at least adequate psychometric properties.

The major strength of the present study lies in the six waves of data – four assessed in adolescence or youth, and two assessed in young adulthood – on theoretically based measures of personality, social environment, and behavior variables. With such comprehensive data, it is possible to describe the course of development from adolescence into young adulthood within each of the three theoretical systems of Problem-Behavior Theory, and to describe variation in development in two separate longitudinal samples. It is also possible to describe development *within* the life-stage of young adulthood itself. Further, the data make possible the study of linkages between adolescence and young adulthood in personality, social environment, and behavior. Finally, the data permit an examination, for the first time, of the usefulness of Problem-Behavior Theory for explaining variation in problem behavior within young adulthood.

References

Bachman, J. G., Johnston, L. D., & O'Malley, P. M. (1981). Smoking, drinking, and drug use among American high school students: Correlates and trends, 1975–1979. *American Journal of Public Health, 71,* 59–69.

Brook, J. S., Lukoff, I. F., & Whiteman, M. (1977). Correlates of adolescent marijuana use as related to age, sex, and ethnicity. *The Yale Journal of Biology and Medicine, 50,* 383–390.

Chassin, L., Presson, C. C., Sherman, S. J., Corty, E., & Olshavsky, R. W. (1984). Predicting the onset of cigarette smoking in adolescents: A longitudinal study. *Journal of Applied Social Psychology, 14*(3), 224–243.

Cronbach, L. J. (1951). Coefficient alpha and the internal structure of tests. *Psychometrika, 16,* 297–334.

DiTecco, D. & Schlegel, R. P. (1982). Alcohol use among young adult males: An application of problem behavior theory. In J.R. Eiser (Ed.), *Social psychology and behavioral medicine* (pp. 199–233). New York: Wiley.

Donovan, J. E., & Jessor, R. (1978). Adolescent problem drinking: Psychosocial correlates in a national sample study. *Journal of Studies on Alcohol, 39,* 1506–1524.

Donovan, J. E., & Jessor, R. (1985). Structure of problem behavior in adolescence and young adulthood. *Journal of Consulting and Clinical Psychology, 53*, 890–904.

Jessor, R., Chase, J. A., & Donovan, J. E. (1980). Psychosocial correlates of marijuana use and problem drinking in a national sample of adolescents. *American Journal of Public Health, 70*, 604–613.

Jessor, R., Donovan, J. E., & Widmer, K. (1980). *Psychosocial factors in adolescent alcohol and drug use: The 1978 national sample study and the 1974–78 panel study.* Boulder: Institute of Behavioral Science, University of Colorado.

Jessor, R., & Jessor, S. L. (1977). *Problem behavior and psychosocial development: A longitudinal study of youth.* New York: Academic Press.

Jessor, R., & Jessor, S. L. (1984). Adolescence to young adulthood: A twelve-year prospective study of problem behavior and psychosocial development. In S.A. Mednick, M. Harway, & K. M. Finello (Eds.), *Handbook of longitudinal research: Teenage and adult cohorts* (Vol. 2, pp. 34–61). New York: Praeger.

McLaughlin, R. J., Baer, P. E., Burnside, M. A., & Pokorny, A. D. (1985). Psychosocial correlates of alcohol use at two age levels during adolescence. *Journal of Studies on Alcohol, 46*, 212–218.

Rachal, J. V., Guess, L. L., Hubbard, R. L., Maisto, S. A., Cavanaugh, E. R., Waddell, R., & Benrud, C. H. (1980). *Adolescent drinking behavior, Vol. 1: The extent and nature of adolescent alcohol and drug use: The 1974 and 1978 national sample studies.* Research Triangle Park, NC: Research Triangle Institute.

Rachal, J. V., Williams, J. R., Brehm, M. L., Cavanaugh, B., Moore, R. P., & Eckerman, W. C. (1975). *A national study of adolescent drinking behavior, attitudes, and correlates* (Report No. PB–246–002; NIAAA/NCALI–75/27). Springfield, VA: U.S. National Technical Information Service.

Scott, W. A. (1960). Measures of test homogeneity. *Educational and Psychological Measurement, 20*, 751–758.

Scott, W. A. (1968). Attitude measurement. In G. Lindzey & E. Aronson (Eds.), *Handbook of social psychology* (2nd ed., Vol. 2, pp. 204–273). Reading, MA: Addison-Wesley.

Part II

Young adulthood

4

The participants as young adults

Before engaging the theory-testing and developmental aspects of this research, we present some qualitative information in this chapter about the young adult participants and about the lives they were living. Young adulthood is usually a time of new experiences and expanded responsibilities: Young adults may enter the labor market for the first time; they may begin to live with a partner or marry, and perhaps have children; they may commit themselves to political and religious philosophies that shape their attitudes and guide their behavior; and they may dissolve old friendship ties and establish new ones. To establish a descriptive overview of the context of young adult life, we include information about the areas of political outlook, religion and morality, family life, sexuality and reproductive behavior, work and leisure, friendships, and health. Since the use of alcohol and involvement with other drugs are key problem behaviors and constitute a major focus of the research, the description of young adult involvement in those behaviors is reserved for presentation in the next chapter.

The chapter is organized around two major aspects of young adult life. The first concerns the sociopolitical views and personal beliefs of the men and women in the study. Under this topic, we describe their political attitudes and affiliations as well as their moral beliefs, religious outlooks, and religious memberships. The second aspect refers to the social roles or social locations occupied by the study participants. We characterize their involvement and activities in several life areas: family, sexuality, work and leisure, friendship relationships, and personal health.

The information was obtained in 1981 when members of the High

School sample were 25–27 years old, and members of the College sample were about 30 years old. The wide range of data available is of intrinsic interest, and it yields a picture – for these participants – of their young adult lives at the beginning of the decade of the 1980s. There is, of course, no presumption of describing young adult life, in general, in America.

Political outlook and behavior

The respondents in this study came of age during a time of notable political turmoil in the United States. Governmental policies and institutions were called into question to an unprecedented extent. Challenges to the legitimacy of governmental authority and the wisdom of governmental decisions, particularly around the Vietnam War, were especially intense among youth. With that background as part of their personal history, their orientation to politics and government when they had matured and entered young adulthood is of special interest.

Large percentages of the respondents described their political affiliation in 1981 as either Independent or unaffiliated (59% of the High School men, 51% of the High School women, 39% of the College men, and 47% of the College women). Smaller percentages reported they were Republicans (24%, 26%, 22%, and 23% of the respective subgroups) or Democrats (12%, 19%, 20%, and 25%, respectively).

Between 1979 and 1981, turnover in political party membership ranged from 10 percent to 40 percent. Among those who described themselves as Republicans or Democrats in 1979, most of the shift was toward a self-described Independent affiliation in 1981. Among 1979 Independents who had shifted affiliation by 1981, most of the shift was toward the Republican Party; four times as many High School men shifted to a Republican affiliation as to a Democratic one, twice as many High School women and College men shifted to a Republican affiliation as to a Democratic one, and half as many College women did likewise.

There was a fairly even spread across the political continuum from conservatism to liberalism. In the High School sample, somewhat more of the respondents described their political point of view as conservative than as liberal or radical. In the College sample, the reverse was true. Of the High School men, 40 percent described themselves as politically conservative, 38 percent reported being "middle of the road," and 20 percent reported being liberal or radical. Comparable percentages for the High School women were 33, 41, and 25 percent; for the College men – 32, 29, and 39 percent; and for the College women – 25, 29, and 45 percent. Although the majority of the participants reported that their political point of view had remained stable between 1979 and 1981, more reported change in the direction of greater conservatism than greater liberalism (29% vs. 8% for High School men; 23% vs. 14% for High School women; 42% vs. 8% for College men; and 28% vs. 6% for College women).

The great majority of the respondents reported having voted in the 1980 presidential election. Voter participation was slightly higher in the College sample than in the High School sample: Seven out of ten High School men and women and eight out of ten College men and women voted in the election. Ronald Reagan received the largest percentage of the votes in the High School sample, and Jimmy Carter received the largest percentage of the votes in the College sample. In the High School sample, however, the proportion of men and women who voted for Reagan was lower than the combined proportions of those who voted for Jimmy Carter or John Anderson. Forty-three percent of High School men voted for Reagan, 23 percent for Carter, and 25 percent for John Anderson. For High School women, the respective percentages were 41 percent for Reagan, 33 percent for Carter, and 15 percent for Anderson. In the College sample, about 30 percent of the men and women voted for Reagan, 38 percent voted for Carter, and about 20 percent voted for Anderson.

Summary

On the basis of their participation in the 1980 presidential election, these samples of young adults appear to be more involved than average in the processes and duties of citizenship. On the basis of their 1980 presidential votes, it seems that a more liberal political outlook had a slight edge over a more conservative outlook in these groups. Nevertheless, the *changes* in political point of view they reported as occurring during their young adult years were primarily in the direction of greater conservatism.

Religiosity and moral attitudes

Allegiance to institutional religion and its associated moral beliefs reflects an identification with a body of traditional values and standards of behavior. Such an affiliation often provides a sense of community, stability, and support. Indications from our data suggest that ties to institutionalized religion were, for many, intact, and that belief in God or a Higher Power was important.

Fully two-thirds of the men and women in the High School sample and more than half of the College men and women reported some religious affiliation, whereas a little over 20 percent of the High School sample and nearly a third of the College Sample reported that they had no religious affiliation, were atheist, or were agnostic. The religious affiliations reported by the respondents covered a wide range of denominations. The three most popular denominations in each subgroup were as follows: for High School men – Roman Catholic (9%), Methodist (8%), and Presbyterian (8%); for High School women – Methodist (12%); Roman Catholic (11%), and Presbyterian (8%); for College men – Roman Catholic (11%), American Council Lutheran (10%), and Methodist (7%); for College women – Methodist (9%), Jewish (9%), and Episcopalian (7%). When the full range of denominational membership was classified by degree of fundamentalism, it could be determined that relatively few of the men and women in either sample belonged to highly fundamentalist religious groups (only about 10% of High School men and women and 5% or less of College participants). Despite these nominal ties to institutionalized religion, many of the young adults either had not attended religious services in the past year (32–38%) or had attended only once or twice (19–27%).

Although not attending religious services very often, many of the participants retained some investment in a religious outlook. The majority of the High School respondents (56% of men and 64% of women) said that it was personally very important for them to believe in God, as did about four in ten of the men and women in the College sample. In addition, whereas most respondents reported that the role of religion in their lives had not changed in the interval between the 1979 and 1981 questionnaires, quite a few (14–26%) said that religion had come to play a more important role in their lives over these two years. A few people – ten High School participants and one College woman – reported that they had been "born again" since taking the 1979 questionnaire.

Many of the respondents had relatively strong opinions on a number of moral issues, including heavy drinking, drinking and driving, extramarital sexual behavior, and abortion. Women were somewhat more moralistic about alcohol issues and about extramarital sexual activity than were men. There was also a general tendency for members of the High School sample to express stricter attitudes on these subjects than members of the College sample. About 60 percent and 40 percent of the women in the High School and College samples, respectively, thought that it was very wrong for a person to be a heavy drinker, compared with 40 percent and 30 percent of the men in these respective samples. Similarly, whereas nearly 60 percent of the women in the two samples thought it was very wrong to drive after having a good bit to drink, only 41 percent of the High School men and 29 percent of the College men thought so. With respect to extramarital sex, about two-thirds of the High School women and 44 percent of the College women thought that such behavior was very wrong, compared with half of the High School men and about a quarter of the College men. On the other hand, only small percentages of both men and women thought that young people should wait until they are married to initiate sexual intercourse (19% of High School men and women, 4% of College men, and 11% of College women).

Moral attitudes regarding abortion in the event of an unplanned pregnancy were less stringent among College respondents than among High School respondents. More than half of the men and women in the College sample believed that it is not wrong to have an abortion when a pregnancy was not planned, compared with one third of the High School men and women. Furthermore, 28 percent of the High School respondents believed that to have an abortion under these circumstances is very wrong, whereas only about one in ten of the College men and women took that position.

Summary

With respect to religiosity and moral outlook, then, these young adults appeared generally to be somewhat conventional. Most identified themselves as having a specific religious affiliation, and a great number attached personal importance to having a belief in God. In addition, considerable numbers had strong moral opinions regarding excessive alcohol use and extramarital sexual behavior. On the other hand, actual attendance at religious services was generally low, and moral judgments regarding abortion and premarital sexual behavior were somewhat lenient.

Family life

For many young adults, family structure and family relationships are obviously in transition. Some are acquiring partners and working out the terms of a committed relationship; some have had children and are discovering the responsibilities of parenthood; and many are, as adults, in evolving relationships with their parents. The nature of these various family relationships, including the stresses and satisfactions that characterize them, are the focus of this section.

Interpersonal commitment

By 1981, the majority of the participants were living in committed relationships, either marital or nonmarital. In both samples, more than half of the men and women (53–60%) were married and living with spouse. The average length of marriage was about four years in the High School sample and five years in the older, College sample.

About one in ten of the men and women were single and involved in a cohabitational relationship. Almost all of the unmarried cohabitors were heterosexuals. Among the people who were cohabiting, there tended to be some longevity to the relationships: About half of the men and two-thirds of the women who were cohabiting had been living with that person for a year or more.

A sizable proportion of the study participants had been through a divorce. Among those who had ever been married, up to one in five

(13–22%) had experienced a divorce. Most of those who had been divorced, however, had remarried. By 1981, about half of the men and two-thirds of the women who had ever been divorced had married again.

Among the married or cohabiting respondents, many expressed satisfaction with various aspects of their relationship with their partner. For example, three-quarters were satisfied with the amount of affection and support received from their spouse or partner and with the degree to which their spouse or partner respected their feelings and opinions. Only a little more than 10 percent said they were dissatisfied with these aspects of their relationship. The remainder said they were neither satisfied nor dissatisfied. Dissatisfaction with the quality of communication in the relationship was somewhat more common; about 16 percent of the men and 25 percent of the women reported they were dissatisfied in this area of their relationship. On the other hand, two-thirds of the men and women were satisfied with the quality of communication in their relationship.

Consistent with the generally high levels of reported satisfaction, few people acknowledged experiencing frequent stress in their relationship with spouse or partner. Less than 10 percent of the married or cohabiting participants indicated that their spouse or partner had made frequent demands on them that they couldn't possibly meet during the past year. Fewer than one in ten said they couldn't find things that they and their partner enjoyed doing together because they have such different interests in life. However, a small but notable proportion of the married or cohabiting young adults (up to 15% in the different samples) reported frequent, serious disagreements in the previous year about crucial aspects of their relationship.

Decision-making responsibilities were generally shared in these young adults' relationships. The great majority of married or cohabiting respondents reported that both partners made the decisions, together, about which friends to spend time with, whether or not both partners should have a job, how to spend shared leisure time, and how to allocate family finances. The only area of decision-making in which an imbalance of responsibility was noticeable was with regard to allocation of household chores. About a third of the women said they almost always handled such decisions, compared with 5 percent or less of the men.

A majority of those participants who had never been married said they would like to get married some day. Among the never-married, eight out of ten of the High School men and women, half of the College men, and two-thirds of the College women would like to marry someday. Still, quite a few of the never-married young adults in our study were unsure about whether they would like to be married at some future time; this included about 20 percent of the High School men, High School women, and College women, and fully 40 percent of the College men. Such uncertainty may reflect an alienation from or distrust of the traditional social patterns or structure defined by marriage. Only a few of the never-married participants said they definitely did not want to marry, and women were more likely to say this than men (7% vs. 2% in the High School sample; 10% vs. 3% in the College sample).

Parenthood and childrearing

About a quarter of the men and a third of the women had one or more children by 1981. The average number of children for both High School and College men and women was just under two. No one in the study had more than three children, and few people had stepchildren or adopted children (6–11% of those with children). A small proportion of respondents were pregnant or had a pregnant partner at the time they took the 1981 questionnaire (12% of College women and 5–8% of the remaining groups). Of those who were expecting a child, about half had no other children.

The great majority – about nine out of ten – of those people who had children were married and living with spouse. Only 5 percent or fewer of the parents in our samples had never been married.

High levels of reported satisfaction with various aspects of parenting were more characteristic of mothers than of fathers. Women were twice as likely as men to say that they were very satisfied with their parenting abilities (30% vs. 16% in the High School sample, and 34% vs. 19% in the College sample) and with the kind of relationship they had with their children (55% vs. 37%, and 53% vs. 24% in the respective samples). Mothers were also much more likely than fathers to say that they were very satisfied with the amount of time they were able to spend with their children (39% of the mothers vs. 7% of the fathers in the High School sample; 53% vs. 19%, respectively, in the College sample). More than a third of the fathers were dissatisfied with the limited amount of time they were able to spend with their children, as were 21 percent of the High School mothers and 9 percent of the College mothers.

Some stresses associated with childrearing were more common than others. About a fifth of the High School fathers, a quarter of the High School mothers, and a third of the College parents reported that there were frequently things they were not able to do just because they had children. In contrast, frequent problems in their relationship with spouse or partner because of the children were less common; they were reported by less than 10 percent of the parents. Relatively more women than men said that having children around often interfered with their getting their work done (19% vs. 7% in the High School sample, and 34% vs. 10% in the College sample).

Among those who had children, the desire to have more children was most typical of those with only one child; about three-quarters of these people wanted to have more children. About 30 percent of the High School parents who had two children wanted to have more, as did 58 percent of College men and 29 percent of College women with two children. Of the 13 people who had three children, only one, a High School father, wanted to have more. Most of those who had no children were looking forward to being parents; about two thirds of them wanted to have children someday. Uncertainty about someday having children was less characteristic of those who were married than of those who were cohabiting but not married. About 13 percent of the married men who did not have children were not sure whether they would ever like to have children, as were 24 percent and 15 percent of their female counterparts in the High School and College samples, respectively. Among the unmarried cohabitors, 43 percent of High School men, 35 percent of High School women, 20 percent of College men, and 71 percent of College women were not sure whether they ever wanted to have children. Only 4–14 percent of married or partnered participants who did not have children said they did not want to have any children.

A number of women in the samples had had abortions, a topic discussed later in the chapter.

Young adults' relationship with their parents

The great majority of the young adults – about 85 percent – had two living parents. Three percent to 6 percent reported that their mother was dead, and about 10 percent reported that their father was dead. Only one respondent (a High School man) reported that both his mother and father were dead. In 80–85 percent of those families where both parents were still alive, the parents were still married to each other. In other words, quite a large proportion of the young adults came from intact families.

Women were more likely to have frequent contact with their parents, especially their mothers, than were men. About half of the young adult women said that they had a lot of contact with their mothers, compared with 25–30 percent of the men. Nearly half of the High School women also had a lot of contact with their fathers, as did 25–30 percent of the other subgroups. About 3 percent of participants said they had almost no contact with their mothers, and 7 percent of women and 9 percent of men had almost no contact with their fathers.

Almost all (91–97%) of the respondents said they got along well with their mothers and fathers. In addition, most of the young adults were satisfied with various aspects of their relationships with their parents, including the amount of affection received from parents, the amount of respect parents showed for their children's opinions, parents' willingness to help out when their children had problems, and parents' confidence in their children's ability to handle their own lives. About 75–90 percent of the men and women were satisfied with these facets of their maternal relationship, and 70–80 percent were satisfied with these aspects of their paternal relationship. Young adults' relationships with their parents were not completely benign, however. Roughly one out of ten respondents expressed dissatisfaction with these different dimensions of their relationships with their parents. About one in ten of the young adults said they often experienced difficulties in communicating with their mothers, and 13–18 percent frequently had communication problems with their fathers.

Summary

Overall, most members of the young adult samples seemed to be making a positive transition to adult family life. In 1981, the great majority were in committed relationships – either marital or cohabitational – and, in general, these relationships were characterized by relatively high satisfaction and low stress. By the time the men and women in the High School and College samples had reached their mid-twenties and the age of thirty, respectively, many had families of their own. Family size was relatively small – an average of two children – and almost all parents were married. Men's lesser satisfaction with various aspects of parenting may reflect changes in social and personal expectations regarding sex roles and male involvement in childrearing. The majority of these young adults had regular contact with their own parents, and these relationships were generally positive.

Sexuality and sexual and reproductive behavior

Sexuality and sexual activity obviously have different meanings in adulthood from those they may have had in adolescence. For most adults, sexual activity is not an experimental or transitional experience; rather, it has become a normative part of life. Sexuality involves psychological as well as behavioral dimensions, including the stress, satisfaction, and meanings attached to sexual activity. The description of sexuality in the lives of the young adult participants encompasses these psychological aspects as well as more objective dimensions of sex and reproduction, such as sexual identity, nature of relationship with partner, use of contraception, and abortion experience.

Most of the participants identified themselves as heterosexual (about 86% of the men and women in the High School sample and 82% of the members of the College sample). Less than 5 percent reported a gay or lesbian sexual identity, and only 1–7 percent described themselves as bisexual.

Most of the unmarried individuals were sexually active in 1981. Some – one-fifth of the unmarried High School respondents and

one-quarter of the unmarried College respondents – were in cohabitational relationships. Others described their relationship with their
sexual partner as serious, but they were not living with that person
(about 15% of High School men and College men and women, and
29% of High School women), and a smaller proportion (8–12%)
described their sexual partner only as a "friend." Among the unmarried, relatively more men than women indicated that their sexual
activity took place outside the context of a relationship (26% vs. 16%).
A very small number of the unmarried respondents were virgins: eight
men and seven women in the High School sample, and one man and
one woman in the College sample.

As might be expected, sexual monogamy was more characteristic
of married than of single respondents. Among those who were sexually
active in 1981, nearly all of the married men and women were sexually
monogamous. Only about one in ten of the married respondents and
the unmarried, cohabiting women said that they were sexually involved
with more than one person; more than one in four single, cohabiting
men were sexually involved with more than one person. Of the unmarried respondents who were not living with someone in a committed
relationship, about a third of all groups except College men were
sexually involved with only one person; only 15 percent of the single
College men were sexually monogamous. Forty percent and 50 percent of the single, noncohabiting, sexually active men in the High
School and College samples, respectively, reported they had had three
or more partners in the preceding six months, as did 30 percent of
the single, noncohabiting, sexually active women.

Rather sizable proportions of respondents reported dissatisfaction
with their recent sexual experience (about one-quarter of the High
School sample and one-third of the College sample), whereas a little
more than half of the High School men and women and about 43
percent of the College participants said they were satisfied with their
sex life over the past six months. Stress in this area was relatively
low. Less than 20 percent described their recent sexual experience
as involving a fair or a large amount of stress. Slightly more than half
of the men and women indicated that they experienced little or no
stress or pressure in this area of their lives. Three-quarters of the
High School men and women and 62 percent of the College men
and women were sure that things would work out as they wanted as
far as their sex life was concerned.

Consistent use of contraception was the rule among those participants who were neither pregnant nor trying to become pregnant. In
both samples, about 70 percent of these men and women reported
that contraception was *always* used in the past year. Nineteen percent
of the men and 12 percent of the women in the High School sample
and 17 percent of the men and 19 percent of the women in the
College sample reported that they usually (but not always) took measures to prevent pregnancy. Only a small percentage were relatively
careless about contraception. Ten percent of the women in each
sample, 9 percent of High School men, and 5 percent of College
men stated that they either rarely or never used birth control.

We asked respondents what type of birth control was generally used
"when *you* use." Of those who answered this question, 32 percent of
High School women and 22 percent of College women used birth
control pills; 31 and 38 percent respectively, used a diaphragm or
cervical cap; 9 and 16 percent, respectively, used an intrauterine
device (IUD). Among the men, about a third in each sample reported
using condoms, and another third of each sample indicated that their
partner was always responsible for birth control. About 5 percent of
the men had had a vasectomy. We also asked what type of contraception was generally used "when *your partner* uses." Of those who
answered, about a third of the men in both samples reported that
their partner used oral contraceptives; between a fifth and a quarter
reported that their partner used a diaphragm or a cervical cap; and
11–15 percent said that their partner used an IUD. Among the
women, about half reported that they themselves were always responsible for contraception; about one in ten depended on their partner's vasectomy; and just under a third reported that their partner
used condoms.

Respondents were generally satisfied with their usual method of
contraception, with men reporting higher satisfaction than women. A
little more than 70 percent of the men were satisfied with their usual
method of contraception, compared with only slightly more than half
of the women. In addition, 13–14 percent of the men were dissatisfied
with their usual birth control method, compared with about a quarter
of the women.

A final issue worth noting with respect to sexuality is the reported
prevalence of abortion experience among the sexually experienced
women. By 1981, 22 percent of the women in the High School sample

and 28 percent of the women in the College sample reported having had one or more abortions. Among those women who reported an abortion, 24 percent said they had had more than one.

The reasons mentioned most often for having an abortion were "not being ready" to have a child, or being unable to care for a child at that time. Included among these reasons were financial limitations and being "too young" to have a child. Nearly two-thirds of the High School women and 86 percent of the College women cited reasons such as these for having an abortion. The second most frequently cited category of reasons referred to problems with or lack of a partner – for example, being unmarried, being unready to marry, problems in or dissolution of the relationship with partner in conception, or not being in the "right" relationship for having a child. In both samples, just under half of the women with abortion experience said that such relationship issues contributed to their decision to abort. In the High School sample, 17 percent of the women said they had the abortion because having a child would have interfered with their progress toward educational and/or career goals, as compared with 7 percent of the College women. Some factors were mentioned by only a few (4% or less) of the women; these included parental pressure, the possibility of birth defects, not wanting children ever, and pressure from partner.

Perceived social support for having an abortion was relatively strong for these women. The majority of them (57% in the High School sample and 56% in the College sample) reported that they received a great deal of support for their decision to abort. Twenty-two percent of the High School women and 30 percent of the College women who had had an abortion said that they had had at least some support when they chose to have the abortion. The remaining women reported that they had either little or no support (22% in the High School sample; 15% in the College sample). A more detailed account of abortion experience in these young adult samples is presented in Costa, Jessor, and Donovan (1987).

Summary

By young adulthood, then, sexual experience and sexual involvement were common among most participants in the study. A very small number of these predominantly heterosexual men and women were still virgins. Sexual activity was the rule rather than the exception among the single people in the samples. Although most of these people said that their sexual activity took place within the context of an interpersonal relationship, more than half of them had had more than one sexual partner in the recent past.

Although most respondents described the sexual aspects of their lives as high in satisfaction and low in stress, dissatisfaction and stress were not uncommon in this life area. Indeed, up to a third of these young adults were not satisfied with their recent sexual experiences. Satisfaction with contraception was generally high, more so for men than for women. Since women typically assumed responsibility for contraception and therefore were more likely to experience the inconveniences of different methods, this is not surprising.

A significant number of women – 22–28 percent – reported that they had had an abortion. Considering that such behavior is typically underreported, the actual proportions are likely to be higher. For most of these women, the decision to have an abortion was based on a sense of personal inability to care for a child – often due to financial limitations or young age at pregnancy. Nearly all of these women who had had an abortion reported that they experienced social support for their decision.

Work life and leisure time

By young adulthood, the transition from being dependent on parents for material support to being responsible for one's own expenses is expected. Many young adults have completed their formal education by then and are working at paying jobs. Some are establishing careers. We present information in this section about the work world for the young adult samples, including level of educational preparation, income, and number of hours worked each week, as well as certain psychological aspects of work, such as satisfactions and stress. We also provide a brief description of the availability and use of leisure time in these young adult groups.

Only a small proportion of the men and women were in school in 1981. Five to 10 percent of the participants were either full-time or part-time students. Many of the participants had attained high levels of education. In the High School sample, about half of the men and women were at least college graduates by 1981; 30 percent had a bachelor's degree only, and an additional 20 percent had earned higher degrees or had had at least some postgraduate education. In the College sample, the proportion of college graduates was, of course, higher. Nearly nine out of ten of these men and women had completed college by 1981; 46 percent had a bachelor's degree only; 18 percent of the men and 14 percent of the women had a master's degree; 11 percent of the men and 7 percent of the women had a Ph.D. or other professional degree; and 12 percent of the men and 20 percent of the women had completed some postgraduate education without attaining a degree.

Full-time employment was widespread, although it was more prevalent among the men than the women. Whereas 78 percent of the High School men and 88 percent of the College men had full-time jobs in 1981, 55 and 61 percent of the women in these respective samples were employed full-time. Among the women, about three-quarters of those who were single were working full time, compared with less than half of those who were married. The men tended to work longer hours than the women; one-fifth of the employed men worked 50 or more hours a week, compared with 4 and 10 percent, respectively, of the employed High School women and College women.

Except for the College men, nine out of ten of those working were in someone else's employ; eight out of ten College men were employed by another. Seventeen percent of College men were self-employed, as were 4–6 percent of the other subgroups. Only 1–4 percent described themselves as employers or owners. More than a quarter of the respondents said that between 1979 and 1981 they had had two or more different jobs.

Among the women, 16 percent of the High School sample and 20 percent of the College sample identified themselves as full-time homemakers. Another 10 percent of the High School sample women and 6 percent of the College sample women were homemakers who worked part-time outside the home.

The greater general level of educational attainment in the College sample was accompanied by higher income levels. About half of the College men and one-quarter of the College women reported annual incomes of $18,000 or more. In comparison, one-third of the men and 12 percent of the women in the High School sample reported personal incomes of at least $18,000 a year. Less than 20 percent of the men reported annual incomes below $7,500, compared with about a third of the women. Of those in this lower income bracket, 44 percent of High School men, 66 percent of High School women, 33 percent of College men and 88 percent of College women were married. Among these married, lower-income people, 8 percent of High School men, two-thirds of College men, and about three-quarters of women in both samples reported that their spouse earned $10,000 or more per year.

Quite a few participants had experienced a recent change in financial status. About one out of three reported a major improvement in financial status in the past year. On the other hand, one in ten reported a severe financial or property loss during that time.

For many of the participants, their career accomplishments fell short of their expectations for themselves. When asked to rate their progress as far as work or career was concerned, 29–43 percent said they were behind where they thought they should be at this stage of life. Men were more apt than women to perceive that they were *ahead* of where they should be in their careers (32% vs. 21% in the High School sample, and 24% vs. 11% in the College sample). Although many of the young adult respondents were optimistic about their work situations, one-quarter of them were not sure that things would work out as desired as far as work and career were concerned.

Overall satisfaction with work was generally high: Fifty-seven percent of High School men, 49 percent of High School women, and about 60 percent of College men and women were satisfied with their work. Nevertheless, that leaves a considerable number who were dissatisfied with their jobs (24%, 32%, and 20% of these respective groups). With respect to important material and psychological aspects of work, satisfaction was more common than dissatisfaction. Of those who had worked in the preceding year, half said they were satisfied with salary and benefits, whereas about a third reported dissatisfaction with salary and benefits. Half to two-thirds said that they were satisfied with the interest or challenge of their jobs, compared with 16–20 percent who were dissatisfied. Satisfaction with the sense of usefulness or accomplishment that one's work provides was high, characterizing about two-thirds of High School respondents and Col-

lege men and three-quarters of College women. Dissatisfaction with
this aspect of job or career was reported by 13 percent of High School
men, 26 percent of High School women, 18 percent of College men,
and 13 percent of College women. Information from the earlier, 1979
wave of the follow-up study suggests, too, that lower levels of adjustment at work are significantly related to greater general feelings
of alienation (Hays, 1980).

Work was stressful for many of the respondents. Seventeen to 27
percent of the young adults said that they were under a great deal of
pressure at work. In addition, 20–30 percent indicated that in the
past year they often had to ignore responsibilities to family or friends
because of the time demands of their job.

Some respondents reported serious problems at work. Between
1979 and 1981, 16 percent of the men and about 10 percent of the
women had been given a serious warning because their supervisor
was dissatisfied with their work. However, only a few respondents
(4–9%) were denied a raise or promotion or were fired or laid off
from work due to a supervisor's dissatisfaction with their work in that
interval.

Reported use of alcohol or drugs while at work varied considerably
across the sex-by-sample subgroups. Sixteen percent of the men in
the High School sample reported drinking at work at least several
times in the past year, compared with 2 percent of the High School
women and 8 percent of the College men and women. Similar proportions reported having used marijuana at work at least several times
in the past year (15%, 4%, 7%, and 3% of the respective groups).

Many of the young adult men and women felt that they did not
have enough leisure time. About 40 percent of High School men and
women and nearly half of College men and women were dissatisfied
with the amount of free time that they had.

Leisure time was used in a variety of ways. Sixteen to 24 percent
of the men and women indicated that they often took part in physical
activities like sports, running, and other forms of exercise during their
free time. A smaller proportion of respondents – about one in ten –
said they frequently watched television during leisure hours. Twenty
to 25 percent of respondents indicated that they rarely spent their
free time watching television. About 17 percent of the men and 26
percent of the women often used their leisure time for reading. In-

volvement in hobbies and other such pastimes was more characteristic of women's use of free time than men's; half of the women often engaged in such pastimes, compared with 30 percent of the men.

Alcohol was frequently used as part of free-time activities, especially by men. Thirty-seven percent of the men in the High School sample and 44 percent of those in the College sample said that drinking was often a part of their leisure activities, compared with 22 and 30 percent of the women in these respective samples. Relatively fewer of the young adults reported frequent use of marijuana during leisure activities, about 10 percent of all subgroups except 2 percent for College women.

Summary

By 1981, when members of the High School sample were aged 25–27 and members of the College sample had reached the age of 30, almost all participants had full-time jobs. With the exception of married women, eight out of ten of these men and women were employed full-time. The majority of working young adults were satisfied with their jobs or careers. Nevertheless, roughly one in five of these working adults described their work situations as being high in stress, and similar numbers of respondents reported that work responsibilities frequently interfered with their ability to attend to family responsibilities. In a related matter, nearly half of the study participants were dissatisfied with the amount of leisure time that they had.

Substance use at work was relatively rare in most of the subgroups, with the exception of the High School men. More than one in ten of these men said that they used alcohol on the job, and more than one in ten said they used marijuana while at work. Alcohol use was also often a part of leisure-time pursuits for many of the young adult participants. Fully four out of ten of the men frequently included alcohol use as part of their leisure activities, as did a fifth to a third of the women.

Friendship

Among the key primary relationships in life are those with friends. Such relationships are, of course, complex with both positive and negative aspects. Friends can be sources of socialization, learning, and support throughout life, but disruptions in friendships, like disruptions in other important relationships, can also be disturbing and unsettling. Various aspects of young adult friendships, including satisfaction, stress, and support, are described in this section.

In 1981, very nearly all of the participants claimed one or more close friends; only 1 percent of the men and 2 percent of the women said they had no close friends. A small proportion – 14–19 percent – were dissatisfied with the number of friends that they had. A somewhat larger proportion – about a third – expressed dissatisfaction with the amount of time they could spend with friends. Satisfaction with the affective or emotional aspects of friendships was the rule. Anywhere from 71 percent to 86 percent of respondents in each subgroup were satisfied with the amount of warmth and affection they received from their friends, with their friends' ability to understand them and their feelings, with the extent to which they and their friends were open with one another, and with the amount of support and encouragement they received from their friends. Except for the College women, single people living alone attributed a greater proportion of their overall life satisfaction to friendships than did married people or single, cohabiting people (Costa, 1983).

Relationships with friends were relatively free of stress for many of the participants. About three-quarters of the men and women said that they experienced very little stress or pressure in their relationships with friends. A surprisingly high proportion of men in the High School sample (14%) reported the death of a close friend in the preceding year. Less than half as many of the other respondents (4–5%) lost a close friend to death in that interval.

The majority of the young adults felt that their friends were very often supportive and helpful. Women generally reported experiencing such support more often than men. Relatively more women than men indicated that their friends frequently encouraged them and showed interest in their ideas, plans, and feelings (69% vs. 52% in the High School sample; 75% vs. 54% in the College sample) and that their friends very often tried to understand their problems and give them the help they needed (73% vs. 56% in the High School sample; 80% vs. 64% in the College sample). In addition, about three-quarters of the women in both samples felt free to talk to their friends about personal problems, whereas only half the men felt the same. Men and women did not differ, however, in feeling able to depend on friends to help out with a job that they couldn't handle themselves: About 75 percent of the respondents reported that they could frequently count on friends to help in those circumstances. Although these data provide a generally positive picture of young adult friendships, it is nevertheless worth noting that as many as 20–50 percent of our respondents perceived that their friends did not often provide them with the fundamental types of support typically expected from friends.

Sizable percentages of the men and women had doubts about the future of their friendships. Eighteen percent to 25 percent of the young adults were not sure that things would work out the way they would like them to as far as their friendships were concerned.

Summary

In general, friendships were a very positive aspect of life for the young adults in the study. The majority of respondents were satisfied with the emotional aspects of their friendships, and most felt that they could usually count on friends for help and support. The most frequently voiced complaints with regard to this area of life concerned the more objective dimensions of friendships – number of friends and availability of time to spend with friends – dimensions that are generally likely to suffer in a population that is also busy establishing families and careers.

Health and health-related behavior

Good health is often a highly valued and important element in people's overall sense of well-being and life satisfaction. In recent times there has been a growing emphasis on preventive medicine and health-promoting behavior as a way to ensure and sustain good health. This trend toward a preventive outlook on health care has occurred both among health professionals and in the popular media. The data in this study permit a description of the general health status reported by this group of young adults, and they indicate the extent to which health-promoting activities have been adopted in this age group.

In 1981, about three-quarters of the respondents described their physical health as either very good or excellent. Most of the remaining 25 percent reported that their health was good, while a very small number described their health as either fair or poor. Quite a few of the young adults said that they gave more attention to taking care of their health than they used to (a third of High School men, nearly half of College men, and almost 60% of women in both samples).

The assessment of health-promoting behavior in young adulthood surveyed physical exercise, dietary habits, and stress avoidance. Regular exercise was more characteristic of members of the College sample than the High School sample. About half of the former and one-third of the latter reported that they generally exercised on a regular basis; 25 percent of the High School sample and 17 percent of the College sample said that they rarely exercised. One third to one half of the respondents reported that they usually limited salt, sugar, and preservatives in their diets, watched their weight, and avoided eating "junk food." Such health-promoting dietary behavior was more common among women than men. With respect to stress avoidance, about 30 percent of the men and less than 20 percent of the women reported they rarely avoided stressful situations when it was possible for them to do so.

Two primary risks to health are overweight and tobacco use. Very few of the participants could be classified as overweight or obese on the basis of their reported height and weight. Using criteria applied in the First National Health and Nutrition Examination Survey conducted in 1971–74 (National Center for Health Statistics, 1983), we could classify about 6 percent of the men and women as overweight and 1 percent as obese. Despite the low proportion of respondents who were overweight by these objective standards, considerable percentages said they wanted to lose weight: Fourteen percent of High School men, 23 percent of College men, and fully a third of the women in both samples reported that they would like to lose ten or more pounds.

About a third of the High School men and women and a fourth of the College men and women were cigarette smokers in 1981. Of those who smoked, roughly half smoked a pack of cigarettes or more each day. Among the smokers, 12 percent of the High School men and about one-third of the remaining groups had been advised by their physicians to cut down on their smoking or to quit because it was adversely affecting their health. The majority of the young adults thought that smoking has a serious effect on a person's health (56% of High School men, 73% of High School women, 67% of College men, and 79% of College women). Most of the remaining participants thought that smoking has at least a moderate effect on health. In the High School sample, nonsmokers thought that smoking has a significantly more negative impact on health than did smokers. In the College sample, smokers and nonsmokers did not differ in their perceptions of the effects of smoking on health. A negative attitude toward cigarette smoking was very evident in the opinion of over 80 percent of the men and more than 90 percent of the women that young people should never start smoking. (A more detailed account of young adult cigarette smoking is provided in Chapter 5.)

In the two-year interval between the 1979 and 1981 questionnaires, relatively few participants had had major medical problems. Twelve percent to 16 percent reported three or more visits to a physician for reasons of illness or injury. Less than 10 percent of the participants had experienced a serious accident or injury, and less than 7 percent had had a serious illness requiring hospitalization.

Only a few indicators of mental health were available. One third of the men and half of the women in the study reported that in the two-year interval between the 1979 and 1981 questionnaires there had been a period of at least several months when they felt "very lonely, very depressed, or very unsure" of themselves. By any standards, these proportions are substantial for sustained experiences of depression. At the time of the 1981 questionnaire, about 15 percent of the participants felt that most of the things they were doing with their lives did not seem worthwhile or meaningful to them. Very few (8% or less) of the respondents were undergoing therapy at the time of the 1981 testing. Between 1979 and 1981, however, a substantial proportion of the women – nearly 25 percent – had undergone counseling or psychotherapy, compared with about 10 percent of the men.

Summary

The picture of young adult health that emerges is generally a positive one. Nearly all the men and women in the study said that they were in good health, and medical problems were rare. Many of these young adults engaged in exercise and made an attempt to eat a diet that was beneficial to health. Very few were overweight. On the negative side, 25–33 percent were cigarette smokers, and half of these smokers smoked at least a pack a day. Also, considerable numbers of both the men and the women had had sustained feelings of depression in the past two years.

Overall life satisfaction

Although it is clearly valuable to view the various aspects of the participants' lives separately, the picture that emerges from such an approach remains fragmented and incomplete. What it fails to provide is a more integrated perspective on the people on whom the research is based. Although there are a number of ways to describe the intra-individual integration of the lives of the participants, we have chosen to focus on their overall life satisfaction, that is, on the pervasiveness of individual satisfaction or dissatisfaction across the four life areas of family, work, friendships, and sexuality. In order to summarize respondents' feelings about these key domains of their lives, we simply tallied the number of life areas in which participants were dissatisfied – from none to four.[1]

The great majority of participants reported dissatisfaction in either no life areas or only one life area, indicating a rather widespread sense of contentment in these samples of young adults. Sixty percent of High School men, 49 percent of High School women, and half of the College men and women reported being dissatisfied in none of the four life areas. In the High School sample, a fifth of the men and a third of the women were dissatisfied in one life area; in the College sample, about a third of men and women were dissatisfied in one life area.

Nearly a fifth of the men and women were dissatisfied in two or more life areas (19% of High School men, 17% of High School women, 13% of College men, and 21% of College women). In the High School sample, 14 percent of men and 13 percent of women were dissatisfied in two life areas, and 4 percent of both men and women were dissatisfied in three life areas. In the College sample, 11 and 18 percent of men and women, respectively, were dissatisfied in two life areas, while 2 and 1 percent of men and women, respectively, were dissatisfied in three life areas. Only three people, one High School woman and two College women, were dissatisfied in all four life areas.

Of those people who reported dissatisfaction in one life area, the most frequently mentioned areas in both samples were work (reported by 40% of High School men, 44% of High School women, 29% of College men, and 26% of College women) and sex (reported by 33%, 40%, 48%, and 66% of the respective subgroups experiencing dissatisfaction in one life area). With the exception of the College women, these two life areas were also the most frequently mentioned by those who were dissatisfied in two life areas; among College women, sex and family life were the two most often reported, and work was the third. Among men in both samples, family life was the third most often mentioned area of dissatisfaction, whereas for High School women, friendship was. Among those people who reported dissatisfaction in three of the four life areas, work and sex were most often mentioned by all participants. The third most frequently mentioned area of dissatisfaction in the High School sample was friendship, for men, and family, for women. In the College sample, equal proportions of men cited friendship and family as areas of dissatisfaction. There was only one College woman who was dissatisfied in three life areas, which included work, sex, and friendship.

Having established that nearly one out of five participants was dissatisfied in two or more central areas of young adult life, we were interested in considering the implications of that dissatisfaction – that is, whether people characterized by greater dissatisfaction differed from those who were less dissatisfied. When the mean scores of these two groups on a number of psychosocial and behavioral measures were compared, the results generally indicated few significant differences between the groups.

As would be expected, the two groups differed significantly on other indicators that were closely related to reported satisfaction–dissatisfaction. Those who were dissatisfied in a greater number of life areas reported experiencing significantly greater stress in those life areas, and, except for the High School men, reported having recently experienced a significantly greater number of negative life events than those with lesser dissatisfaction. Men and women who were more dissatisfied with their lives were also characterized by significantly lower self-esteem ($p \leq .10$ for College men), by a greater sense of alienation (except for College men), and, again except for College men, by lower expectations that things would work out well for them, both in general ($p \leq .10$ for High School men), and with reference to the combined life domains of family, work, friendship, and sex.

There are a few other differences between those who reported dissatisfaction in a greater number of life areas and those who were dissatisfied with fewer areas of their lives. Most of these differences have to do with work lives or friendships. For all groups but College men, those people who were more dissatisfied across the four life areas rated themselves as significantly further behind where they thought they should be as far as work or career was concerned ($\leq .10$ for College women). Except for the High School men, those who were dissatisfied in more life areas reported having had a significantly greater number of different jobs in the interval between 1979 and 1981. Women with greater life-area dissatisfaction reported more frequent involvement in negative behavior at work, such as not working up to one's ability or staying away from work for no good reason. With respect to friendships, High School men and women with a greater number of life-area dissatisfactions reported having fewer close friends ($p \leq .10$ for women), and men in both samples who were more dissatisfied reported having fewer other, or nonclose, friends ($p \leq .10$ in the College sample).

A few other differences obtain between the less-satisfied and the more-satisfied participants. In the High School sample only, there was a modest link between higher life dissatisfaction and weaker ties to institutionalized religion. Those men and women with a greater number of life-area dissatisfactions were less religious ($p \leq .10$) and attended religious services less often ($p \leq .10$) than did those with fewer life-area dissatisfactions. For all groups but High School men, those who were dissatisfied in a greater number of life areas had significantly lower expectations of receiving affection from others ($p \leq .10$ in the College sample) than did those who were dissatisfied with fewer life areas. Women who were dissatisfied in a greater number of life areas had significantly lower expectations for achievement. And High School respondents who were higher in dissatisfaction attached a greater importance to using alcohol as a way of coping with problems ($p \leq .10$ for men).

It is important to point out the many ways in which these two groups did *not* differ from each other. Compared with their more satisfied peers, the high-dissatisfaction people were no different in terms of their status attainments. The two groups did not differ in levels of educational attainment, job prestige, or levels of personal income. Nor did they differ on a variety of indicators of social support, including perceived support from friends, perceived parental support, positive relationship with parents, and perceived support from co-workers. The two groups did not differ on personal belief measures of social criticism or internal–external locus of control, on personal control measures of intolerance of deviance or morality, on perceived friends controls against deviance, or on coping functions attached to sexual behavior or marijuana use. Finally, the groups differentiated on the basis of number of life-area satisfactions showed almost no differences on problem-behavior involvement, including cigarette smoking, general deviant behavior, drunkenness, negative consequences of drinking, driving after drinking alcohol, marijuana use, and use of other illicit drugs. The exception to this overall pattern occurred with respect to reported frequency of high-volume drinking – that is, drinking five or more drinks at a sitting. In both samples, men with a greater number of life-area dissatisfactions reported engaging in such behavior more often ($p \leq .10$ in the High School sample).

Summary

Among the participants in the study, there was a small but not insubstantial group whose lives were colored by a pervasive sense of dissatisfaction, stress, and pessimism. Although these people experienced dissatisfaction in more of the different domains of their lives, there appeared to be few pervasive implications of that dissatisfaction. They were characterized by greater job instability, slower progress toward personally established career goals, and smaller friendship networks. Although they also differed from more satisfied peers on a few other characteristics, including expectations for achievement and affection, coping functions for alcohol use, religiosity, and church attendance, these differences were often not significant across all four gender-by-sample subgroups. Furthermore, the high-dissatisfaction people had accomplished no less in the areas of education, income, and job prestige, they experienced equivalent levels of social support, and they were no more likely to engage in substance use or other problem behaviors.

Conclusion

This descriptive overview of the lives of the young adult participants engages a variety of life domains and reveals a variety of outlooks and life-styles. Their political, religious, and moral viewpoints and attitudes reflected a mix of liberalism and conventionality. Whereas most cast their votes in 1980 for the Democratic or Independent presidential candidates, quite a few described a personal evolution toward a more conservative political point of view. Also, although many were very moralistic regarding excessive alcohol use and extramarital sex, most were relatively tolerant of premarital sexual activity and of abortion.

With respect to family life and work, the picture that emerges is one of transition to and involvement in the realms of intimate relationships (both marital and nonmarital), parenthood, and jobs and careers. Intimate relationships were generally positive, and dissatisfactions with childrearing experiences most typically reflected perceived limits on time available to spend with children. Most of those who were not married did want to marry someday, and most of those who had no children said that they would like to have children at some time in their lives. Many of the men and women had maintained contact with and had good relationships with their parents, and many had satisfying and supportive relationships with friends.

Eight out of ten men, eight out of ten single women, and around 40 percent of married women had full-time jobs. Although work experiences were generally satisfying, a sizable proportion of the working adults described their jobs as high in stress and as demanding a great deal of time.

Nearly all of the young adult men and women in the study were sexually experienced by 1981. Among those who were single, most were sexually active, and a significant proportion had multiple sexual partners. Relative to this fact, it is important to bear in mind that these behavior patterns predated a general awareness of the existence and seriousness of acquired immune deficiency syndrome (AIDS).

Finally, with respect to health, the situation among these young adult men and women was generally positive. The great majority were in good physical health, and a large number made an effort to maintain good health by exercising and by monitoring their diet. With respect to mental health, however, the picture was somewhat less positive. A sizable proportion of the young adults in our study had experienced a prolonged interval when they were very depressed. In addition, approximately one out of five participants reported dissatisfaction in half or more of the four life areas of family, work, friendship, and sex. Despite this relatively pervasive dissatisfaction, these people differed in only a few ways from the other, more satisfied respondents.

In brief, these qualitative, descriptive data make clear that the young adult participants in this study were sampled from a normal rather than a clinical population. The men and women were generally optimistic, healthy, and somewhat conventional. Nevertheless, a not insubstantial number of the men and women could be characterized as unconventional, liberal, and "off-track" with respect to fulfilling traditional adult roles, and a significant proportion of the participants were unhappy or dissatisfied with their lives.

Note

1 Respondents had been asked how they felt, in general, about each of these areas of their lives. With respect to friendship, for example, they were asked: "Think of the friendships you now have. How do you feel about them in general?" Response options for each of the four general satisfaction items are "very satisfied," "satisfied," "neither satisfied nor dissatisfied," "dissatisfied," and "very dissatisfied." A response of "dissatisfied" or "very dissatisfied" was scored as a "1," and all other responses were scored as "0."

An alternate, less stringent version of this measure of life-area dissatisfaction was also created. For that other measure, the response "neither satisfied nor dissatisfied" was scored as "1" instead of as "0." On that indicator, a third of High School men and women, 42 percent of College men, and a third of College women were classified as dissatisfied in half or more of the life areas. Results of analyses using both versions of the measure were very similar.

References

Costa, F. (1983). Friendship patterns in young adulthood: A social psychological approach. Unpublished doctoral dissertation, University of Colorado, Boulder.

Costa, F., Jessor, R., & Donovan, J.E. (1987). Psychosocial correlates and antecedents of abortion: An exploratory study. *Population and Environment, 9* (1), 3–22.

Hays, R. (1980). A social-psychological analysis of alienation in young adulthood. Unpublished manuscript, Institute of Behavioral Science, University of Colorado, Boulder.

National Center for Health Statistics (1983). Obese and overweight adults in the United States. *Vital and Health Statistics*, Series 11, No. 230. DHHS Publ. No. 83–1680. U.S. Public Health Service. Washington, DC: U.S. Government Printing Office.

5

Problem behavior in young adulthood

There is a paucity of information about the extent, the patterning, and the structure of problem behavior in the life stage of young adulthood. In this chapter, we examine a number of different forms of young adult problem behavior and the linkages among them.

As defined in Chapter 2, the concept of problem behavior includes those behaviors that are considered a problem, a source of concern, or undesirable by the social or legal norms of conventional society, behaviors that usually elicit negative social sanctions when they occur. Five different areas of young adult problem behavior are described in this chapter; they include problem drinking, marijuana use, the use of other illicit drugs, general deviant behavior, and cigarette smoking.

Problem behavior in young adulthood

Before considering the structure of interrelations among the five problem behaviors, it is useful to describe their assessment and prevalence based on the 1979 and 1981 young adult questionnaires.

Involvement in problem drinking

Our concept of "problem" drinking has consistently focused on alcohol consumption to the point of drunkenness and on the negative social and interpersonal consequences associated with drinking. This perspective echoes Cahalan's (1970) emphasis on drinking-related problems rather than on the amount of drinking per se. Young adult drinkers were classified as problem drinkers if they reported being drunk more than six times in the past six months, *or* if they reported three or more (out of eight) negative consequences due to their drinking in the past six months. The possible negative consequences include criticism from friends, missing work or calling in sick, difficulties with spouse or partner, problems on the job, trouble with the police, accidents at home or at work, driving after drinking, and parents or siblings expressing concern over the respondent's drinking.[1]

On the basis of this operational definition, 16 percent ($N = 89$) of the young adults were classified as problem drinkers in 1981. Men in both samples were nearly three times as likely as women to be classified as problem drinkers: In the High School Study sample, 27 percent of the men and 10 percent of the women met the criteria for designation as problem drinkers; in the College Study sample, 20 percent of the men and 7 percent of the women were designated problem drinkers.

Problem drinkers and "nonproblem" drinkers differed markedly, as expected, on the two classification criteria: the number of times in the past six months they had been drunk, and the number of areas of negative consequences of drinking they had experienced in the past six months. In regard to frequency of drunkenness, the great majority of the nonproblem drinkers reported they had not been drunk at all in the past six months or that they had been drunk only once or twice (82% of High School sample men, 86% of High School sample women, 74% of College sample men, and 94% of College sample women). In contrast, in three of the four subsamples of problem drinkers, a majority had been drunk *ten* or more times in the past six months (61% of High School sample problem-drinker men, 55% of High School sample women, 65% of College sample men, and 43% of College sample women).[2] With regard to negative consequences due to drinking, the great majority of those classified as nonproblem drinkers either had experienced no negative consequences or had experienced them in only one area of their lives (78%, 90%, 79%, and 93%, respectively, for the High School sample men and women and College sample men and women). Among those classified as problem drinkers, however, the majority of each subsample reported negative consequences due to drinking in *three or more* areas (56% of High School sample men, 86% of High School sample women, 59% of College sample men, and 87% of College sample women).

The criteria used to establish the category of problem drinkers yielded a group significantly more involved with alcohol than the nonproblem drinkers on a variety of other measures as well. Problem drinkers reported drinking from two to four times as much a day, on the average, as the nonproblem drinkers. They also reported significantly more frequent occasions of high-volume drinking (five or more drinks per occasion), more frequent hangovers, and more frequent lapses of memory about events that occurred during their drinking episodes. The majority of those classified as problem drinkers also acknowledged that their drinking had been a problem for them over the past six months (54% of High School male problem drinkers, 59% of High School female problem drinkers, 59% of College male problem drinkers, and 86% of College female problem drinkers). In contrast, only a few of those classified as nonproblem drinkers thought their drinking had been a problem for them (8%, 5%, 8%, and 6% in the same four subsamples, respectively).

The gender and sample differences are also consistent across a variety of other drinking behavior measures as well. In regard to high volume drinking, 18 percent of the High School sample men reported high-volume drinking 20 or more times in the past six months, as did 5 percent of the High School sample women, 17 percent of the College sample men, and 6 percent of the College sample women. With respect to reported driving after having had "a good bit to drink," 16 percent of the High School sample men had done this six or more times in the past six months, in contrast to 5 percent of the High School sample women, 10 percent of the College sample men, and 5 percent of the College sample women. Young adult males in the High School Study sample emerge on all measures as the group most heavily involved in alcohol use and problem drinking.

Further conviction about the construct validity of the classification of young adult problem drinking derives from correlations of the two measures of "times drunk" and "negative consequences due to drinking" with a variety of other measures of young adult drinking behavior. Both criterion measures correlate significantly with average daily intake of alcohol, frequency of drinking first thing in the morning, number of lapses of memory of drinking episodes, number of times drinking continued over a period of several days ("binges"), and proportion of drinking that is solitary. The measures of times drunk and of negative consequences also correlate *negatively*, as expected, with church attendance frequency and participation in church-sponsored activities in both of the High School subsamples, and the times-drunk measure correlates negatively with these two conventional behaviors for both of the College subsamples.

Involvement in marijuana use

Since the two samples of young adults were either in high school or in college at the height of the "pot and protest" years, it is not surprising that the great majority of them had had at least some experience with marijuana. By 1981, about three-fourths of the High School sample (77% of men, 73% of women) reported having used marijuana at least twice in their lives. An even greater percentage of the College sample (87% of men, 84% of women) reported at least that amount of experience with marijuana.

About 40 percent of the young adults were current users in 1981 (i.e., had used marijuana within the past six months). Although there was no real difference between the genders in the percentage who had *ever* tried marijuana (lifetime prevalence), there was a gender difference in the percentage who were classified as current users of marijuana as young adults. In the High School sample, 44 percent of the men and 34 percent of the women were current users of marijuana; in the College sample, 50 percent of the men and 38 percent of the women were current users. (By way of contrast, in Wave IV [1972/73] of the adolescent/youth phase of the research, current use of marijuana was reported by 30% of the males and 32% of the females in the High School sample, and by 75% of the males and 63% of the females in the College sample.)

The amount of current use of marijuana in young adulthood also tended to be higher among men than women, and higher for the younger, High School Study participants than for the older, College Study participants. Among current users of marijuana in 1981, the average frequency of use in the previous month was 20 times for the High School sample men, 15 times for the High School sample women, 9 times for the College sample men, and 4 times for the College sample women.

Substantial numbers of participants in each subsample reported having used marijuana at some earlier point in time but no longer using it: By 1981, this included 29 percent of the High School sample men, 39 percent of the High School sample women, 33 percent of the College sample men, and 46 percent of the College sample women. Overall, 36 percent of the young adults were former users. Discontinuation of use, defined as no use in the past six months, was more common for the young adult women than for the young adult men. The reasons most frequently cited by these respondents for stopping marijuana use included the following: It's against their religion, or now they "get high on Christ"; it's not healthy; it's wrong to do; they don't like not being in control; it's against the law; they didn't like feeling paranoid when they used it; they just don't need it anymore; they don't enjoy the high or its effects anymore; they prefer alcohol; their spouse or friends don't use it. Lack of availability was rarely mentioned.

Two different approaches were used to differentiate heavier current use of marijuana in young adulthood from lower levels of current use. The first approach classified participants into three categories: *Heavier Users*, those who had used marijuana ten or more times in the previous month and who usually used it twice a week or more often when it was available; *Occasional Users*, those who had used marijuana between three and nine times in the previous month, *or* who had used it ten or more times in the previous month but who did not *usually* use it twice a week or more; and *Nonusers or Infrequent Users*, which included never users, quitters, noncurrent users, and those who had used marijuana only once or twice in the previous month. On the basis of these definitions, a small percentage of each subsample was classified as heavier users of marijuana (the rates of heavier use being 23% of the High School sample men; 13% of the High School sample women; 12% of the College sample men; and 4% of the College sample women). The great majority of young adults were classified in the "nonuser/infrequent user" category in 1981 (67% of High School sample men, 79% of High School sample women, 63% of College sample men, and 87% of College sample women).

The second approach relied on a four-item summative scale of involvement with marijuana; scores ranged from o (never tried marijuana) to 8 (heavier current use of marijuana). The four component items assessed ever use of marijuana, subjective experience of the drug's effects, availability of a personal supply of the drug, and use twice a week or more when it's available. The psychometric properties of the scale were satisfactory: In the High School sample, its alpha estimate of reliability was .79 and its homogeneity ratio was .49; in the College sample, its alpha reliability was .73, and its homogeneity ratio was .41.

The validity of our assessments of marijuana use is suggested by the comparability of the rates of experience found in our samples in 1981 with rates of use found in other samples of about the same age and birth-cohort. For example, the rates of *lifetime prevalence* – that is, ever experience with marijuana – were 77 and 73 percent for our 25- to 27-year-old men and women, respectively, in 1981; these rates are nearly identical to the rates of "ever use" found by Kandel (1984) in 1980–81 in her sample of New York State 24- to 25-year-old men and women (78% and 69%, respectively). They are somewhat higher than the rates found in the 1982 National Household Survey on Drug Abuse (Miller et al., 1983) – 64 percent of 18- to 25-year olds, and 60 percent of 26- to 29-year-olds – but household interviews have consistently yielded lower prevalence estimates. Our rates of *current use* of marijuana in 1981 are also quite similar to those found by Kandel (1984): 44 and 34 percent for our 25- to 27- year-old men and women, respectively, and 53 and 35 percent for the slightly younger men and women, respectively, in Kandel's sample.

In addition to the similarity of our rates of marijuana use to rates found by others, other data support the validity of the measures of marijuana use we have used. For example, the four-item scale of involvement with marijuana correlates positively and significantly with a measure of negative consequences due to marijuana use during the past six months and also with a measure of the frequency of driving after using marijuana (except among the College sample women). It also correlates negatively, as expected, with measures of church attendance and of involvement in church-sponsored activities for all four gender-by-study groups.

As with problem drinking, it is the 25- to 27-year-old males from the High School Study sample who were most heavily involved with marijuana as young adults.

Use of illicit drugs other than marijuana

Given the substantial percentage of young adults in our samples who had had experience with marijuana use, it is not surprising to find sizable percentages who had had experience with other illicit drugs as well. With respect to the nonmedical use of *stimulants* or "uppers" by 1981, 37 percent of the men and 31 percent of the women in the High School sample reported more than one such experience in their lifetime; rates for the College sample were comparable: 39 percent of the men and 30 percent of the women had used stimulants more than once without a doctor's prescription. Similar levels of use of psychedelic drugs and of cocaine were also reported by the young adults: Thirty-six percent of the High School sample men and 25 percent of the High School sample women had used *psychedelic drugs* more than once in their life, and 41 and 25 percent of the College sample men and women, respectively, had also done so; with reference to lifetime use of *cocaine* by 1981, 43 percent of the High School sample men, 30 percent of the High School sample women, 42 percent of the College sample men, and 33 percent of the College sample women reported such use.

Far fewer of the young adults in our samples were engaged in *current use* of these other illicit drugs. Only 13 percent had used a stimulant drug in the past six months (18% of High School sample men, 13% of High School sample women, 14% of College sample men, and 6% of College sample women); and only 7 percent had used a psychedelic drug in the past six months (12% of High School sample men, 4% of High School sample women, 12% of College sample men, and 3% of College sample women).

Current use of cocaine was about twice as prevalent among the young adults as stimulant use or psychedelic drug use. Thirty-four percent of the High School sample men, 21 percent of the High School sample women, 31 percent of the College sample men, and 21 percent of the College sample women had used cocaine in the past six months.

In addition to the categories of stimulants, psychedelic drugs, and cocaine, the young adult questionnaire also included questions about the use (or nonmedical use) of four other categories of drugs: barbiturates, tranquilizers, heroin, and other narcotics (morphine, codeine, etc.). Use of these drugs, however, was minimal in the young adult samples.

Two different measures were developed to represent levels of young adult involvement with these other illicit drugs. The first measure is simply the *number of categories* of illicit drugs (out of seven) that the young adult had used *in the past six months*. Seventy percent of the entire sample had not used any of the other illicit drugs in the past six months (65% of High School sample men, 75% of High School sample women, 61% of College sample men, and 75% of College sample women). Fifteen percent had used drugs from one of the categories (16%, 13%, 21%, and 15%, respectively), 6 percent had used drugs from two of the seven categories (5%, 6%, 10%, and 5%, respectively), and 9 percent had used drugs from three or more categories in the past six months (14% of the High School sample men, 7% of the High School sample women, 8% of the College sample men, and 5% of the College sample women).

The second measure of involvement in other illicit drug use summarized the *frequency of current use* of whichever illicit drug the respondent used most frequently in the past six months. In contrast with the first measure, this one reflects the *highest intensity* of involvement a respondent reported with respect to his/her "favorite" illicit drug. Thirty percent of the young adults had used an illicit drug other than marijuana in the past six months: While 17 percent had used their favorite drug only between one and five times in the past six months (18% of High School sample men, 14% of High School sample women, 24% of College sample men, and 16% of College sample women), 13 percent had used their favorite illicit drug six or more times in the past six months (18% of High School sample men, 11% of High School sample women, 15% of College sample men, and 9% of College sample women). Scores on this measure varied from 0 to 6 ("never" to "21 or more times").

As with marijuana use, one indicator of the validity of these data is their comparability with the rates of illicit drug use found in the National Institute on Drug Abuse 1982 National Household Survey on Drug Abuse (Miller et al., 1983) and in Kandel's young adult follow-up of New York State adolescents (Kandel, Davies, Karus, & Yamaguchi, 1986). In our High School sample, 49 percent of the men and 44 percent of the women had used one or more of the illicit drugs other than marijuana in their lives; in Kandel's young adult data, the analogous rates were 51 percent for the men and 38 percent for the women. In the NIDA national survey data, 22 percent of the 26- to 34-year-olds reported some use of cocaine, while 36 percent of our somewhat younger sample (25–30 years old) had used cocaine more than once. The rates of other illicit drug use observed in our samples were quite comparable to those found in other samples of similar age tested at about the same time.

As expected, the number of other illicit drugs used, and the highest frequency of use of an illicit drug during the previous six months, both correlated negatively with frequency of church attendance in the past year. These findings support the construct validity of these measures of other illicit drug use in young adulthood.

Involvement in general deviant behavior

The measure of general deviant behavior encompasses a variety of behaviors that violate social or legal norms but that do not involve substance use or abuse. The 12-item scale includes items that asked about damaging public or private property (reported by 2% in past year), giving false information on job or loan applications (reported by 15% in the past year), shoplifting (5%), starting fights (6%), lying to cover up something the respondent did (43%), writing bad checks (16%), breaking into a place that was locked (2%), taking things of value that belong to other people (4%), and similar items. Although the scale has satisfactory psychometric properties (alpha reliability = .73, homogeneity ratio = .22), it was treated as an index owing to the low rates of involvement reported for many of the behaviors. An index score was constructed by summing the *number of different deviant behaviors* engaged in once or more in the past year (range, 0–12).

Of the total sample, 25 percent had engaged in none of the deviant behaviors in the past year (26% of High School sample men, 20% of High School sample women, 30% of College sample men, and 32% of College sample women), 29 percent had engaged in *one* of the behaviors (27% of both High School sample men and women, 32% of College sample men, and 31% of College sample women), 21 percent had engaged in *two* of the behaviors (18% of High School sample men, 25% of High School sample women, 24% of College sample men, and 16% of College sample women), and 25 percent had engaged in *three or more* of the 12 behaviors in the past year (28% of both High School sample men and women, 14% of College sample men, and 21% of College sample women). There were no significant differences among the four gender-by-study subsamples in the mean number of different deviant behaviors engaged in during the past year (means were 1.75, 1.75, 1.43, and 1.42 for the four subsamples, respectively).

A dichotomous measure of higher involvement in general deviant behavior was also developed for use in contingency table analyses. This measure divided the young adults into lower involvement and higher involvement groups by assigning approximately the top 30 percent of the sample to the higher involvement group.

The construct validity of the general deviant behavior measure was established by using several approaches. One indicator of its validity is the strong negative Spearman rank-order correlation between mean scores on the deviant behavior items and the mean levels of rated "wrongness" of these behaviors (rho = −.96, −.97, −.96, and −.97 for the four gender-by-study subsamples). The more wrong a behavior was rated by the young adult participants, the lower was the reported involvement in that behavior over the past year. A second indicator of construct validity is the negative correlation between general deviant behavior index scores and church attendance frequency in the past year; these correlations were statistically significant for the two High School subsamples, but not for the College subsamples.

Involvement in cigarette smoking

Twenty-eight percent of the young adults were current smokers in 1981. Smoking was slightly more prevalent in 1981 among members of the High School sample (30% of the men and women) than it was within the older College sample (25% of the men and 24% of the women). Within the group of current smokers, 12 percent smoked only one cigarette a day, on the average, during the past month; 15

percent smoked two to five cigarettes a day; 18 percent smoked half a pack of cigarettes a day; 25 percent smoked about one pack of cigarettes a day; 21 percent smoked a pack and a half a day; and 8 percent smoked two or more packs of cigarettes a day.

Relatively few (13%) of the young adults had not at least tried smoking by the time of the 1981 data collection. "Never smokers" comprised 14 percent of the High School sample men and women, 13 percent of the College sample men, and 10 percent of the College sample women.

Many of those who had had some experience with cigarettes, however, had tried smoking only one or two times in their life. Forty-two percent of the High School sample men, 32 percent of the High School sample women, 35 percent of the College sample men, and 37 percent of the College sample women had had just this minimal level of involvement with smoking.

A good percentage of these young adults (17%) were considered "ex-smokers" in 1981, that is, they were once regular smokers but had not smoked for at least six months. Smoking cessation was less prevalent in the High School sample (9% of the men, 17% of the women) than it was in the College sample (24% of the men, 22% of the women). A somewhat smaller percentage (6%) of the young adults were classified as noncurrent smokers, meaning they had smoked in the past six months, but had not had a cigarette in the past month.

In the analyses that follow, two measures of cigarette smoking are used. The first measure is ordinal in nature; it assesses the number of cigarettes smoked per day in the past month, and it orders the young adults from never smokers to current smokers who smoked two or more packs of cigarettes a day. Never smokers, ex-smokers, and noncurrent smokers had scores of zero on this measure. The second measure is simply a dichotomous status index differentiating between current smokers (smoked in the past month) and everyone else.

There is a fair amount of support in the data for considering cigarette smoking a problem behavior. First, the great majority of the young adults in our samples perceived that the general public's attitude about smoking has changed in recent years; 76 percent felt the general public's attitude had become less accepting of smoking, and

14 percent felt the general public had become strongly opposed to
it. Second, the great majority were bothered by smoking in public
places; 38 percent said it bothered them "a little," and 42 percent
said it bothered them "a great deal." Lastly, all 568 young adults
thought that smoking has an effect on a person's health; 3 percent
thought it has a mild effect, 27 percent thought the effect is moderate,
and 68 percent thought that smoking has a serious effect on health.

Several lines of evidence support the construct validity of the measure of involvement with smoking. First, among the current smokers,
the greater the reported number of cigarettes smoked per day, the
more often respondents reported lighting up a cigarette first thing in
the morning, the more often they "chain-smoked" (lighting up another cigarette immediately when they finished smoking one), and the
more often they felt that they "must" have a cigarette. Second, in
the larger sample which includes never smokers and noncurrent
smokers, involvement with smoking correlated negatively, as expected,
with church attendance frequency and with self-ratings of overall
health.

Summary

There is still considerable variation in involvement in different problem behaviors in young adulthood: Sixteen percent of the young adult
participants could be classified as problem drinkers; 40 percent were
currently using marijuana, with 14 percent classified as *heavier* users;
30 percent had used one or more illicit drugs other than marijuana
in the past six months, and 13 percent had used their favorite illicit
drug six or more times in the past six months; 25 percent had engaged
in three or more general deviant behaviors in the past year; and 28
percent were current smokers.

The young adults from the High School sample tended to have
greater current involvement in the different problem behaviors than
did those from the College sample, and men tended to have greater
current involvement in problem behaviors than did women (except
for current smoking). College sample women tended to be the least
involved in the different problem behaviors.

In general, the levels of young adult involvement in the different
problem behaviors are quite consonant with those found in other

studies, and the problem behavior measures typically correlate with other measures as expected theoretically. Such findings support the construct validity of the measures of problem behavior.

Interrelations among problem behaviors in young adulthood

On the basis of previous research in this area, our own and that of other investigators, it was anticipated that the measures of young adult problem behavior would covary, that is, be associated in a positive direction. Young adults more heavily involved in one area of problem behavior were expected to be more involved in other areas of problem behavior as well.

In order to examine whether this expectation, well established among adolescents, holds also in young adulthood, we undertook several different types of analyses. As a first step, the measures of involvement in each of the five different problem behavior areas were intercorrelated. In these correlational analyses, the following *continuous* measures of the various problem behaviors were used: times drunk in the past six months; frequency of marijuana use in the past month; highest frequency of use of any other illicit drug in the past six months; the general deviant behavior index; and number of cigarettes smoked per day in the past month. A continuous measure of conventional behavior, church attendance frequency, was also included in the correlational analyses as an indicator of discriminant validity.

The Pearson correlations among these young adult behavior measures in 1981 are presented in Table 5.1 for the High School sample men and women, and for the College sample men and women, separately. In the High School Study data, 19 of the 20 correlations among the different problem behaviors are statistically significant ($p < .05$) and in the expected positive direction. Greater reported involvement in one form of problem behavior is associated with greater involvement in other forms of problem behavior in young adulthood, and this holds for both men and women. The sole nonsignificant correlation is between general deviant behavior and cigarette smoking for the women. All five of the problem behaviors also correlate negatively, and at a significant level, with the conventional behavior mea-

Table 5.1. *Pearson correlations among continuous measures of problem behavior and conventional behavior, by study and gender, 1981 young adult data*

	Times Drunk	Marijuana Use	Other Illicit Drug Use	Deviant Behavior	Cigarette Smoking	Church Attendance
High School Study						
Problem behavior measures						
Times Drunk/Past 6 Months		.27***	.41***	.21**	.15*	−.21**
Frequency of Marijuana Use/Past Month	.48***		.59***	.14*	.23***	−.18**
Highest Frequency Other Illicit Drug Use/ Past 6 Months	.53***	.57***		.29***	.24***	−.23***
General Deviant Behavior Frequency/ Past Year	.37***	.36***	.32***		.04	−.13 +
Number Cigarettes Smoked per Day/ Past Month	.30***	.34***	.31****	.22**		−.18**
Conventional behavior measure						
Church Attendance Frequency/Past Year	−.32***	−.25***	−.38***	−.19**	−.29**	

College Study

Problem behavior measures

	1	2	3	4	5	6
Times Drunk/Past 6 Months		.15	.45***	.53***	.24*	−.15
Frequency of Marijuana Use/Past Month	.34**		.19+	.07	.15	−.08
Highest Frequency Other Illicit Drug Use/Past 6 Months	.31**	.47***		.30**	.22*	−.21*
General Deviant Behavior Frequency/Past Year	.16	.39***	.11		.01	−.10
Number Cigarettes Smoked per Day/Past Month	.19	.02	−.03	.01		−.20*

Conventional behavior measure

	1	2	3	4	5	6
Church Attendance Frequency/Past Year	−.15	−.07	−.24*	−.06	−.20+	

Note: For both the High School and College studies, the correlations for the men are below the diagonal, and the correlations for the women are above the diagonal.

***$p \leq .001$ (two-tail test); **$p \leq .01$; *$p \leq .05$; +$p \leq .10$.

sure of church attendance frequency for the High School sample men, and four of the five problem behaviors (all but general deviant behavior) correlate negatively with church attendance for the High School sample women.

In the College Study data shown in the bottom half of the table, all but one of the correlations are in the expected direction, and almost half (9 out of 20) are statistically significant. For the College sample men, times drunk, marijuana use, and other illicit drug use are positively correlated with each other, and marijuana use frequency is correlated with involvement in general deviant behavior. The measures of cigarette smoking and of general deviance generally do not correlate significantly with the other problem behaviors for this subsample.

For the College sample women, a different pattern of correlations obtains among the problem behaviors. In this subsample, the measures of times drunk and of other illicit drug use correlate significantly with all of the other problem behavior measures except for marijuana use, which does not correlate significantly with any of the other problem behaviors. The measures of other illicit drug use and of cigarette smoking both correlate significantly and negatively with the conventional behavior measure of church attendance.

One possible reason why the correlations among the problem behaviors are weaker and less consistent in the College sample data than they are in the High School sample data is that both the means and standard deviations on the measures were smaller in the College sample data; this could have attenuated their correlations. The means and standard deviations are lowest for the College sample women, which is consistent with the fact that the lowest intercorrelations among the behaviors are found in this subsample.

The intercorrelations in the 1981 data replicate in the young adult data collected in 1979, two years earlier. The replication is the strongest for the High School sample: Of the correlations that are statistically significant ($p < .05$) in the 1981 data, all but three were also significant in the 1979 data as well. In the College sample, the replication of the 1981 correlations in the 1979 data is stronger for the men than for the women; in the men's data, two-thirds of the correlations are similar between 1981 and 1979, whereas for the women, only one-third of the correlations are similar between the two data waves.

The intercorrelations among the 1981 young adult behavior measures shown in Table 5.1 are as strong as or stronger than the intercorrelations observed in the earlier, adolescent/youth phase of the research (see Donovan & Jessor, 1985, Table 1). For example, the correlations between times drunk and frequency of marijuana use were .25, .07, .26, and .12 in the 1972/73 data for the High School sample males and females and the College sample males and females, respectively; in the 1981 young adult data, the analogous correlations are .48, .27, .34, and .15, respectively (see Table 5.1). It should also be noted that all of these correlations are attenuated by measurement error. Later in this chapter, in Table 5.3, we present disattenuated correlations based on latent-variable measures of the problem behaviors. As will be seen, those correlations are considerably larger in magnitude.

Interrelationships among the various problem behaviors can be examined in another way, using the dichotomous status measures of involvement. In the High School male sample, for example, *problem drinkers* exhibited the following rates of involvement in the other behaviors: Fifty-three percent were heavier users of marijuana, 40 percent used other illicit drugs with some frequency, 54 percent had high scores on general deviant behavior, 47 percent were current smokers, and only 9 percent were church attenders. In contrast, the rates of involvement for High School sample males who were *not* problem drinkers are the following: Only 13 percent were heavier marijuana users, only 9 percent used another illicit drug with some frequency, only 21 percent had high scores on general deviance, only 23 percent were current smokers, and fully 43 percent were church attenders. Results for the High School sample women were similar.

With regard to the College sample male *problem drinkers*, 25 percent were heavier marijuana users, 18 percent used another illicit drug with some frequency, 35 percent had high scores on general deviance, 47 percent were current smokers, and 29 percent had attended church. In contrast, among the College sample males who were *not* problem drinkers, only 10 percent were heavier users of marijuana, 15 percent used another illicit drug with some frequency, 17 percent had higher involvement in general deviant behavior, 19 percent were current smokers, and 35 percent were churchgoers.

Cross-tabulations between the other dichotomous status measures of involvement show much the same pattern of differences between those young adults involved in one area of problem behavior and those who were not. For instance, among the High School males who were *heavier marijuana users*, 60 percent were problem drinkers, 86 percent used other illicit drugs, 56 percent had high scores on general deviance, 61 percent were current smokers, and only 17 percent were churchgoers. In contrast, among the High School males who were not heavy marijuana users, only 17 percent were considered problem drinkers, only 20 percent had used other illicit drugs in the past six months, only 21 percent had high general deviance scores, only 20 percent were current smokers, and 41 percent were churchgoers. Similar results obtain when current smokers were compared with those who were not current smokers, when those with high scores on general deviance were compared with those with low scores on general deviance, and when those who used other illicit drugs with some frequency were compared with those who did not.

The correlational analyses demonstrate that all of the problem behaviors are positively correlated with one another and negatively correlated with the measure of conforming behavior, church attendance frequency, in young adulthood. In general, the magnitude and consistency of these correlations are higher in the High School sample than in the College sample, and they are higher for men than for women. These associations among the different categories of problem behavior provide initial support for the concept of a *syndrome* of problem behavior in young adulthood, a syndrome parallel to that established earlier for adolescence (Donovan & Jessor, 1985; Donovan, Jessor, & Costa, 1988; Jessor & Jessor, 1977).

This finding that different problem behaviors are correlated in samples of young adults has also been reported by several other studies, both local and nationwide (see Burke, Hunter, Croft, Cresanta, & Berenson, 1988; Elliott, Huizinga, & Menard, 1989; Gove, Geerken, & Hughes, 1979; Johnston, O'Malley, & Eveland, 1978; Kandel, Simcha-Fagan, & Davies, 1986; Newcomb & Bentler, 1986; O'Donnell, Voss, Clayton, Slatin, & Room, 1976).

Testing for a single common factor

The syndrome concept suggests that a single common factor may underlie the different forms of problem behavior and be responsible for their intercorrelations. To test that proposition, we employed the Jöreskog (1967) maximum-likelihood factor analysis procedure. The test involves a comparison of the observed correlations among the behaviors with the correlations that would be predicted from the single-factor model. If a one-factor model were appropriate, the observed correlation between any two problem behaviors would be equal to the product of the estimated loadings of these behaviors on the common factor.[3]

Maximum-likelihood factor analyses were carried out on the 1981 data for each of the gender-by-study groups with the same set of five problem behaviors used in the preceding correlational analyses. In all four of the subsamples, the obtained chi-square values were clearly *non*significant, as expected, indicating that there were few differences between the observed and the predicted correlation matrices. In all cases, therefore, a single common underlying factor was able to account for the observed correlations among the different problem behaviors. (Probability levels for the chi-square tests were .84 for the High School sample men, .50 for the High School sample women, .24 for the College sample men, and .26 for the College sample women.)

According to the Burt–Banks formula for determining the significance of factor loadings, all of the problem behaviors loaded significantly on the underlying factor for both the High School sample men and women. In the College sample data, all of the behaviors loaded significantly except for cigarette smoking for the men and frequency of marijuana use for the women.

Analyses based on the 1979 young adult data replicate the 1981 results reported above. In three of the four gender-by-study subsamples (all except the High School sample women), the chi-square values were again *non*significant, confirming further support for a single underlying common factor and, therefore, for the notion of a syndrome of problem behavior in young adulthood.

The present results extend those reported earlier (Donovan & Jessor, 1985); the problem-behavior syndrome in these young adult data includes one additional behavior not taken into account in the earlier analyses: cigarette smoking. Both the bivariate correlational analyses and the maximum-likelihood factor analyses provide a warrant for considering problem behavior in young adulthood as a multiple-component composite variable.

Testing for a second-order latent variable

The analyses thus far suggest that a single common factor can explain the correlations among the five different young adult problem behaviors examined. A drawback to these analyses, however, is their reliance on a single item, or a single composite measure, to represent involvement in each area of problem behavior. The conclusion that there is a single factor underlying all five problem behaviors would be strengthened if each area of problem behavior were represented by multiple measures. That would allow examination of the relations among latent variable constructs representing "true scores" on the problem behaviors. Structural equation modeling techniques can be used to determine whether there is a second-order factor that accounts for the correlations among latent variables (first-order factors), reflecting involvement in the five areas of young adult problem behavior.

The Jöreskog and Sörbom (1989) program, LISREL 7, was used. For these analyses, each area of problem behavior was represented by several measures assessed in 1981. *Problem Drinking* was represented by times drunk, frequency of high-volume drinking, and a summative score reflecting frequency of negative personal and social consequences of drinking, all in the past six months. *Marijuana Use* was represented by two items: frequency of marijuana use in the past month, and average intake of marijuana per occasion. *Other Illicit Drug Use* was represented by three items, reflecting frequency of use of stimulants, psychedelic drugs, and cocaine in the past six months; these were the drugs used most often by the young adults. *General Deviance* was represented by three subscales reflecting different aspects of nonnormative behavior; these were a four-item subscale assessing lying, a three-item subscale assessing aggression, and a two-item subscale assessing theft. *Cigarette Smoking* was represented by two items that asked about lifetime experience with smoking, and number of cigarettes smoked per day in the past month. Because all of these indicator measures are ordinal, polychoric correlations were calculated for the analyses.

The first step in the process of testing for a second-order factor was to determine whether these 13 indicator measures do in fact assess five separate areas of problem behavior involvement in young adulthood. This "measurement model" was tested by using LISREL 7 to perform a confirmatory factor analysis of the five-factor model. Weighted least squares estimation procedures were used (Browne, 1984) since this is the most appropriate method for the analysis of ordinal data. According to the various measures of fit provided by LISREL, this measurement model provides an excellent fit to the data for both the High School and College Study samples. The likelihood ratio chi-square, the first measure of fit provided by LISREL, was 27.8 (with 55 degrees of freedom) for the High School Study and 23.1 for the College Study. These chi-square values indicate that there was no significant lack of fit between the measurement model and the data in either study. The goodness-of-fit index (GFI), which should be greater than .90 for satisfactory fit (see Cole, 1987), was .997 for the High School Study sample and .993 for the College Study sample. The goodness of fit adjusted for degrees of freedom (AGFI), which should exceed .80 for a well-fitting model, was .995 for the High School Study sample and .989 for the College Study sample. Bentler and Bonett's (1980) Normed Fit Index (NFI), the most popular fit index, was .996 for the High School Study and .990 for the College Study sample. These four different indexes all indicate an excellent level of fit between the measurement model and the data.

The factor loadings for each of the 13 indicator measures on their respective latent variables, for both the High School Study and College Study samples, are presented in Table 5.2. For both samples, every one of the indicators loaded significantly on its latent variable (i.e., each loading was at least twice the size of its standard error). The loadings were all substantial in magnitude.

In addition to confirming the measurement model, these analyses also provide estimates of the correlations among the five latent-variable measures of involvement in problem behavior. These are, in essence, correlations between "true score" measures of the problem

Table 5.2. *Standardized loadings of indicator measures on latent-variable measures of problem behavior, by study, 1981 young adult data*

Factor/Indicators	Standardized loadings	
	High School Study	College Study
Problem Drinking		
Times Drunk/Past 6 Months	.94	.93
Frequency High-Volume Drinking/Past 6 Months	.93	.90
Total Negative Consequences of Drinking	.88	.85
Marijuana Use		
Frequency Marijuana Use/Past Month	.95	.96
Average Intake of Marijuana per Occasion	.94	.89
Other Illicit Drug Use		
Frequency Stimulant Use/Past 6 Months	.82	.90
Frequency Psychedelics Use/Past 6 Months	.81	.80
Frequency Cocaine Use/Past 6 Months	.89	.82
General Deviant Behavior		
Lying/Past Year	.59	.52
Aggression/Past Year	.56	.85
Theft/Past Year	.55	.83
Cigarette Smoking		
Experience with Smoking/Lifetime	.89	.94
Number Cigarettes Smoked per Day/Past Month	.99	.90

Note: All estimates are greater than twice their standard error.

behaviors, analogous to correlations corrected for attenuation due to unreliability. As might be expected, the correlations among the latent-variable measures of problem behavior shown in Table 5.3 are considerably larger than those among the observed variable measures seen earlier in Table 5.1. The average intercorrelation for the High School Study sample is .55, and for the College Study sample it is

.44, and all but one of the correlations are significant. For both samples the highest correlation is between Marijuana Use and Other Illicit Drug Use (.87 for the High School sample, .81 for the College sample). For both samples, the Cigarette Smoking latent variable correlated least well with the other latent-variable measures of problem behavior involvement.

With the establishment of a satisfactory measurement model, the next step was to carry out a second set of LISREL analyses. These were to determine how well the data supported a second-order latent variable of problem behavior involvement, and to determine the loading of each of the first-order latent-variable measures of specific problem behaviors on the second-order latent variable. Overall, the second-order model fits the data almost as well as the measurement model did. Chi-square measures of fit (with 60 degrees of freedom) were 37.5 for the High School Study and 30.8 for the College Study. In the High School Study sample, the goodness-of-fit index (GFI) was .996; in the College Study sample, it was .991. Adjusted goodness-of-fit indexes (AGFIs) were .994 and .987, respectively, for the two samples. Bentler and Bonett's (1980) Normed Fit Index (NFI) was .994 and .987 for the two samples, respectively.

A further test of the second-order factor model was made by performing a LISREL analysis of the matrix of correlations among just the latent-variable measures of problem behavior. The GFI from this analysis estimates the ability of the underlying factor to account for the latent-variable correlations in Table 5.3, and is not biased upward by the fit of the measurement model. For the High School Study, this GFI was .952. For the College Study, it was .972. These results confirm that even when the fit of the measurement model is not allowed to influence the overall fit, a single underlying factor can still account for the correlations among the latent-variable measures of problem behavior.

As can be seen in Figure 5.1, all five latent variables of involvement in the different problem behaviors loaded significantly on the second-order latent variable. In both studies, Other Illicit Drug Use loads most strongly on the underlying factor, followed in decreasing order by Marijuana Use, Problem Drinking, General Deviant Behavior, and Cigarette Smoking. This second-order latent variable is best interpreted as behavior system proneness for problem behavior. As

Table 5.3. *Correlations among latent-variable measures of problem
behavior, by study, 1981 young adult data*

	PROB-DRK	MJUSE	OTH-DRUG	DVB	SMOKE
High School Study (N = 365)[a]					
Problem Drinking					
(PROBDRK)	1.00				
Marijuana Use					
(MJUSE)	.68	1.00			
Other Illicit Drug Use					
(OTHDRUG)	.72	.87	1.00		
General Deviant					
Behavior (DVB)	.61	.52	.66	1.00	
Cigarette Smoking					
(SMOKE)	.37	.43	.39	.26	1.00
College Study (N = 181)[a]					
Problem Drinking					
(PROBDRK)	1.00				
Marijuana Use					
(MJUSE)	.55	1.00			
Other Illicit Drug Use					
(OTHDRUG)	.58	.81	1.00		
General Deviant					
Behavior (DVB)	.48	.49	.47	1.00	
Cigarette Smoking					
(SMOKE)	.28	.30	.32	.11[ns]	1.00

Note: All correlations but one are significant (i.e., greater than twice their
standard error); ns = not significant.
[a]Participants missing scores on any of the 13 items used in establishing the
5 latent variables were not included in these LISREL analyses. The N
omitted from the High School Study was 19; from the College Study, 3.

implied by the model in Figure 5.1, involvement in any one of the
problem behaviors in young adulthood is influenced by involvement in
the other problem behaviors. These results, the first using structural equation modeling, strongly confirm the earlier correlational and

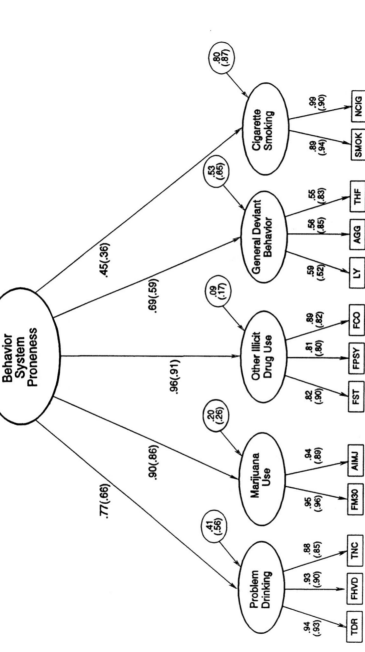

Figure 5.1. The second-order latent variable of Behavior System proneness for problem behavior, showing the High School Study and College Study loadings of the five different problem-behavior latent variables. (Loadings for College Study are in parentheses.) Acronyms: TDR = Times Drunk; FHVD = Frequency of High-Volume Drinking; TNC = Total Negative Consequences of Drinking; FM30 = Frequency of Marijuana Use in Past Month; AIMJ = Average Intake of Marijuana per Occasion; FST = Frequency of Stimulant Use; FPSY = Frequency of Psychedelic Drug Use; FCO = Frequency of Cocaine Use; LY = Frequency of Lying; AGG = Frequency of Aggression; THF = Frequency of Theft; SMOK = Lifetime Smoking Experience; NCIG = Number of Cigarettes Smoked per Day.

factor-analytic findings, and provide additional support for the validity of the concept of a syndrome of problem behavior in young adulthood. It is important to point out, however, that there is considerable residual variance in each of the measures of problem behavior that is not accounted for by the latent variable. That fact indicates the importance of looking at each of the behaviors in its own right as well.

The Multiple Problem Behavior Index

The analyses presented thus far have established that the various categories of young adult problem behavior are interrelated and constitute a coherent behavioral syndrome. That the five different problem behaviors reflect a single underlying common factor is particularly compelling. This evidence provides the rationale for constructing a composite measure to reflect variation in degree of young adult involvement in the class or syndrome of problem behavior. An index of multiple problem behavior involvements was constructed to reflect the level of intensity of *current involvement* in the five problem behavior areas considered simultaneously. It is based on within-group standardized scores (*T*-scores) on the same continuous-variable measures of the problem behaviors that were used in the foregoing correlational analyses. Psychometric scale properties for the Multiple Problem Behavior Index are presented in Table 5.4 for each of the four young adult subsamples.

As may be seen in Table 5.4, the Multiple Problem Behavior Index has satisfactory scale properties for both the High School sample men and women (alpha reliabilities are .76 and .65, respectively), and somewhat weaker scale properties for the College sample men and women (alphas are .55 and .60, respectively). For an index based on only five components, these properties are acceptable. The item-total correlations are all acceptable, with only one exception (Cigarette Smoking for the College Study men).

The Multiple Problem Behavior Index will serve as a key criterion measure for the young adult correlational analyses presented in later chapters of this book. It will be relied upon in testing the adequacy of Problem-Behavior Theory as an account of variation in young adult problem behavior. It will also serve as a criterion measure *in young*

Table 5.4. *The Multiple Problem Behavior Index psychometric properties, by study and gender, 1981 young adult data*

	High School Study		College Study	
	Men	Women	Men	Women
Scale properties				
Alpha reliability	.76	.65	.55	.60
Homogeneity ratio	.39	.27	.20	.23
Mean scale score	249.74	249.49	250.01	250.00
Standard deviation	35.51	31.98	29.88	30.95
N	160	222	84	100
Item-total correlations (item removed)				
Times Drunk	.60	.45	.42	.58
Frequency of Marijuana Use	.62	.48	.52	.21
Highest Frequency of Other Illicit Drug Use	.61	.62	.34	.47
General Deviant Behavior	.43	.25	.26	.34
Number Cigarettes Smoked per Day	.39	.25	.07	.23

adulthood to be predicted from variation in psychosocial proneness to problem behavior *in adolescence*.

Summary

The extent and the patterning of young adult involvement in five different categories of problem behavior have been the focus of this chapter. In the initial section, the measures of problem behavior were described, and information on prevalence and construct validity was presented. Sizable proportions of the young adults were involved in the various problem behaviors, with the High School Study males being most involved of the four subsamples. The key findings are that involvements in the different problem behaviors covary, and that their intercorrelations reflect a single underlying common factor. The data support the notion of a syndrome of problem behavior in young adulthood, a notion that had previously been shown to hold for adolescence.

Notes

1 This definition differs in two respects from the one used in the adolescent phase of the research (Jessor & Jessor, 1977): It requires twice as frequent drunkenness for a drinker to be considered a problem drinker, and it is concerned with a larger number of areas of potential negative consequences of drinking than was true of the earlier criterion.

2 In the 1979 questionnaire, drunkenness was assessed by an open-ended item. In those data, the average number of "times drunk" for the non-problem drinkers ranged from 1.5 to 3 times in the past six months for the four subsamples; for the problem drinkers, the average number of times drunk ranged from 14 to 35 times in the past six months.

3 The Jöreskog program computes a large-sample chi-square test of the discrepancy between the matrix of observed and the matrix of predicted correlations among the behaviors. A *non*significant ($p >. 05$) chi-square value provides support for the hypothesis of a single common factor, whereas a significant chi-square would suggest that more than a single common factor underlies the relations among the different problem behaviors.

References

Bentler, P. M., & Bonett, D. G. (1980). Significance tests and goodness of fit in the analysis of covariance structures. *Psychological Bulletin, 88,* 588–606.

Browne, M. W. (1984). Asymptotically distribution free methods for the analysis of covariance structures. *British Journal of Mathematical and Statistical Psychology, 37,* 62–83.

Burke, G. L., Hunter, S. MacD., Croft, J. B., Cresanta, J. L., & Berenson, G. S. (1988). The interaction of alcohol and tobacco use in adolescents and young adults: Bogalusa Heart Study. *Addictive Behaviors, 13,* 387–393.

Cahalan, D. (1970). *Problem drinkers: A national study.* San Francisco: Jossey-Bass.

Cole, D. A. (1987). Utility of confirmatory factor analysis in test validation research. *Journal of Consulting and Clinical Psychology, 55,* 584–594.

Donovan, J. E., & Jessor, R. (1985). Structure of problem behavior in adolescence and young adulthood. *Journal of Consulting and Clinical Psychology*, *53*, 890–904.

Donovan, J. E., Jessor, R., & Costa, F. M. (1988). Syndrome of problem behavior in adolescence: A replication. *Journal of Consulting and Clinical Psychology*, *56*, 762–765.

Elliott, D. S., Huizinga, D., & Menard, S. (1989). *Multiple problem youth*. New York: Springer.

Gove, W. R., Geerken, M., & Hughes, M. (1979). Drug use and mental health among a representative national sample of young adults. *Social Forces*, *58*, 572–590.

Jessor, R., & Jessor, S. L. (1977). *Problem behavior and psychosocial development: A longitudinal study of youth*. New York: Academic Press.

Johnston, L. D., O'Malley, P. M., & Eveland, L. K. (1978). Drugs and delinquency: A search for causal connections. In D. B. Kandel (Ed.), *Longitudinal research on drug use* (pp. 137–156). New York: Wiley.

Jöreskog, K. G. (1967). Some contributions to maximum likelihood factor analysis. *Psychometrika*, *32*, 443–482.

Jöreskog, K. G., & Sörbom, D. (1989). *LISREL 7: A guide to the program and applications* (2nd ed.). Chicago, IL: SPSS Inc.

Kandel, D. B. (1984). Marijuana users in young adulthood. *Archives of General Psychiatry*, *41*, 200–209.

Kandel, D. B., Davies, M., Karus, D., & Yamaguchi, K. (1986). The consequences in young adulthood of adolescent drug involvement. *Archives of General Psychiatry*, *43*(8), 746–754.

Kandel, D., Simcha-Fagan, O., & Davies, M. (1986). Risk factors for delinquency and illicit drug use from adolescence to young adulthood. *Journal of Drug Issues*, *16*, 67–90.

Miller, J. D., Cisin, I. H., Gardner-Keaton, H., Harrell, A. V., Wirtz, P. W., Abelson, H. I., & Fishburne, P. M. (1983). *National Survey on Drug Abuse: Main findings 1982* (DHHS Publication No. ADM 83-1263). Rockville, MD: National Institute on Drug Abuse.

Newcomb, M. D., & Bentler, P. M. (1986). Frequency and sequence of drug use: A longitudinal study from early adolescence to young adulthood. *Journal of Drug Education*, *16*, 101–120.

O'Donnell, J. A., Voss, H. L., Clayton, R. R., Slatin, G. T., & Room, R. G. W. (1976). *Young men and drugs: A nationwide survey* (NIDA Research Monograph No. 5). Rockville, MD: National Institute on Drug Abuse.

6

Psychosocial correlates of problem behavior in young adulthood

From the perspective of Problem-Behavior Theory, the explanatory account of behavior depends on the joint consideration of variables in the different systems of the conceptual framework. The multivariate logic of the theory, summarized by the concept of *psychosocial proneness* described in Chapter 2, has been supported by the findings from the earlier phase of this research (Jessor & Jessor, 1977). The earlier data demonstrated that the key measures in the Personality, Perceived Environment, and Behavior Systems of Problem-Behavior Theory were able to account for substantial amounts of variance in a variety of specific problem behaviors among adolescents and college-age youth. The measures of those psychosocial risk factors mapped overall proneness to involvement in problem behavior, and reflected an underlying dimension of conventionality–unconventionality.

In this chapter, we examine the relation of young adult personality, perceived environment, and behavioral characteristics to young adult involvement in problem behavior. Two main objectives are addressed. The first is to establish the specific psychosocial risk factors that are related to greater problem-behavior involvement in this young adult stage of the life course. The primary focus is on those variables or risk factors that were identified in the earlier, adolescent phase of the research and that best represent the concept of psychosocial proneness. In addition, other personality and perceived environment characteristics that are unique to this young adult phase of the research will also be examined. These include, in particular, measures of stress and satisfaction associated with the different life areas of young adulthood.

The second objective of this chapter is to carry out a multivariate appraisal of Problem-Behavior Theory in young adulthood. The extent to which the various personality, perceived environment, and behavioral risk factors, taken together, can account for variation in problem behavior in young adulthood will be explored. Both objectives have the goal of determining whether the psychosocial variables that were identified in the earlier, adolescent phase of the research remain relevant to variation in involvement in problem behavior during this later, young adult stage of the life course as well.

Psychosocial correlates of problem behavior in young adulthood

The question addressed in this section is whether the various psychosocial measures of Problem-Behavior Theory are related to young adult involvement in problem behavior. Level of involvement in problem behavior was established on the basis of scores on the Multiple Problem Behavior Index described in Chapter 5. The Multiple Problem Behavior Index is a continuous measure that reflects intensity of current involvement in five different areas of problem behavior: problem drinking, marijuana use, use of other illicit drugs, general deviance, and cigarette smoking. Scores on the personality, perceived environment, and behavior system measures that summarize the concept of psychosocial proneness were correlated with scores on the Multiple Problem Behavior Index. The six personality system proneness measures used include two from the Motivational-Instigation Structure – Value on Achievement and Expectation for Achievement; two from the Personal Belief Structure – Social Criticism and Alienation; and two from the Personal Control Structure – Attitudinal Intolerance of Deviance and Religiosity. Proneness to problem behavior in the Perceived Environment System was represented by one measure taken from the Distal Structure – Friends Controls – and three from the Proximal Structure – Friends' Approval of Drug Use, Friends Models for Drug Use, and Friends Models for Religiosity. One measure of proneness in the Behavior System was used, the measure of Church Attendance in the Past Year.

In addition to these measures of psychosocial proneness, two measures of *stress* in young adult life – Total Stress Across Life Areas and Negative Life Events (both described in Chapter 3) – were also examined in relation to the Multiple Problem Behavior Index. Of the new concepts added to the explanatory framework of Problem-Behavior Theory for this phase of the research, the concept of stress was considered to be especially relevant. Stress in critical areas of life can constitute an interference with the attainment of goals or satisfactions, and that can serve as a source of instigation to problem behavior (Jessor, Graves, Hanson, & Jessor, 1968). Greater stress is also assumed to increase the likelihood that alcohol and other drugs may be used as ways of coping. In addition, the stress associated with negative life events has been advanced by others as a risk factor for psychiatric problems, physical illness, and problem behavior (Finney & Moos, 1984; Rodin, Morton, & Shimkin, 1982; Vinokur & Selzer, 1975).

Analyses of the relation between the psychosocial measures and the summary measure of problem behavior involvement were done separately for the four gender-by-study groups. The relevant bivariate correlations are presented in Table 6.1. As can be seen in Table 6.1, those individuals who are characterized by personality, perceived social environment, and behavioral risk factors that represent greater psychosocial proneness to problem behavior are, indeed, more intensely involved in problem behavior. This conclusion holds for both the High School Study and the College Study. Although neither of the two motivational-instigation measures in the Personality System shows a consistent relationship with problem behavior, more socially critical attitudes, greater alienation, lower intolerance of deviance, and lower religiosity all relate significantly to greater involvement in problem behavior. For these young adults, personality proneness to problem behavior involvement is reflected most consistently and most strongly in personal controls against problem behavior – intolerance of deviance and religiosity.

With respect to perceived environment proneness, lesser friends controls against problem behavior, greater friends' approval of drug use, more friends models for drug use, and fewer friends models for religious involvement are all significantly correlated with greater involvement in problem behavior. In short, perception of the social environment as less controlling and less conventional is associated with more intense involvement in problem behavior in young adulthood.

Table 6.1. *Pearson correlations of measures of psychosocial proneness and of life stress with the summary measure of problem behavior involvement in young adulthood (1981), by group*

Measures of psychosocial proneness and life stress in young adulthood	Multiple Problem Behavior Index			
	High School Study		College Study	
	Men (N = 160)	Women (N = 222)	Men (N = 84)	Women (N = 100)
Personality System				
Motivational-Instigation Structure				
Value on Achievement	.05	.09 +	.05	.21*
Expectation for Achievement	−.08	.03	−.10	−.16*
Personal Belief Structure				
Social Criticism	.20**	.04	.42***	.14 +
Alienation	.24***	.20***	.26**	.20*
Personal Control Structure				
Attitudinal Intolerance of Deviance	−.44***	−.32***	−.18*	−.18*
Religiosity	−.31***	−.24***	−.25**	−.24**
Perceived Environment System				
Distal Structure				
Friends Controls	−.30***	−.16**	−.16 +	−.17*
Proximal Structure				
Friends' Approval Drug Use	.38***	.45***	.29**	.45***
Friends Models Drug Use	.69***	.68***	.68***	.46***
Friends Models Religiosity	−.31***	−.24**	−.20*	−.32***
Behavior System				
Conventional Behavior Structure				
Church Attendance/ Past Year	−.40***	−.29***	−.24**	−.25**

Table 6.1 (*cont.*)

Measures of psychosocial proneness and life stress in young adulthood	Multiple Problem Behavior Index			
	High School Study		College Study	
	Men (N = 160)	Women (N = 222)	Men (N = 84)	Women (N = 100)
Life Stress				
Total Stress Across Life Areas	.21**	.16**	.06	.32**
Negative Life Events	.22**	.14*	.08	.15 +

***$p \leq .001$ (one-tailed test); **$p \leq .01$; *$p \leq .05$; +$p \leq .10$.

With respect to behavior system proneness, lower involvement in conventional behavior, as measured by less frequent attendance at religious services, is related to more intense problem behavior involvement. Overall, then, measures of problem behavior proneness from all three systems of Problem-Behavior Theory are significantly related to young adult problem behavior, just as they were to problem behavior in adolescence/youth. The correlations, modest in magnitude, are generally consistent across the four subgroups.

In the lower portion of Table 6.1, it can be seen that measures of life stress also bear a significant relationship to variation in young adult problem behavior. Greater total stress across life areas (family, friendship, work, and sexuality) is related to greater intensity of involvement in problem behavior for all groups but the College Study men. Also, for all groups but the College men, the greater the number of self-rated negative life events in the preceding two years, the greater the problem behavior involvement ($p \leq .10$ for College women). These findings are new to our research; they suggest that the experience of stress may represent an additional source of influence on young adult problem behavior, an influence that would extend the scope of the present theoretical framework. This possibility will be examined further later on in this chapter.

In addition to the measures of psychosocial proneness and of stress shown in Table 6.1, a number of other measures were also correlated with the Multiple Problem Behavior Index. Although the data are not tabled, several generalizations can be made from these other analyses. First, although the relationship between personality proneness and problem behavior involvement is supported by the data in Table 6.1, a number of the other measures of personality proneness contained in the Problem-Behavior Theory framework (see Figure 2.1) relate only inconsistently or not at all to problem behavior involvement in young adulthood. These include Internal–External Locus of Control (for the men but not the women in both samples, a more external locus of control *is* significantly related to greater involvement in problem behavior), Self-Esteem, Value on Independence, and Expectation for Independence. In the earlier, adolescent phase of the study, both the self-esteem measure and the internal–external control measure were only weakly related or were unrelated to problem behavior. The conceptual remoteness of these variables from the underlying dimension of conventionality–unconventionality may well account for this outcome and for its consistency across the two life stages. As for the motivational-instigation measures relevant to independence, it may be that independence is more strongly linked to unconventionality in adolescence/youth, when issues of being free of adult regulation and control are very salient, than it would be in adulthood.

Second, there are several other findings in the young adult data that provide further support for the association of greater psychosocial unconventionality with greater involvement in problem behavior. For example, a measure of political liberalism is significantly and positively related to involvement in problem behavior. Third, a few findings from the measures of specific life areas are consistent enough to be of interest. With respect to family life, lower satisfaction in this life area (for all groups but College women) is significantly correlated with greater problem behavior involvement. With respect to friendship, having relatively lower proportions of friends who are married is significantly related to greater involvement in problem behavior (except for High School men). With respect to health, lower self-rated physical health is significantly correlated with greater involvement in problem behavior for all groups except the College men. With respect to work, lower satisfaction with work (men only), lower-perceived co-worker controls against deviant or illegal behavior (men only), higher perceived co-worker pressure to engage in deviant behavior (except College men), and more frequent supervisor dissatisfaction with one's work (except College women), are all related significantly to greater involvement in problem behavior.

Finally, there are modest relations between status attainment in young adulthood and problem behavior involvement. In the High School Study, educational attainment is negatively and significantly correlated with greater involvement in problem behavior, $r = -.20$ and $-.14$ for the men and women, respectively. And, for men in both samples, lower income level and lower job prestige are also significantly related to greater problem behavior involvement. The correlations for income level are $-.16$ for the High School men and $-.19$ ($p \leq .10$) for the College men; the correlations for job prestige are $-.14$ ($p \leq .10$) and $-.27$ for the respective groups.

The measures of psychosocial proneness presented in Table 6.1 were also correlated with each of the five component problem behaviors that comprise the Multiple Problem Behavior Index. Those correlations can be found in Table 6.2. The pattern of relationships that was shown in Table 6.1 is generally replicated for each of the individual problem behaviors in Table 6.2. As was true for the overall Multiple Problem Behavior Index, findings were somewhat weaker for the College Study women than for the other three groups. In addition, the pattern of relationships is not as strong in relation to the measure of cigarette smoking as it is to the other problem behaviors.

The bivariate findings presented thus far provide modest but consistent support for the linkage between psychosocial variables in the Personality, Perceived Environment, and Behavior Systems of Problem-Behavior Theory and involvement in problem behavior in young adulthood. For the young adult men and women in both studies, the following are all associated with greater involvement in problem behavior: values, beliefs, and attitudes that are less in keeping with traditional social norms; perceived environments that present greater social support for and fewer controls against normative departures; and behavior that fails to affirm a bond to conventional institutions. As was the case in adolescence/youth, the characteristics that are associated with greater problem behavior involvement in young adult-

Table 6.2. *Pearson correlations of measures of psychosocial proneness and life stress with measures of specific problem behaviors in young adulthood (1981), by group*

Measures of psychosocial proneness and life stress in young adulthood	Times Drunk/Past 6 Months				Marijuana Use/Past Month			
	High School Study		College Study		High School Study		College Study	
	Men ($N=160$)	Women ($N=222$)	Men ($N=84$)	Women ($N=100$)	Men ($N=160$)	Women ($N=222$)	Men ($N=84$)	Women ($N=100$)
Personality System								
Value on Achievement	.07	.11+	−.07	.15+	−.01	.05	.17+	.15+
Expectation for Achievement	−.18*	.09+	−.14+	−.09	−.11+	.06	−.04	−.04
Social Criticism	.15*	.07	.30**	.11	.25***	.04	.33***	.15+
Alienation	.20**	.12*	.24*	.12	.14*	.05	.15+	−.04
Intolerance of Deviance	−.37***	−.18**	−.11	−.14+	−.33***	−.16**	−.26**	.00
Religiosity	−.23**	−.19**	−.29**	−.11	−.17**	−.18**	−.07	−.13+
Perceived Environment System								
Friends Controls	−.29***	−.13*	−.20*	−.12	−.20**	−.13*	−.03	−.17*
Friends' Approval Drug Use	.26***	.31***	.18*	.25**	.38***	.33***	.13	.22*
Friends Models Drug Use	.47***	.31***	.31**	.10	.72***	.70***	.68***	.42***
Friends Models Religiosity	−.35***	−.24***	−.32**	−.13+	−.14*	−.11*	−.06	−.26**
Behavior System								
Church Attendance/ Past Year	−.32***	−.21**	−.15+	−.15+	−.25***	−.18**	−.07	−.08
Life Stress								
Total Stress Across Life Areas	.16*	.04	−.02	.30**	.08	.02	.08	−.01
Negative Life Events	.11+	.10+	−.06	.11	.14*	−.01	.10	−.02

***$p \leq .001$ (one-tailed test); **$p \leq .01$; *$p \leq .05$; +$p \leq .10$.

hood again reflect what we have termed "greater psychosocial unconventionality." Our findings in this latter regard are similar to those reported by Kandel from her own follow-up study focused specifically on drug use: "The social psychology of marijuana use . . . is much the

Table 6.2. (*cont.*)

	Other Illicit Drug Use/Past 6 Months				General Deviance/Past Year			
	High School Study		College Study		High School Study		College Study	
	Men (N=160)	Women (N=222)	Men (N=84)	Women (N=100)	Men (N=160)	Women (N=222)	Men (N=84)	Women (N=100)
	.04	.04	.09	.11	.12+	−.00	.02	.09
	−.10	.06	−.08	−.16+	.02	−.07	−.03	−.10
	.22**	−.03	.11	.11	.08	.08	.23*	−.01
	.17*	.07	.14	.22*	.20**	.28***	.25**	.09
	−.29***	−.22***	.06	−.03	−.43***	−.40***	−.24**	−.43***
	−.28***	−.19**	−.25**	−.26**	−.15*	−.07	.02	−.13+
	−.33***	−.14*	−.10	−.13+	−.09	−.02	−.06	−.20*
	.35***	.36***	.35***	.38***	.18**	.27***	.15+	.28**
	.55***	.54***	.47***	.44***	.33***	.25***	.42***	.19*
	−.29**	−.22***	−.11	−.28**	−.18**	−.15**	−.01	−.13
	−.38***	−.23***	−.24**	−.21*	−.19**	−.13*	−.06	−.10
	.04	.14*	−.03	.23**	.35***	.23***	.17+	.41***
	.14*	.05	−.11	.01	.22**	.15**	.30**	.18*

(*continued on next page*)

same in young adulthood as in adolescence" (1984, p. 208), including lower participation in conventional roles and lower social achievement. Similarly, Newcomb and Bentler (1988) report a strong association, in young adulthood, between drug use and what they term "social

138   *Young adulthood*

Table 6.2 (*cont.*)

Measures of psychosocial proneness and life stress in young adulthood	Cigarette Smoking Involvement				Church Attendance/Past Year			
	High School Study		College Study		High School Study		College Study	
	Men (N=160)	Women (N=222)	Men (N=84)	Women (N=100)	Men (N=160)	Women (N=222)	Men (N=84)	Women (N=100)
Personality System								
Value on Achievement	−.02	.09+	−.07	.15+	−.05	−.07	.01	−.12
Expectation for Achievement	.05	−.02	−.00	−.12	.06	.01	.16+	.13+
Social Criticism	.02	−.02	.30**	.06	−.22*	−.10+	−.09	−.29**
Alienation	.15*	.12*	−.01	.19*	−.25***	−.12+	−.13	−.25**
Intolerance of Deviance	−.14*	−.02	−.00	.05	.29***	.29***	.05	.13+
Religiosity	−.25***	−.12*	−.18*	−.08	.75***	.78***	.69***	.73***
Perceived Environment System								
Friends Controls	−.13*	−.08	−.16+	.10	.38***	.22***	.15+	.39***
Friends' Approval Drug Use	.18**	.16**	.07	.25**	−.43***	−.38***	−.13	−.34***
Friends Models Drug Use	.40***	.35***	.16+	.24**	−.35***	−.29***	−.12	−.22*
Friends Models Religiosity	−.20**	−.05	−.10	−.16+	.49***	.50***	.24***	.49***
Behavior System								
Church Attendance/ Past Year	−.29***	−.18**	−.20*	−.20*	—	—	—	—
Life Stress								
Total Stress Across Life Areas	.10	.08	−.03	.04	−.13+	−.13*	.03	−.09
Negative Life Events	.16*	.12*	.01	.17*	−.23**	−.20**	.13	−.12

***$p \leq$ .001 (one-tailed test); **$p \leq$ .01; *$p \leq$ .05; +$p \leq$ .10.

conformity," a latent variable based on law abidance, liberalism, and religious commitment. In addition, O'Donnell, Voss, Clayton, Slatin, and Room (1976) found drug use related to greater attitudinal unconventionality among young adult men.

Although the various psychosocial measures of Problem-Behavior

Theory are associated with problem behavior involvement in young adulthood in a theoretically predictable way, the magnitude of the relationship between overall psychosocial proneness and problem behavior remains to be determined. This issue – the extent to which the Problem-Behavior Theory measures, taken together, can account for cross-sectional variation in young adult involvement in problem behavior – is addressed in the next section.

The multivariate appraisal of Problem-Behavior Theory in young adulthood

In the earlier, adolescent phase of the research, the key analytic strategy involved combining measures of risk factors within the Personality System, within the Perceived Environment System, and within the Behavior System as predictor sets. In addition to assessing the explanatory usefulness of these three systems separately, the strategy also involved combining measures from all three systems in order to yield a more comprehensive and theoretically exhaustive account of adolescent problem behavior involvement (see Jessor & Jessor, 1977, chap. 7). In assessing the relevance of Problem-Behavior Theory for the life stage of young adulthood, a similar multivariate analytic approach was employed.

The personality, perceived environment, and behavior measures shown in Table 6.1 were selected for the multivariate analyses. Most of these measures were the same ones used in the multivariate appraisal of Problem-Behavior Theory during the earlier phase of the research. Multiple regression analyses were carried out for the Multiple Problem Behavior Index, for each of its component problem behaviors, and for the conventional behavior of attendance at religious services. For each behavioral criterion, the analysis was replicated in both genders in both the High School and the College studies. The regression analyses were also replicated, as closely as possible, using the earlier, 1979 data wave.

A sequence of five separate multiple regressions was employed with each criterion behavior. The measures included in each regression, or "run," are the following:

Run I   *Personality system proneness* (6 measures): Value on Achieve-
         ment, Expectation for Achievement, Social Criticism, Al-
         ienation, Attitudinal Intolerance of Deviance, and
         Religiosity.
Run II   *Perceived environment system proneness* (4 measures): Friends
         Controls, Friends' Approval of Drug Use, Friends Models
         for Drug Use, and Friends Models for Religiosity.
Run III *Psychosocial proneness* (10 measures): all of the preceding
         measures.
Run IV   *Behavior system proneness* (1 measure): Church Attendance
         in the Past Year.
Run V   *Overall psychosocial proneness* (11 measures): all measures
         from Runs III and IV combined.

Multiple correlation coefficients from these regression analyses, for
the Multiple Problem Behavior Index criterion measure, are presented in Table 6.3 for both men and women in the High School
and the College studies. The results from the combined personality,
perceived environment, and behavior measures in Run V provide
strong support for the relevance of Problem-Behavior Theory as an
account of problem behavior involvement in young adulthood. In all
four groups, the Run V multiple correlations are significant and substantial: .76, .75, .77, and .63 for the High School men and women
and the College men and women, respectively. For all but the College
women, more than half of the variance in the Multiple Problem
Behavior Index is accounted for by the 11 measures of overall psychosocial proneness. The general robustness of these findings is evident in their replication in the 1979 data wave (not tabled); the
multiple Rs for the respective groups in 1979 are .78, .69, .60, and
.67.
    These multiple Rs are also comparable to the level found in the
earlier, parallel analyses during adolescence and youth. When 14 Year
IV (1972) measures of personality, perceived environment, and behavioral proneness (and also socioeconomic background) were used
to predict multiple problem behavior involvement in adolescence, the
multiple correlations for the High School men and women, respectively, were .74 and .77. This level of multiple R is almost identical
to that obtained in young adulthood for the same samples. In the

Table 6.3. *Multiple correlations of psychosocial proneness with the summary measure of problem behavior in young adulthood (1981)*

	Multiple Problem Behavior Index			
	High School Study		College Study	
Psychosocial proneness in young adulthood	Men (N = 155)[a]	Women (N = 181)	Men (N = 75)	Women (N = 87)
Run I. Personality System proneness (6 measures)	.53***	.44***	.55***	.40*
Run II. Perceived Environment System proneness (4 measures)	.71***	.71***	.70***	.58***
Run III. Psychosocial proneness – Field Pattern (10 measures)	.75***	.75***	.77***	.62***
Run IV. Behavior System proneness (1 measure)	.40***	.34***	.27*	.22*
Run V. Overall psychosocial proneness (11 measures)	.76***	.75***	.77***	.63***

[a] N values in all groups are smaller as a consequence of the listwise deletion procedure used in these analyses.

***$p \leq .001$ (by F-test); **$p \leq .01$; *$p \leq .05$.

College Study, the comparable figures for Year IV (1973) were .68 for the men and .68 for the women. For this latter sample, the multiple R is somewhat stronger in young adulthood than it was for youth among the men ($R = .77$ vs. .68), and slightly weaker among the women ($R = .63$ vs. .68).

Given the effectiveness of the overall set of measures in Run V, and the comparability of the young adult findings to those obtained in adolescence, it is of theoretical interest to examine the separate contributions that personality proneness, perceived environment proneness, and behavior proneness make to the psychosocial account of young adult problem behavior. With respect to personality proneness, Run I shows that personality system measures alone account for significant amounts of the variance in problem behavior for all groups. Personality has a slightly stronger relationship to behavior for the men than the women. Multiple correlations are .53 for High School men, .44 for High School women, .55 for College men, and .40 for College women. These multiple Rs are similar to those from the replication in the 1979 data; the latter were .53, .51, .46, and .35 for the respective groups. In analyses of the 1972/73 adolescent/youth data, multiple regressions using a similar set of five measures of personality proneness resulted in similar Rs for all but the College men. Multiple correlations for the four respective groups were .57, .58, .29, and .41. At both life stages, therefore, the personality concepts employed appear to be relevant and to play comparable roles in accounting for variation in problem behavior.

In young adulthood, as was also the case in adolescence, the perceived environment system measures play a stronger role in relation to problem behavior than do the personality system measures. The greater strength of the former seems due primarily to their proximal nature, although, of course, measurement error and differential construct validity cannot be ruled out. Data from Run II show that, for all groups but the College women, perceived environment proneness accounts for roughly half the variance in problem behavior; for the College women, the perceived environment measures account for 34 percent of the variance in problem behavior. Again, the multiple Rs for the 1979 data are generally comparable, although they are slightly lower for the High School women and the College men than they are in 1981. The multiple correlations from the analyses of the 1981 data are also quite similar in magnitude to those from the earlier analyses carried out on the 1972/73 data. For example, among the High School men, the 1981 R is .71, compared with .67 from the earlier data; for the High School women, the comparable figures are .71 and .69.

When the six personality system measures are added to the four perceived environment measures in Run III, there is an increment in the multiple Rs over those that obtained for the Perceived Environment System alone. For all groups, except the College women, the increase in the multiple R is significant. Measures from both theoretical systems, therefore, contribute toward an account of variation in problem behavior involvement in young adulthood.

With respect to behavior proneness, the data from Run IV (actually a bivariate correlation) show that conventional behavior (i.e., church attendance) in young adulthood is significantly related to problem behavior involvement. As was also true in the earlier 1972/73 data, the relationship is not as high as the relationships of personality proneness or perceived environment proneness to problem behavior involvement. The parallel 1979 analyses closely replicate the 1981 findings, and the 1972/73 data are very comparable in the High School Study; for the College respondents, the 1981 correlations are somewhat lower than those obtained in the earlier analyses. Although the behavior system measure of church attendance yields significant relationships, it adds nothing to the strength of the combined personality and perceived environment measures in Run III. A similar situation obtains in the regression analyses of the 1979 data.

In summary, the findings presented in Table 6.3 are generally consistent across the two genders and across the two young adult data waves, 1979 and 1981. The results indicate, also, that the relationship between psychosocial proneness and variation in problem behavior involvement is similar at two very different stages of the life course: adolescence/youth and young adulthood. At both stages, measures of Problem-Behavior Theory account for similar proportions of the variance in problem behavior.

The relevance of the Problem-Behavior Theory measures in young adulthood was examined further by employing the same sets of regression analyses with each of the component problem behaviors in the Multiple Problem Behavior Index – frequency of drunkenness, marijuana use, use of other illicit drugs, general deviant behavior, and cigarette smoking – as well as with the conventional behavior of church attendance. For these analyses, two measures of behavior system proneness, rather than one, were available for use in Runs IV and V. In addition to Church Attendance Frequency, a summary measure

Table 6.4. *Multiple correlations of psychosocial proneness with measures of specific problem and conventional behaviors in young adulthood (1981)*

Psychosocial proneness in young adulthood	Times Drunk/Past 6 Months				Marijuana Use/Past Month				Other Drug Use/Past 6 Months			
	High School Study		College Study		High School Study		College Study		High School Study		College Study	
	M	W	M	W	M	W	M	W	M	W	M	W
Run I. Personality System proneness (6 measures)	.43	.40	.48	.27[b]	.43	.24[b]	.47	.32[b]	.43	.31	.33[b]	.35[b]
Run II. Perceived Environment System proneness (4 measures)	.54	.41	.46	.28[b]	.73	.73	.73	.56	.58	.55	.49	.53
Run III. Psychosocial proneness – Field Pattern (10 measures)	.58	.49	.57	.35[b]	.75	.73	.78	.61	.60	.60	.53	.57
Run IV. Behavior System proneness (2 measures)[a]	.60	.47	.42	.56	.61	.54	.53	.22[b]	.64	.65	.40	.50
Run V. Overall psychosocial proneness (12 measures)	.65	.55	.62	.64	.78	.75	.79	.63	.68	.69	.54	.62

Note: M = Men; W = Women

[a] In the prediction of Church Attendance, only one Behavior System measure (the Multiple Problem Behavior Index) was used.

[b] This multiple correlation is not significant (by F-test) at the .05 level or better. All correlations without this symbol are significant at the .05 level or better.

of multiple problem behavior involvement was used which *excluded* the specific problem behavior that constituted the criterion behavior. The multiple correlation coefficients from these analyses are presented in Table 6.4 for both men and women in both studies. Again, the results from Run V show that the combined personality, perceived environment, and behavior measures account for significant amounts of variance in all five of the different young adult problem behaviors. The only two exceptions to this generalization are cigarette smoking for the College men and also for the College women. The multiple

Table 6.4 (*cont.*)

General Deviance/Past Year				Cigarette Smoking Involvement				Church Attendance/Past Year			
High School Study		College Study		High School Study		College Study		High School Study		College Study	
Men	Women	Men	Women	Men	Women	Men	Women	Men	Women	Men	Women
.46	.52	.37[b]	.45	.32	.23[b]	.39[b]	.27[b]	.79	.80	.74	.74
.34	.33	.43	.31[b]	.42	.37	.22[b]	.37	.59	.55	.30[b]	.56
.51	.56	.53	.50	.48	.45	.42[b]	.44[b]	.80	.81	.75	.75
.42	.27	.27[b]	.34	.43	.28	.20[b]	.28	.40	.34	.27	.22
.55	.56	.54	.57	.51	.46	.43[b]	.48[b]	.81	.81	.75	.75

*R*s are, in general, slightly higher in the High School Study than in the College Study.

Among the various problem behaviors, the use of marijuana and the use of other illicit drugs are most successfully accounted for. The Run V multiple correlations for frequency of marijuana use are very similar to those just examined for the combined Multiple Problem Behavior Index: .78, .75, .79, and .63 for the High School men, High School women, College men, and College women, respectively. With the exception of the College women, then, the psychosocial proneness variables account for more than half the variance in young adult frequency of marijuana use. Multiple *R*s for frequency of use of other illicit drugs range from .54 to .69, accounting for roughly a third of the variance in that problem behavior. For the remaining three problem behaviors – frequency of drunkenness, deviant behavior, and cigarette smoking – the multiple Rs are somewhat lower. The majority of the multiple correlations range from .50 to .65, accounting for between 25 percent and 40 percent of the variance in these three behaviors. The regression results for most of the problem behaviors are generally similar across the genders and across the two studies.

The relative contributions of personality proneness and perceived environment proneness are illuminated by these analyses. For the criterion behaviors of frequency of marijuana use and the use of other illicit drugs, the measures of perceived environment proneness are generally stronger than are the measures of personality proneness. Differences of this magnitude are not unexpected since the perceived environment measures are clearly more proximal to these problem behaviors than are the personality measures, and, indeed, two of the four environmental measures actually refer to the behavior of marijuana use. With respect to the general deviance criterion, however, the situation is reversed; here the personality measures are stronger than the perceived environment measures (with the exception of the College men). This outcome reflects the fact that now the personality set includes a highly proximal measure, Attitudinal Intolerance of Deviance, a measure that not only is proximal to but actually parallels the content of the deviant behavior measure. These examples of variation in the relative strength of personality system versus perceived environment system proneness illustrate the fact that differential explanatory strength is not inherent in the theoretical systems per se. Rather, it is, at least in part, a function of the degree of proximality of the measures employed in each system to the particular criterion behavior being analyzed.

The behavior system proneness findings from Run IV show that, with a few exceptions, the measures yield significant multiple Rs for young adult involvement in the various specific problem behaviors. The exceptions are marijuana use among the College women, and both general deviance and cigarette smoking among the College men. For all behaviors but the use of other illegal drugs, behavior system proneness is more strongly related to problem behavior involvement among the High School men than among the other three groups. When behavior system proneness measures are added to the other measures of psychosocial proneness, they do add a significant increment to the multiple R in many of the cases. For High School men and women, the behavior measures significantly increase the multiple R for drunkenness, marijuana use, and use of other illicit drugs. For men in the High School Study, the behavior measures also contribute to a significantly higher R for general deviance and cigarette smoking. In the College Study, the behavior measures significantly increase the multiple R for drunkenness for both men and women, and for use of illicit drugs other than marijuana and for general deviance for women only. These findings are important because they indicate that involvement in *other* problem behaviors often plays a significant role in accounting for involvement in any specific problem behavior, a role above and beyond that played by the personality and perceived environment measures.

A criterion measure of *conventional* behavior, Church Attendance, is also shown in Table 6.4. Multiple Rs predicting church attendance from overall psychosocial proneness (Run V) are unusually high: .81 for both the High School men and women, and .75 for the College men and women. From the results of Runs I and II, it can be seen that personality proneness is a far stronger predictor of Church Attendance than is perceived environment proneness. In fact, the personality measures alone account for nearly as much variance as the combined set of measures in Run V. This is another example of how a specific, proximal measure can create an explanatory advantage for one system over another. In this case, the personality measure of Religiosity is very proximal to the criterion behavior of Church Attendance.

A final issue concerns the particular measures that are entering the regression equations and contributing significantly to the multiple Rs in Table 6.3. Of special interest is whether, when personality and perceived environment measures are combined, variables from *both* systems contribute significantly to the multiple R. With respect to the Multiple Problem Behavior Index, the significant personality measures in Run I are Religiosity, Social Criticism, and Attitudinal Intolerance of Deviance for the High School men; Religiosity, Alienation, and Attitudinal Intolerance of Deviance for the High School women; Religiosity and Social Criticism for the College men; and Value on Achievement for the College women. For the set of perceived environment measures in Run II, Friends Models for Prob-

lem Behavior is significant for all four samples; in addition, Friends'
Approval of Drug Use is significant for the High School women.

When the psychosocial measures are combined in Run III, the
significant measures in the High School samples are Friends Models
for Drug Use and Attitudinal Intolerance of Deviance for men; and
Friends Models for Drug Use and Alienation for women. In the
College samples, the significant measures are Religiosity and Friends
Models for Drug Use for men; and Expectations for Achievement
and Friends Models for Drug Use for women. These findings support
the field theory perspective of Problem-Behavior Theory: In all cases,
measures from *both* the personality and the perceived environment
system contribute significantly to the multiple R. With respect to
personality, measures of personal controls (Attitudinal Intolerance of
Deviance and Religiosity), of personal beliefs (Alienation), and of
motivational-instigations (Expectation for Achievement) are involved
in accounting for variation in problem behavior among the four different subgroups. From the perceived environment, Friends Models
for Drug Use is relevant to problem behavior involvement for all four
subgroups.

When the overall set of 11 measures is used in the regressions in
Run V, the significant measures are Attitudinal Intolerance of De-
viance and Friends Models for Problem Behavior for the High School
men; Alienation and Friends Models for Problem Behavior for the
High School women; Friends Models for Problem Behavior for the
College men; and Value on Achievement and Friends Models for
Problem Behavior for the College women.

The concept of stress in relation to involvement in problem behavior

Although the Problem-Behavior Theory framework has been useful
in accounting for variance in young adult problem-behavior involvement, the proportion of variance that is *un*accounted for remains
substantial. At best, Problem-Behavior Theory accounts for about
50–60 percent of the variance in multiple problem behavior involvement in the young adult samples reported here. In considering ways
to strengthen this account and also to entertain alternative etiological
influences, we added the domain of psychosocial stress to the frame-

work for the Young Adult Follow-Up Study. The measures of stress that were included provide at least a preliminary opportunity to evaluate its role in accounting for variation in problem-behavior involvement in young adulthood. The data in Table 6.1 showed that there is a significant, though modest, relation between the measures of stress and problem behavior. In the following section, the magnitude of the relation of stress to young adult problem-behavior involvement is explored further, and the question of whether stress provides an *independent* account of variation in young adult problem behavior – that is, whether it reflects an area of risk not already captured by the measures in the conceptual framework of Problem-Behavior Theory – is examined.

Examining the independence of the concepts of psychosocial proneness and stress

It is important, first, to establish that the two categories of risk – psychosocial proneness and stress – are relatively independent of each other. Bivariate correlations were employed to assess the relationship between the 11 measures of psychosocial proneness and the two measures of stress. Correlations of the 11 proneness measures with the two stress measures generally ranged from 0 to .3 for the High School men and from 0 to .4 for the other three groups. For the High School men, only seven of the 22 bivariate correlations reached significance; for the High School women, ten correlations reached significance. In the College samples, the number of correlations reaching significance were four and six for the men and women, respectively. These findings indicate that, at best, there is only a small positive relationship between the measures of the concepts of proneness and of stress and that they share only a small portion of common variance.

Stress as an account of young adult problem behavior

In order to assess the relationship of stress to young adult problem behavior, multiple regression analyses were again employed. Two stress measures were included: Total Stress Across Life Areas, and Negative Life Events (the content and psychometric properties of

Table 6.5. *Multiple correlations of stress with measures of problem and conventional behavior in young adulthood (1981)*

	Life stress			
	High School Study		College Study	
	Men (N = 160)	Women (N = 222)	Men (N = 84)	Women (N = 100)
Problem Behaviors				
Multiple Problem Behavior Index	.28**	.19*	.06	.33**
Times Drunk/Past 6 Months	.17	.13	.08	.32*
Marijuana Use/Past Month	.14	.05	.09	.06
Other Drug Use/Past 6 Months	.14	.17	.12	.22
General Deviance/Past Year	.39***	.23**	.26	.43***
Cigarette Smoking Involvement	.19	.14	.03	.14
Conventional Behavior				
Church Attendance/Past Year	.24*	.20*	.11	.08

Note: The measurement of stress included the measures of Total Stress Across Life Areas and Negative Life Events.
***$p \leq .001$; **$p \leq .01$; *$p \leq .05$.

these measures were described in Chapter 3). One multiple regression run was applied to each of the same behaviors presented in Tables 6.3 and 6.4. The results are presented in Table 6.5 for the regressions of the various problem behavior and conventional behavior criterion measures on the two stress measures.

Stress makes a significant contribution to the explanation of variation in young adult problem behavior for all but the College men when the criterion measure is the Multiple Problem Behavior Index. The multiple correlations are .28 and .19 for the High School men and women, respectively, and .06 and .33 for the College men and women, respectively. The actual amount of variance accounted for by the stress measures, however, is very small, ranging only from 1 percent to 11 percent. The pattern of these findings shows no meaningful gender differences or study differences in the linkage between stress and multiple problem behavior involvement. Parallel analyses performed on the 1979 data[1] yield quite comparable outcomes. The 1979 multiple correlation coefficients for the respective groups are .38, .23, .16, and .22; these Rs are significant in the High School sample only. The multiple Rs for the two stress measures are considerably smaller than those resulting from the six personality proneness measures in Run I or the four perceived environment proneness measures in Run II in Table 6.3. In other words, personality proneness alone or perceived environment proneness alone is a considerably stronger predictor of problem behavior involvement than is stress, at least as measured here.

When multiple correlations are run between stress and the specific behaviors, for four of the five problem behaviors and for the conventional behavior of church attendance, stress is either not significant or, when it is significant, it accounts for only a small amount of the variance in behavior. Stress is significant for the College women in relation to frequency of drunkenness ($R = .32$), and for the High School men and women in relation to church attendance ($R = .24$ and .20, respectively). The one exception to this pattern of weak and erratic relationships is found with regard to the measure of general deviant behavior. For this criterion, stress is significant for all groups but the College men, accounting for up to 18 percent of the variance in those groups.

Although its contribution as measured appears to be weak, the question still remains whether stress reflects a source of variance not already encompassed by the measures of psychosocial proneness. In order to answer this question, regression analyses were run in which the two stress measures were added after the measures of overall psychosocial proneness, in Run V, had been entered. The significance level of the R^2 change between the overall proneness run, without

Table 6.6. *Hierarchical multiple correlations of overall psychosocial proneness and stress with measures of problem and conventional behavior in young adulthood (1981), by group*

	High School Study		College Study	
	Men	Women	Men	Women
Problem behaviors				
Multiple Problem Behavior Index				
Overall psychosocial proneness	.76***	.75***	.77***	.63***
Stress alone	.28**	.19*	.06	.33**
Overall proneness plus stress	.76***	.75***	.78***	.64***
R^2 Change between overall run				
with and without stress	.01	.00	.02	.02
Times Drunk/Past 6 Months				
Overall psychosocial proneness	.65***	.55***	.62***	.64***
Stress alone	.17	.13	.08	.32*
Overall proneness plus stress	.65***	.56***	.62***	.67***
R^2 Change between overall run				
with and without stress	.00	.01	.01	.04
Marijuana Use/Past Month				
Overall psychosocial proneness	.78***	.75***	.79***	.63***
Stress alone	.14	.05	.09	.06
Overall proneness plus stress	.78***	.75***	.81***	.64***
R^2 Change between overall run				
with and without stress	.00	.01	.02	.02
Other Drug Use/Past 6 Months				
Overall psychosocial proneness	.68***	.69***	.54*	.62***
Stress alone	.14	.17 +	.12	.22
Overall proneness plus stress	.69***	.70***	.60*	.63***
R^2 Change between overall run				
with and without stress	.01	.01	.06	.01
General Deviance/Past Year				
Overall psychosocial proneness	.55***	.56***	.54*	.57**
Stress alone	.39***	.23**	.26 +	.43***
Overall proneness plus stress	.59***	.57***	.56*	.62***
R^2 Change between overall run				
with and without stress	.05**	.00	.02	.07*

Table 6.6 (*cont.*)

	High School Study		College Study	
	Men	Women	Men	Women
Cigarette Smoking Involvement				
Overall psychosocial proneness	.51***	.46***	.43	.48 +
Stress alone	.19 +	.14	.03	.14
Overall proneness plus stress	.52***	.48***	.44	.49
R^2 Change between overall run				
with and without stress	.00	.01	.01	.01
Conventional behavior				
Church Attendance/Past Year				
Overall psychosocial proneness	.81***	.81***	.75***	.75***
Stress alone	.24*	.20*	.11	.08
Overall proneness plus stress	.81***	.82***	.75***	.75***
R^2 Change between overall run				
with and without stress	.01	.01*	.00	.00

***$p \leq .001$ (by *F*-test); **$p \leq .01$; *$p \leq .05$; +$p \leq .10$.

the stress measures, and the run with the stress measures added was computed. The relevant data are shown in Table 6.6 for the four subsamples.

When the two stress measures are entered into the regression equation after the psychosocial proneness measures, there is generally no increase at all in the R^2 or only a very minimal increase over the R^2 for the proneness measures alone. The increment in the regression coefficients is typically of a magnitude of .00–.02, and it is generally not significant. With respect to the Multiple Problem Behavior Index criterion, for example, the multiple correlations are .76, .75, .78, and .64 for the High School men, High School women, College men, and College women, respectively, when stress is added to the equation, compared with .76, .75, .77, and .63 for these respective groups when the 11 psychosocial proneness measures alone are used. For four of the specific problem behaviors – drunkenness, marijuana use, use of other illicit drugs, and cigarette smoking – and for church attendance, stress makes no additional contribution at all. With respect to the general deviance criterion, however, there are modest increases – up to 7 percent – in the amount of variance accounted for when stress is added. It is worth nothing, however, that even on this criterion, the stress variables contribute significantly to the final *R*s only for the High School men and the College women. These findings indicate that, although stress does bear a small and significant relationship to problem behavior, the magnitude of its linkage is tenuous compared to that of psychosocial proneness, and it seems not to engage a source of variance that is not already subsumed by the measures of psychosocial proneness.

Summary

Several major conclusions can be drawn about the social psychology of problem behavior in young adulthood from the analyses presented in this chapter. First, Problem-Behavior Theory appears to be relevant as an account of problem behavior during this life stage. The psychosocial measures of the key variables in the theory account for significant and substantial portions of the variation in young adult problem behavior across a variety of behavioral indicators. More than half of the variance in multiple problem behavior involvement and also in marijuana use is explained, while 25–40 percent of the variance in the other individual problem behaviors – deviant behavior, cigarette smoking, frequency of drunkenness, and use of illicit drugs other than marijuana – is accounted for. In addition, over half the variance in a conventional behavior – church attendance – is explained. The replication of the findings across two waves of data collection (1979 and 1981), across both genders, and across the High School and College studies, gives them greater compellingness. In a number of instances, however, the outcomes were weaker for the College women. Among the College women, both the means and the standard deviations on the problem behavior measures were lower than in any of the other subsamples, and that may have influenced their results.

A second important conclusion that can be drawn from these findings is about the continuity of the explanatory account at two separate stages of the life course – adolescence/youth and young adulthood. Despite the fact that some of the meaning and content of problem behavior may have changed between these two developmental stages, and despite the fact that a number of the measures of psychosocial proneness were modified to make them more applicable to the later stage of development, the Problem-Behavior Theory framework accounts for nearly identical proportions of the variance in multiple problem behavior involvement at both life stages. In both life stages – adolescence/youth and young adulthood – the link between psychosocial conventionality–unconventionality and engaging in problem behavior appears to be a relatively invariant one.

A third major conclusion is that both personality and perceived environment variables continue to be influential, on their own, in accounting for young adult problem behavior involvement. Personality proneness and perceived environment proneness are consistently significant predictors of all of the problem behaviors examined here, and of the conventional behavior of church attendance, as well, among the High School Study men. The same can be said for the High School Study women with only two exceptions, for personality proneness and marijuana use and cigarette smoking. In the College Study, personality proneness plays a somewhat lesser role, especially among the women; for them, personality proneness is a significant predictor, at the specific behavior level, only of deviant behavior and church attendance. Perceived environment proneness accounts for significant amounts of variation in all of the behaviors, except drunkenness, deviant behavior, and church attendance for the College women; for the College men, the perceived environment accounts for significant proportions of the variance in all of the problem behaviors but cigarette smoking, and also in church attendance.

Finally, it seems clear from the analyses that psychosocial stress is significantly linked to young adult problem behavior – particularly to the Multiple Problem Behavior Index and to the specific measure of deviant behavior. The linkage, however, is a very modest one. In general, stress as measured adds essentially nothing to the account of young adult problem behavior beyond that attributable to psychosocial proneness alone. Although the measurement of stress was not carried as far as the measurement of psychosocial proneness, stress, as measured, neither extends nor provides an alternative to psychosocial proneness as an account of young adult problem behavior.

Note

1 The 1979 measure of Negative Life Events differs somewhat from the 1981 measure. In 1981, the degree of negativity of the reported life events was rated by the respondents along a five-category Likert scale; this was not done in the 1979 data collection.

References

Finney, J. W., & Moos, R. H. (1984). Life stressors and problem drinking among older adults. In M. Galanter (Ed.), *Recent developments in alcoholism* (Vol. 11). New York: Plenum.

Jessor, R., Graves, T. D., Hanson, R. C., & Jessor, S. L. (1968). *Society, personality, and deviant behavior: A study of a tri-ethnic community*. New York: Holt, Rinehart, & Winston.

Jessor, R., & Jessor, S. L. (1977). *Problem behavior and psychosocial development: A longitudinal study of youth*. New York: Academic Press.

Kandel, D. B. (1984). Marijuana users in young adulthood. *Archives of General Psychiatry, 41*, 200–209.

Newcomb, M. D., & Bentler, P. M. (1988). *Consequences of adolescent drug use: Impact on the lives of young adults*. Newbury Park, CA: Sage.

O'Donnell, J. A., Voss, H. L., Clayton, R. R., Slatin, G. T., & Room, R. G. W. (1976). *Young men and drugs: A nationwide survey* (NIDA Research Monograph No. 5). Rockville, MD: National Institute on Drug Abuse.

Rodin, M. R., Morton, D. R., & Shimkin, D. B. (1982). Beverage preference, drinking, and social stress in an urban community. *The International Journal of the Addictions, 17*(2), 315–328.

Vinokur, A., & Selzer, M. L. (1975). Desirable versus undesirable life events: Their relationship to stress and mental distress. *Journal of Personality and Social Psychology, 32*(2), 329–337.

Part III

Development and change

7

Psychosocial development from adolescence to young adulthood

The Young Adult Follow-Up Study provided a relatively unique opportunity to describe the course of psychosocial growth and the direction of developmental change from adolescence/youth into young adulthood. Severely underresearched in any systematic sense, this transition segment of the life course has rarely been subjected to descriptive scrutiny or to the delineation of characteristic kinds of change.

Reasons for this lacuna in developmental knowledge are several, including, of course, the difficulty of access to samples of young adults after they have left high school or college. More fundamentally, there is a paucity of longitudinal studies that have bridged the adolescent and young adult life stages and that have been able to monitor the changes associated with passage from one stage to the other. Most important, perhaps, has been the long-term scientific indifference to adult development, an apparent cost of the almost exclusive preoccupation with growth in the earlier years and, to a lesser extent, with decline in the later years. As Dannefer, a sociologist, has noted, "In the past few years adulthood has become recognized as a neglected ... focus for systematic study in the social sciences" (1984, p. 100). The same theme is echoed by a psychologist: "The study of adult development is, one might say, in its infancy. It has been taken seriously in the human sciences for only the past 30 years or so" (Levinson, 1986, p. 3). In the Young Adult Follow-Up Study, one of our aims was to help right the balance with respect to knowledge about psychosocial development in young adulthood and about its continuity–discontinuity with adolescence/youth. Happily, other efforts, with similar objectives, have recently begun to appear (e.g., Magnusson, 1988).

The description of intraindividual change and of interindividual differences in intraindividual change – both key concerns of developmental study (Wohlwill, 1973) – is uniquely reserved to research that is longitudinal in design and that undertakes repeated measurements of the same individuals over time. In this chapter, we present descriptive data about psychosocial development between adolescence/youth and young adulthood and also within young adulthood itself. Given the relative absence of descriptive knowledge, such data constitute a useful contribution in their own right. There is an additional yield, however, from the fact that, while only descriptive, the data are based on measures derived from Problem-Behavior Theory. They can thereby reveal not only whether the theory is useful for specifying important directions of young adult development, but also whether the changes observed on the personality and perceived environment measures are consonant with the changes observed in behavior, as the theory would lead us to expect.

Although developmental change is ineluctable, its grasp remains problematic. Two basic premises have guided our own particular approach to studying it, both descriptively, as in this chapter, and predictively, as in the one to follow. First, psychosocial change is seen as the product of person–environment interaction, as much an outcome of the person's embeddedness in a socially organized and structured context of age-related roles, expectations, demands, and opportunities as it is of internal dispositions and intentions. In short, we have sought to avoid what Dannefer (1984) has termed the "ontogenetic fallacy" (p. 101), that is, "the conception of human development as a process of maturational unfolding" (p. 103). Our perspective about development is *interactionist*, the very same perspective that was taken, in Chapter 2, about the determinants of action. The second basic premise is that psychosocial change is neither arbitrary nor adventitious but, rather, a relatively predictable and systematic outcome of what has gone before. Such a perspective about "the stability of change" (Jessor, 1983) makes provision for *both* continuity and change. Rather than an irreconcilable antinomy, continuity and change are best seen as two aspects of a single dialectical process in which even major transformations of individuality emerge consequentially from the interaction of prior characteristics and circumstances. This perspective provides us with the rationale for examining the stability of the variables in Problem-Behavior Theory while demonstrating, at the same time, that many of them have undergone major developmental change; it also provides the rationale for undertaking the prediction of change, the topic of the following chapter.

The aims of this chapter, then, are several. First, we consider the temporal stability, across the adolescence–young adult transition, of the psychosocial attributes that constitute the Personality, the Perceived Environment, and the Behavior Systems in Problem-Behavior Theory. How stable are individual differences on the measures of those attributes? Second, we provide descriptive information about the overall course of development and change on these very same attributes, as growth from adolescence/youth to young adulthood takes place. What are the main directions of change and what is the magnitude of change across these key stages of the life trajectory? How coherent are the changes that take place on the different attributes? And third, we show that, whatever the average direction of developmental change, there are interindividual differences in change; the latter are shown to be linked systematically to antecedent characteristics or precursors that serve to signal variation in the subsequent course of growth and change. What accounts for the fact that the transition into young adulthood involves major changes for some adolescents and little or no change for others?

The developmental stability of psychosocial attributes

There is one window on the issue of continuity or change that provides a uniquely informative view of the stability of individual differences over time and development. When the time interval between two successive measurements of an attribute is long enough to be developmentally significant (and, also, to minimize the influence of mere recall), the correlation coefficient between the two measurements can be interpreted as indexing the degree of invariance of relative position on the measure of that attribute. Irrespective of change in the mean on that measure – change that can be major and marked – the size of the correlation indicates whether the position of an individual in the distribution of scores is stable, that is, conserved across the two measurements. For related inquiries about the stability of individual differences, see Costa and McCrae (1988), Dusek and Flaherty (1981) and, for adolescents and preadolescents, Stein, Newcomb, and Bentler (1986) and Backteman and Magnusson (1981).

Stability coefficients for the interval between adolescence/youth (Wave IV, 1972/73) and young adulthood (Wave VI, 1981), and for the two-year interval between the two measurements within young adulthood (Wave V, 1979 and Wave VI, 1981), are presented for both men and women in the High School and College samples in Tables 7.1 and 7.2, respectively.

The data in Table 7.1 provide strong support for the stability of individual differences between adolescence and young adulthood. On nearly all of the measures, in all three of the systems of psychosocial attributes, and for both men and women, the correlations are significant and, in many cases, of substantial magnitude. However, as Mortimer, Finch, and Kumka have reminded us, "There is no agreed-upon baseline, or accepted standard, by which stability can be defined. Whether stability coefficients are 'high' or 'low' seems to depend, to a large extent, on the judgment of the investigator" (1982, p. 268). Inferences about the magnitude of stability need to be drawn, therefore, relative to a variety of qualifying considerations: the length of the time interval spanned by the two measurements; the sociohistorical changes that have occurred in that interval; whether the interval encompasses transitions between major life stages; the pattern of findings across different domains of measurement; and, of course, the unreliability of the measures themselves.

The data for the Wave IV (1972) to Wave VI (1981) interval involve a relatively long time span of nine years for the High School sample, a period in which the youth went from ages 16–18 to ages 25–27, that is, from late adolescence to young adulthood; they are years in which the daily life context shifted, for most of them, from involvement with school and parents to involvement with work and their own family; and it was a time in history, from the early 1970s to the early 1980s, when pervasive and reverberating changes were taking place in the larger social environment. In light of all of these considerations, the stability coefficients for the High School sample in Table 7.1 would seem to be impressive. The correlations for the most part are

Table 7.1. Stability coefficients for the psychosocial measures between Wave IV (1972/1973) and Wave VI (1981) High School and College samples

	Males		Females	
	High School Study (N = 162)	College Study (N = 84)	High School Study (N = 222)	College Study (N = 100)
Personality System				
Motivational-Instigation Structure				
Value on Achievement	.05 (.06)[a]	.33** (.39)	.05 (.07)	.13 (.16)
Value on Independence	.35*** (.59)	.33*** (.46)	.25*** (.39)	.33*** (.54)
Expectation for Achievement	.36*** (.41)	.27** (.38)	.16* (.18)	.18+ (.23)
Expectation for Independence	.33*** (.47)	.23* (.35)	.18** (.25)	.28** (.42)
Personal Belief Structure				
Social Criticism	.34*** (.49)	.59*** (.72)	.36*** (.49)	.50*** (.62)
Alienation	.37*** (.46)	.42*** (.52)	.30*** (.37)	.41*** (.51)
Self-Esteem	.42*** (.54)	.57*** (.68)	.31*** (.39)	.28** (.35)
Internal-External Locus of Control	.40*** (.57)	.35*** (.48)	.27*** (.39)	.37*** (.56)
Personal Control Structure				
Attitudinal Intolerance of Deviance	.35*** (.39)	.53*** (.60)	.32*** (.36)	.55*** (.62)
Moral Attitude	—[b]	—[b]	—[b]	—[b]
Religiosity	.56*** (.61)	.64*** (.73)	.45*** (.49)	.73*** (.83)

(continued on next page)

Table 7.1 (cont.)

	Males		Females	
	High School Study	College Study	High School Study	College Study
	(N = 162)	(N = 84)	(N = 222)	(N = 100)
Perceived Environment System				
Distal Structure				
Parental Controls	.04 (.06)	−.02 (−.03)	.12+ (.19)	.13 (.21)
Friends Controls	.16*	.25*	.02	.31**
Parents vs. Friends Influence	.17* (.28)	.34** (.59)	.12+ (.21)	.23* (.43)
Total Stress Across Life Areas	—b	—b	—b	—b
Proximal Structure				
Friends' Approval of Problem Behavior	.35*** (.67)	.41*** (1.00)	.39*** (.66)	.32*** (.65)
Friends Models for Problem Behavior	.22*** (.31)	.37*** (.66)	.29*** (.42)	.42*** (.76)
Friends Models for Religiosity	.16*	.27**	.18**	.41***
Behavior System				
Problem Behavior Structure	.33*** (.43)	.14 (.25)	.28*** (.43)	.38*** (.59)
General Deviant Behavior	.09		.03	
Times Drunk		.61***		.15
Conventional Behavior Structure				
Church Attendance	.43***	.43***	.34***	.39***

*a*Correlations in parentheses have been corrected for attenuation for those measures that are multiple-item scales for which reliability can be ascertained.

*b*This measure was not available in 1972/1973.

***p ≤ .001; **p ≤ .01; *p ≤ .05; +*p* ≤ .10.

significant and, when corrected for attenuation, account in many cases for a quarter of the variance. Despite the long time interval and the pervasively changing context, the relative position of the individuals in the High School sample tends to be conserved to a significant degree during development out of adolescence and into young adulthood. The data for the eight-year time interval for the College sample are, if anything, still stronger and even more consistent, and, on several of the measures, the coefficients, when corrected for attenuation, account for a third to a half of the variance. Compared with the high school findings, these college-age findings suggest that there is greater stability across this later portion of the age trajectory; while necessarily tentative, that inference is consistent with similar conclusions from other studies using personality questionnaires (Schuerger, Tait, & Tavernelli, 1982).

For both the High School and College samples, the stability of the major personality/attitudinal attributes seems to be greater than that for the attributes in the other two systems, the perceived environment and behavior. A high level of stability of personality has also been reported by Mortimer et al. (1982) in their 14-year follow up study of college freshmen in which the stability of a measure of the self-concept was about .60. "The absolute magnitude of this stability seems to us to be particularly remarkable, given the many role changes and shifts in life experience undergone by this panel during the transition to adulthood" (p. 282). In a more recent panel study of personality stability over an eight-year interval between junior high school and young adulthood, the average stability coefficient across measures of 15 different personality traits was found to be .52, corrected for attenuation, "indicating a high degree of continuity in personality over this . . . period" (Stein, Newcomb, & Bentler, 1986).

When the stability of individual differences *within* young adulthood, that is, between Wave V (1979) and Wave VI (1981), is examined in Table 7.2, the findings are clear, consistent, and compelling for both the High School and College samples and for the men and women within each. The High School Study participants were ages 23–25 in 1979 and 25–27 in 1981; the College Study participants were age 28 in 1979 and age 30 in 1981. Across this two-year interval in the latter part of the third decade of life, stability is uniformly high, even when *un*corrected for attenuation, and relative position in the distri-

Table 7.2. *Stability coefficients for the psychosocial measures between Wave V (1979) and Wave VI (1981) High School and College samples*

	Males		Females	
	High School Study	College Study	High School Study	College Study
	(N = 162)	(N = 84)	(N = 222)	(N = 100)
Personality System				
Motivational-Instigation Structure				
Value on Achievement	.43*** (.60)[a]	.58*** (.86)	.45*** (.70)	.45*** (.77)
Value on Independence	.46*** (1.00)	.50*** (.93)	.48*** (1.00)	.54*** (1.00)
Expectation for Achievement	.51*** (.68)	.58*** (.81)	.39*** (.51)	.53*** (.77)
Expectation for Independence	.54*** (.99)	.56*** (1.00)	.50*** (.96)	.44*** (1.00)
Personal Belief Structure				
Social Criticism	.57*** (.85)	.72*** (.92)	.62*** (.86)	70*** (.92)
Alienation	.57*** (.73)	.65*** (.82)	.66*** (.82)	.63*** (.79)
Self-Esteem	.69*** (.91)	.84*** (1.00)	.64*** (.83)	.62*** (.78)
Internal–External Locus of Control	.59*** (.93)	.61*** (.86)	.53*** (.84)	.52*** (.91)
Personal Control Structure				
Attitudinal Intolerance of Deviance	.67*** (.78)	.72*** (.84)	.66*** (.76)	.69*** (.80)
Moral Attitude	.70*** (.88)	.74*** (1.00)	.73*** (.96)	.80*** (1.00)
Religiosity	.83*** (.88)	.89*** (.95)	.86*** (.91)	.91*** (.96)

Perceived Environment System

Distal Structure

Parental Controls	.53***	(.74)	.42***	(.68)	.32***	(.49)	.26**	(.44)
Friends Controls	.54***		.38***		.37***		.51***	
Parent–Friends Influence	.50***	(.64)	.55***	(.71)	.38***	(.53)	.46***	(.67)
Total Stress Across Life Areas	.51***	(.83)	.62***	(1.00)	.44***	(.77)	.43***	(.72)

Proximal Structure

Friends' Approval of Problem Behavior	.60***	(1.00)	.54***	(1.00)	.57***	(1.00)	.61***	(1.00)
Friends Models for Problem Behavior	.80***	(1.00)	.64***	(1.00)	.76***	(1.00)	.70***	(1.00)
Friends Models for Religiosity	.57***		.17		.49***		.50***	

Behavior System

Problem Behavior Structure

General Deviant Behavior	.69***	(1.00)	.32**	(.78)	.59***	(1.00)	.70***	(1.00)
Times Drunk	.75***		.70***		.61***		.62***	

Conventional Behavior Structure

Church Attendance	.81***		.73***		.77***		.80***	

*a*Correlations in parentheses have been corrected for attenuation for those measures that are multiple-item scales for which reliability can be ascertained.

***$p \leq .001$; **$p \leq .01$; *$p \leq .05$.

bution of scores across most measures in all three systems of
Problem-Behavior Theory is strongly maintained.

This evidence in support of the stability of individual differences
in personality, the perceived environment, and behavior between adolescence and young adulthood, and especially within young adulthood, can be extended downward in age by recalling the evidence,
already presented in our earlier book (Jessor & Jessor, 1977, app. 2
and 4), for stability on many of these same attributes *within adolescence/
youth*. For one example, across the three-year interval between Wave
I (1969/70) and Wave IV (1972/73) for the high school males and
females and the college males and females, respectively, the stability
coefficients for Attitudinal Intolerance of Deviance were .53, .40, .53,
and .61 (uncorrected for attenuation). Thus, the larger design of our
longitudinal research project reveals considerable stability of individual differences across a substantial segment of the life span, that is,
from early adolescence through young adulthood. Psychosocial development, rather than being arbitrary or determined largely by the
vagaries of experience, would seem to be, instead, a systematic process
in which later outcomes tend to be consistent with their earlier adolescent antecedents. Indeed, the degree of stability that has been
demonstrated for such a broad diversity of psychosocial characteristics
would suggest that there is stability of *individuality* across this portion
of the life trajectory.

Psychosocial change from adolescence into young adulthood

Given the relative enduringness of individual differences on many of
the attributes in Problem-Behavior Theory, it is useful to look through
a different window on the issue of psychosocial development from
adolescence into young adulthood. Rather than focusing, as we have
thus far, on the consistency of relative position in the distribution of
scores over time, attention now is on stability or change in the central
tendency or mean of the distribution over time. The distinction is
between what Mortimer et al. term "normative stability..., the
persistence of individual ranks," on the one hand, and "level
stability..., the invariance of group means on successive occasions,"
on the other (1982, pp. 267–269). Mean levels may change markedly

with development even though individual differences are stable, and the interesting question for developmental inquiry is exactly what *does* happen to the psychosocial characteristics or risk factors of adolescence/youth; do they intensify, remain the same, or undergo diminution by young adulthood?

To answer this question, we have plotted trajectories for various psychosocial attributes across the six data points from 1969/70 to 1981 for both the High School and College samples. For some of the measures there were fewer data points, owing to their omission in one or more years of data collection; for some of the measures there was a change in item wording or in response categories over the different measurement occasions; and in a few instances the content of the measure was shifted to maintain conceptual equivalence at different developmental stages (e.g., value on achievement shifted from a focus on school to a more general focus on success in work and in life in general). For the most part, however, the measures were identical across the measurement occasions. Plotting the six different mean scores for the High School Study and College Study men and women makes it possible to generate psychosocial "growth curves" that represent the average course of development followed by our particular cohorts as they made the transition from adolescence to young adulthood in the particular historical era from the beginning of the 1970s to the early 1980s.

The trajectories presented in this section map all three systems of Problem-Behavior Theory: personality, the perceived environment, and behavior. Although a small and selected subset, they involve in all but one or two instances measures with high stability, ones in which comparability across time is maximal, and those with the maximum number of data points. In each figure we have combined the genders and present a single curve for the High School sample and a single curve for the College sample; developmental change for both genders was found to be essentially parallel in nearly all instances. In all cases, also, we have included the adolescent/youth measurements (1969/70 to 1972/73) in order to permit comparison of the direction of development *within* adolescence/youth with that *between* adolescence/youth and young adulthood. As it turns out, such comparison is revealing; it captures something particularly important about the general direction that young adult development takes. It is im-

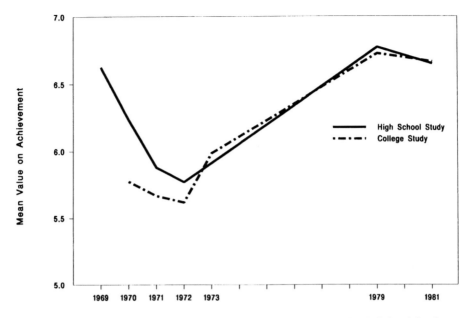

Figure 7.1. Development of Value on Achievement, High School Study
and College Study samples.

portant to recognize, however, that inferences about development
drawn from these trajectories cannot rule out the alternative interpretation that they are reflections of cohort effects or historical change
as well.

The first set of figures, Figures 7.1 through 7.6, represents the
Personality System. Considering for the moment only the adolescence-to-young adult segment of the trajectories, the segment that
lies beyond Wave IV (1972/73), it can be seen that, for both samples,
value on achievement has increased, value on independence has decreased, social criticism has decreased, alienation has decreased, *in*-
tolerance of deviance has increased, and religiosity has decreased (the
latter for the High School sample only, while staying the same for
the College sample). Wherever change has occurred between 1972/
73 and 1981, it has been significant at the .001 level for both samples.
What is more important is that every one of the significant changes
(excepting Religiosity in the High School sample) is, theoretically, *in*

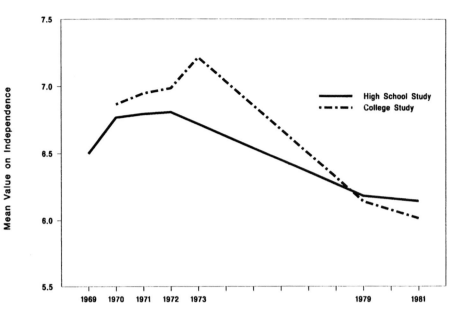

Figure 7.2. Development of Value on Independence, High School Study and College Study samples.

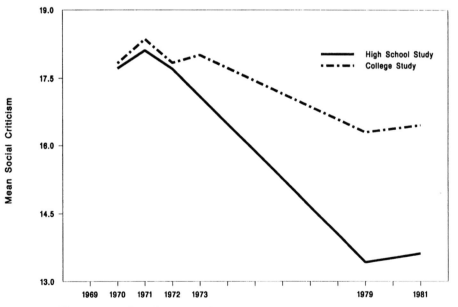

Figure 7.3. Development of Social Criticism, High School Study and College Study samples.

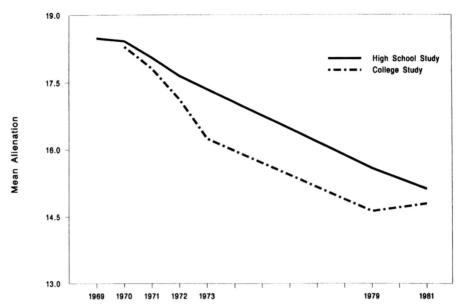

Figure 7.4. Development of Alienation, High School Study and College Study samples.

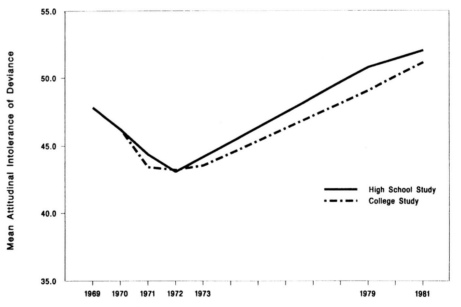

Figure 7.5. Development of Attitudinal Intolerance of Deviance, High School Study and College Study samples.

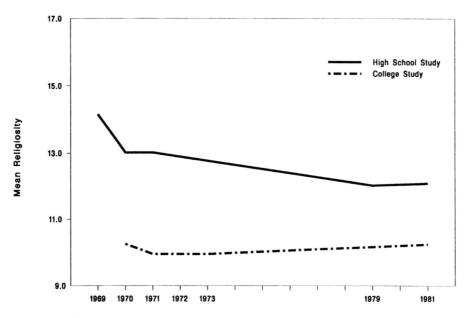

Figure 7.6. Development of Religiosity, High School Study and College
Study samples.

the direction of greater conformity proneness. That is to say, the course
of personality development between adolescence/youth and young
adulthood, at least for these cohorts, and at least in this particular
period of history, is theoretically away from involvement in problem
behavior and toward commitment to conventional behavior.

It is especially instructive to compare this consistent developmental
trend toward conventionality with the trend that obtained earlier
within adolescence/youth – that is, with developmental change in the
preceding segment of the trajectories, that between Wave I (1969/
70) and Wave IV (1972/73). On several of the psychosocial attributes,
a striking shift has taken place: Later development is, to a large extent,
a *reversal* of the earlier developmental trend. For example, value on
achievement was declining in the adolescence/youth phase of the
longitudinal study, but it has increased in the young adult phase; value
on independence was increasing in the earlier phase, but has now
decreased; and attitudinal *in*tolerance of deviance, declining through

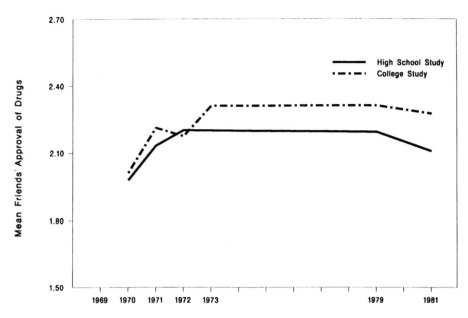

Figure 7.7.   Development of Friends' Approval of Drugs, High School
Study and College Study samples.

adolescence/youth, has now increased beyond even its earliest and,
formerly, highest level. Those earlier directions of change were all,
theoretically, *problem-behavior prone*. Similar problem-behavior prone
developmental changes within adolescence were also observed in an
independent, national sample study cohort of 664 7th and 8th graders
first tested in 1974 and again in 1978 when they had reached grades
11 and 12 (see Jessor, Donovan, & Widmer, 1980, chap. 5). Both of
those earlier studies led us to characterize adolescence as a life stage
prone to problem behavior, and it is that very direction of adolescent
psychosocial development that has now been reversed with development into young adulthood. The decline of social criticism and the
continuing decline in alienation, although not actual reversals of their
own preceding trends, nevertheless buttress the evidence for the
larger developmental shift toward conventionality in young adulthood.
    The next two figures, Figures 7.7 and 7.8, represent the Proximal
Structure of the Perceived Environment System. In Figure 7.7, it can

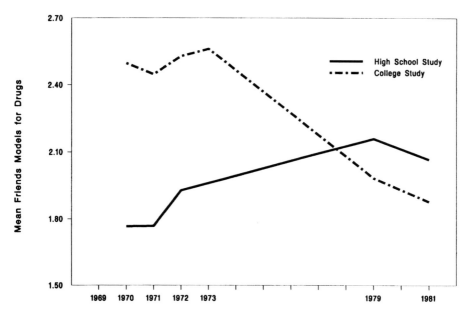

Figure 7.8. Development of Friends Models for Drugs, High School Study and College Study samples.

be seen that there is a leveling off of perceived approval from friends for drug use between adolescence/youth and young adulthood and, for the High School sample, a significant decline within young adulthood. With respect to the perceived prevalence of models for the use of drugs among one's friends, the two samples differ in the change they show between the earlier and later phases of the study, with the High School sample increasing significantly between Waves IV and V and the College sample reversing its earlier direction and decreasing significantly across that same interval. Between Waves V and VI, however, both samples show significant decline. It is clear that the increasing problem-behavior proneness in the perceived environment that characterized earlier development within adolescence/youth is not maintained into young adulthood. Instead, the curves level off or change significantly in the theoretical direction of conformity proneness. This is particularly true for the College sample; for the High School sample, there is some evidence of continuing increase in

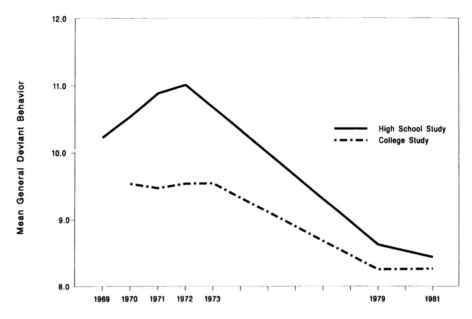

Figure 7.9. Development of General Deviant Behavior, High School
Study and College Study samples.

problem-behavior proneness in the earlier phase of young adulthood
before the decline begins. These contextual findings are generally
consonant with and supportive of the developmental change findings
that were just seen in the personality system.

Turning finally to a consideration of developmental change in the
Behavior System, we have plotted six-wave curves for one of the
problem behaviors, self-reported deviant behavior, and for a conventional behavior, church attendance. These are shown in Figures 7.9
and 7.10.

Theoretically consonant with the changes already seen on the psychosocial measures of personality and the perceived environment,
there is a significant decline ($p \leq .001$) on the measure of deviant
behavior in Figure 7.9 between adolescence/youth and young adulthood for both samples, and, for the High School sample, the decline
is a clear reversal of the earlier direction of developmental change.
With respect to church attendance, as can be seen in Figure 7.10,

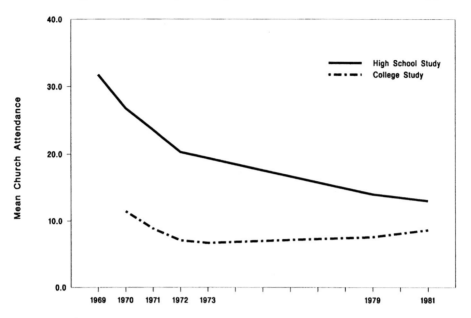

Figure 7.10. Development of Church Attendance, High School Study and College Study samples.

there is a decline in this conventional behavior that is significant for the High School sample from adolescence to young adulthood; this, then, is an exception to the theoretical consistency of the other changes examined thus far. For the College sample, there is a trend toward increased church attendance although it is not significant for the genders combined. (For the females there is a significant increase from 1973 to 1979, while for the males there is a significant decrease over that same interval; between 1979 and 1981, however, the males show a reversal and increase significantly, while the females continue their increase but not significantly.)

Developmental change in the Behavior System from Wave IV (1972/73), to Wave V (1979), to Wave VI (1981) was also examined for two different status measures of problem behavior: Problem Drinker Status, and Heavier Marijuana Use Status. Classification as a problem drinker or as a heavier marijuana user was described in Chapter 5; the classification criteria employed in Waves V and VI in young adulthood were identical but, for both of these status measures, were somewhat more stringent, given the older age involved, than the criteria used in Wave IV in adolescence/youth. With regard to problem drinking, the proportion of problem drinkers in the drinker population declined over the three waves for all four study-by-gender subgroups. For High School sample males and females and College sample males and females, respectively, the Wave IV, V, and VI percentages of problem drinkers are 34, 32, and 28; 20, 15, and 10; 29, 29, and 20; and 10, 8, and 7. Overall, the decline is greatest for the High School sample women and, within young adulthood, for the College sample men, and no group shows an increase. Even conceding that the more stringent classification criteria for Waves V and VI makes their comparison with Wave IV problematic, the consistency of decline *between* Wave V and VI is consonant with the developmental changes already examined in the Personality and Perceived Environment Systems. It is also consonant with the decline just seen in the curve for the continuous measure of problem behavior – that is, the measure of self-reported deviant behavior.

The findings for the proportion of heavier marijuana users among those who have ever used marijuana, while somewhat more complex, parallel the findings for problem drinking. The percentages of heavier marijuana users across the three waves are as follows: for High School sample males – 33, 35, and 30; for High School sample females – 18, 18, and 17; for College sample males – 38, 25, and 14; and for College sample females – 23, 13, and 5. For the High School samples there is no evidence of a decline between Wave IV and Wave V, and indeed, there is a slight increase for the males; both groups do decline but only slightly between Waves V and VI. For the College samples, however, a decline in the proportion of heavier marijuana users is evident across all three waves, and the magnitude of decline is substantial enough to represent a significant diminution in the prevalence of heavy marijuana use in that older group of young adults.

With the exception of the overall decline of the High School sample on church attendance, these developmental findings for the Behavior System are quite consistent with what was seen in the other psychosocial systems: The various attributes tend to reflect change in the theoretical direction of conformity proneness. In light of such findings, it is possible to characterize the transition from adolescence/youth to young adulthood for these samples as, for the most part, *psychosocial development in the direction of conventionality.* That provides a sharp contrast, indeed, with the earlier direction of development within the adolescent period itself.

As noted above, the subset of attributes presented in Figures 7.1– 7.10 is a selected one, and therefore, any characterization has to remain tentative. Among measures not shown here, the developmental changes on expectations for achievement are not theoretically consonant whereas those for expectations for independence are; internal locus of control does increase as expected into young adulthood, but self-esteem is difficult to interpret throughout; friends models for drinking continue to increase for both samples, but this may reflect the institutionalization of alcohol use in adult society rather than an actual increase in problem-behavior proneness. In regard to additional measures of problem behavior itself, it was possible to examine other kinds of change in drinking behavior and marijuana use between adolescence/youth and young adulthood. For those who had begun drinking by Wave IV (1972/73), there is a significant increase in frequency of drunkenness in the past year for the High School sample between 1972 and 1979, and then a significant decrease between 1979 and 1981; for the College sample none of the changes is significant. With regard to average quantity of alcohol per occasion, for both samples there is a significant decline in intake for all three beverages – beer, wine, and liquor – between adolescence and young adulthood. For those who had begun using marijuana by Wave IV (1972/73), there is a slight increase ($p \leq .10$) by Wave V (1979) and then a leveling off by Wave VI (1981) on the measure of frequency of use in the past six months for the High School sample, and a continuous and significant decrease ($p \leq .01$) for the College sample to Wave VI.

With some qualification, these additional data add support for the overall picture that has emerged from reviewing the array of descriptive developmental findings. Where there are exceptions, they occur more for the High School sample than for the College sample (e.g., the increase in friends models for drug use and in frequency of drunkenness, and the decline in church attendance), and they occur more in the Wave IV–V interval than in the Wave V–VI interval. Whether this is due to more general differences between the populations from which the samples were drawn or whether it reflects the actual age difference between the High School sample and the College sample is unclear. The High School sample in Wave IV (1972), it will be recalled, was 16, 17, and 18 years of age. Between Wave IV and Wave V (1979), these young men and young women were traversing an age range, 18–24, that has been identified as highest in prevalence of involvement in alcohol and drug use, an age range of socially organized expectations and increased opportunities for such involvement. The College sample youth, by contrast, were 22 years of age at Wave IV and, therefore, almost beyond that "high-risk" age range. The increases in alcohol- and drug-related problem behavior between Waves IV and V for the High School sample, or at least the absence of clear evidence for decline on some of those measures until the Wave V–VI interval, may well reflect just this age or developmental-stage difference between it and the College sample.

With regard to the lack of theoretical consonance observed among a few of the measures, it may well reflect the existence of a "lag effect"; changes on some of the behaviors may lag changes on some of the psychosocial variables, or vice versa, and their coming into theoretically expected consonance may require that a longer time interval be observed. Although only speculative, it is not at all unreasonable to expect there to be some degree of asynchrony in the timing of differential developmental changes.

The general trend of psychosocial development into young adulthood seems to be quite clear, however; for both of these samples on the variety of measures examined, and at this time in history, it is significantly in the direction of greater conventionality. That trend represents a major shift away from the direction that was seen earlier, within adolescence, of greater proneness toward problem behavior.

Although these findings are merely descriptive, they constitute an important increment in empirical knowledge about the nature and course of young adult development in contemporary American society. They are also in accord with several other follow-up studies of special groups of youth, studies emphasizing that the direction of development into young adulthood for former student activists is toward less radicalism (Nassi, 1981), or in the direction of the *non*activists (Hoge & Ankney, 1982), or, for former hippies, toward "going straight, not staying deviant" (Ramos, 1980).

The theoretical consonance of psychosocial development

What is especially intriguing, beyond the descriptive import of the developmental findings per se, is the theoretical consonance that was observed between the changes in the Personality and Perceived Environment Systems, on the one hand, and those in the Behavior System, on the other. Such consonance provides additional support, albeit indirect, for the developmental relevance of Problem-Behavior Theory.

A different examination of the data on developmental change provides further evidence on this issue. If, indeed, theoretical consonance obtains between changes in the personality and perceived environment "predictors," on the one hand, and changes in the behavioral "criteria," on the other, then increases and decreases in involvement in problem behavior between adolescence/youth and young adulthood should be paralleled by theoretically consonant increases and decreases in problem-behavior proneness or psychosocial conventionality–unconventionality over that same time period. In order to explore this proposition further, we categorized the High School and College samples into three groups based upon whether their Multiple Problem Behavior Index showed an increase in score, a decrease in score, or the same score between Wave IV (1972/73) and Wave VI (1981). For each of those three "criterion" groups, in both samples, we then plotted the direction of change they showed on the Total Conventionality Index, a summary "predictor" measure of personality and perceived environment proneness to problem behavior.' The resulting curves are presented in Figures 7.11 and 7.12 for the High School and College samples, respectively. The findings add further support for a degree of theoretical coherence in developmental change.

As can be seen in Figure 7.11, the High School sample subgroup that did not increase or decrease its Multiple Problem Behavior Index score over the adolescence-to-young adulthood interval also did not change significantly on its Total Conventionality Index score. By contrast, and as theoretically expected, the subgroup that decreased in problem behavior over that same interval significantly increased in psychosocial conventionality, and the subgroup that increased in problem behavior significantly decreased in psychosocial conventionality. Indeed, the significant decrease in conventionality of the latter group is especially noteworthy, given that the overall trend between adolescence and young adulthood is in the opposite direction – that is, toward greater conventionality.

The curves for the College sample in Figure 7.12 show essentially the same pattern, although not as compellingly. The subgroup that does not change in problem behavior shows no significant change in psychosocial conventionality between Wave IV and Wave VI (although there is a significant decline between Wave IV and Wave V); the subgroup that decreases in problem behavior shows, as expected, a significant increase in psychosocial conventionality over the eight-year interval; and the subgroup that increases in problem behavior shows a decrease in conventionality, also as expected, but it does not reach significance in this case.

These findings help strengthen the conviction that developmental changes are, for the most part, theoretically consonant between adolescence/youth and young adulthood although the existence of some asynchronies were noted above. The findings suggest that at least some aspects of psychosocial development proceed in a relatively coherent and integrated way – that is, holistically – rather than taking place through piecemeal changes that are essentially unrelated to each other.

Interindividual differences in psychosocial development

In emphasizing, as we have, that the overall or average trend in our data for development between adolescence/youth and young adult-

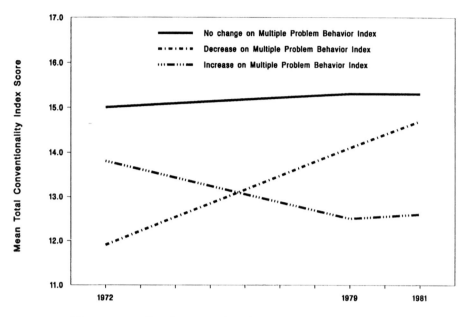

Figure 7.11. Development of psychosocial conventionality, High School Study sample.

hood is in the direction of greater psychosocial and behavioral conventionality, we have not as yet given appropriate attention to what we know to be ubiquitous – namely, *individual differences* in amount and in direction of change. Attention to the latter was long ago urged by Wohlwill (1973), and, more recently, Montada and Schmitt have included this concern in their very definition of developmental psychology: "The object of developmental psychology is the description and explanation of intraindividual change and interindividual differences in…change" (1982, p. 15). Although the focus of the immediately preceding section was on the theoretical consonance of developmental change, it nevertheless provided an initial demonstration of the existence of individual differences in both amount and direction of psychosocial and behavioral change as well. Further ex-

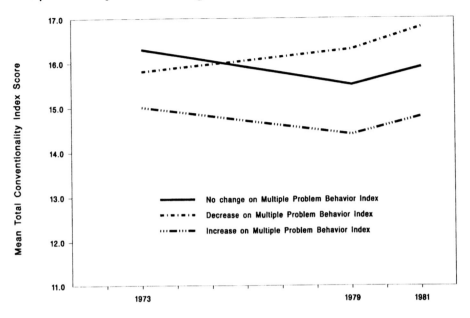

Figure 7.12.   Development of psychosocial conventionality, College Study sample.

ploration of individual differences in change is the concern of the present section.

The window that we have chosen for these explorations is one that enables us to see, simultaneously, the role played by individual differences in development, and their particular relevance for differential developmental change toward greater conventionality. Our general approach was to partition the samples into groups based upon some characteristic or attribute *in adolescence/youth*, and then to examine whether the subsequent course of development into young adulthood was demonstrably different for the different groups. As it turns out, such a strategy can be very illuminating about individual differences in prospective change.

The exploration was focused on individual differences in anteced-ent adolescent conventionality–unconventionality and on the role of such prior differences in the course and magnitude of later developmental change into young adulthood. Employing, once again, the Total Conventionality Index as the summary measure of personality and perceived environment conventionality *in adolescence/youth* (Year IV, 1972/73), we established three groups in each sample: a High Conventionality group, a Medium Conventionality group, and a Low Conventionality group. For each of the three groups, in both samples, it was then possible to plot the trajectory of its subsequent development on a variety of different attributes between 1972/73 and 1981. (Some of the attributes plotted are components that went into the construction of the 1972/73 Total Conventionality Index: measures of Social Criticism, Attitudinal Intolerance of Deviance, and Friends Models for Drug Use.) The questions that can be addressed by such an approach are of intrinsic interest: Are the trajectories of development for the three groups similar or different? If different, are the developmental differences linked systematically to the antecedent differences in conventionality, or are they arbitrary? Do those adolescents who were most unconventional in 1972/73, the Low Conventionality group, remain unconventional into young adulthood or do they, too, get caught up in the overall pendulum swing toward greater conventionality?

An initial answer to those questions is apparent in Figure 7.13. The curves in Figure 7.13 are most interesting; they provide clear evidence of individual differences in developmental change that are linked to variation in antecedent psychosocial conventionality in both the High School and the College samples. If we consider, first, the trajectories of development of value on achievement in the High School sample, it can be seen that the group that was most conventional in adolescence, the High Conventionality group, had the highest value on achievement in 1972, and it remains high; there is no significant developmental change between 1972 and 1981. By contrast, the Low Conventionality group had the lowest value on achievement in 1972 (significantly lower than that of both other groups); but it has increased significantly since 1972, and, by 1981, its mean is virtually identical with that of the High group.

The Medium group was in between the other two initially, and, by 1981, it also has converged on the mean of the High group. Essentially the same pattern is apparent in the curves for the College sample,

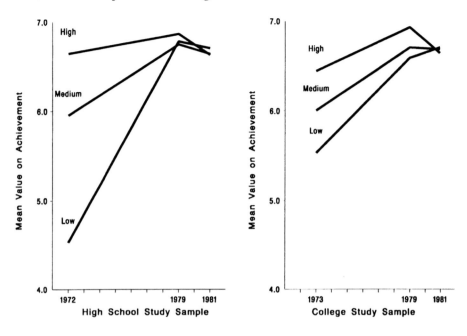

Figure 7.13.   Adolescent conventionality (High, Medium, and Low groups in 1972/1973) and subsequent development of Value on Achievement.

also shown in Figure 7.13. The High group shows no significant developmental change on value on achievement between 1973 and 1981; it is high initially and remains so. Both the Medium and the Low groups do change significantly, both of them converging on the High group by 1981, thereby replicating, in an independent sample, the pattern observed for the high school youth.

These findings are important for several reasons: First, they show that initial individual differences do implicate differential subsequent developmental change. The group initially high in conventionality shows no significant developmental change over the eight- or nine-year interval on value on achievement, whereas the groups initially medium or low in conventionality change significantly in the direction of higher value on achievement, with the mean of the High Conventionality group as their apparent asymptote. Second, the curves show that developmental change is in the direction of greater psychosocial conventionality – here, greater value on achievement – especially for those who were least conventional as adolescents: the Low Conventionality group. Rather than holding on to their unconventionality into young adulthood, the Low group shows the greatest rate of change, and its curve has the steepest slope in both the High School and the College samples. Third, the data suggest that the overall developmental trend toward conventionality emphasized earlier in this chapter is a composite of major individual differences in change; it is contributed to largely by the changes in the initially Low group, and also in the initially Medium group, with the High group holding its original position and not changing at all.

The nature of these differential developmental changes is not explainable simply as the outcome of "regression toward the mean" across multiple occasions of measurement. Although that phenomenon could well be a factor in the changes that have been shown across these three-occasion observations, it fails to account for the key characteristics of those changes: first, that there has been a significant increase in the mean value on achievement for the total sample; second, that significant change occurs for the extreme group that was initially low on value on achievement but not for the extreme group that was initially high; and third, that there is a significant decrease in the variance in value on achievement from the adolescent to the young adult measurement occasions. This same argument also applies, for the most part, to the other attributes that were examined.

The pattern seen in Figure 7.13 emerges in relation to a number of other attributes in the three systems of Problem-Behavior Theory, although not all of them. There is a sufficient degree of generality, however, to strengthen the conviction that the pattern is robust. In Figure 7.14, the curves for change in Social Criticism reveal a similar although not as compelling pattern of convergence in the direction of greater conventionality, that is, toward lower scores on social criticism; in this case, all three groups – High, Medium and Low – have changed significantly in the same direction.

The curves for change in Attitudinal Intolerance of Deviance, shown in Figure 7.15, represent a paradigm example. Here the High Conventionality group does not change significantly; initially most intolerant, it remains intolerant. The Low Conventionality group, initially least intolerant, changes the most and in the direction of

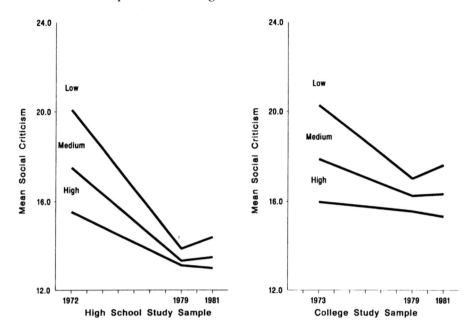

Figure 7.14.   Adolescent conventionality (High, Medium, and Low groups in 1972/1973) and subsequent development of Social Criticism.

greater intolerance of deviance. And the Medium Conventionality group also changes significantly toward greater conventionality. The convergence by 1981 around the mean of the High Conventionality group is evident in both samples.

The curves for a measure of the perceived environment, Friends Models for Drug Use, shown in Figure 7.16, also indicate differential change and convergence in the direction of greater conventionality; the same pattern is also evident in Figure 7.17 on the behavior system measure of General Deviant Behavior.

In regard, then, to individual differences in antecedent conventionality during adolescence (represented by the High, Medium and Low groups on the Total Conventionality Index), it is clear that there is systematic variation in the course of subsequent psychosocial development. Those initially most conventional show the least change; those initially most unconventional show the most change; and where

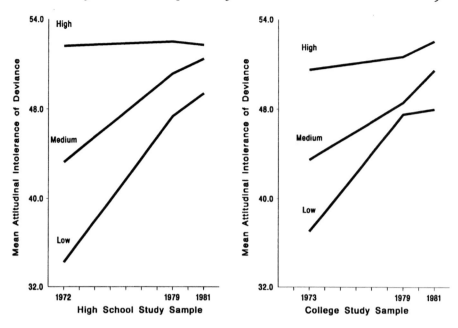

Figure 7.15. Adolescent conventionality (High, Medium, and Low groups in 1972/1973) and subsequent development of Attitudinal Intolerance of Deviance.

change occurs it is in the direction of greater conventionality. Further, the convergence of the curves shown in Figures 7.13 through 7.17 suggests that, with growth from adolescence into young adulthood, there is a trend toward psychosocial and behavioral homogenization, with a significant diminution of the variation in conventionality–unconventionality that was seen in adolescence, as well as an increase in conventionality itself.

Conclusion

In this chapter, we have presented a considerable amount of data – all of it descriptive – on psychosocial and behavioral development from adolescence/youth to young adulthood. Our primary aim has been to exploit the unique contribution of longitudinal design in

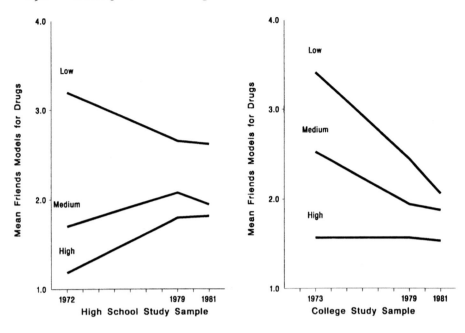

Figure 7.16.   Adolescent conventionality (High, Medium, and Low groups in 1972/1973) and subsequent development of Friends Models for Drugs.

enabling us to examine stability and change over time, and to begin to fill in the long-standing lacuna in knowledge about development into young adulthood. In this effort, several things have emerged with a good deal of clarity. First, evidence for the stability of individual differences across the adolescence-to-young adult transition is compelling. It tends to support a continuity perspective on psychosocial and behavioral development, and, in relation to personality stability in particular, it repudiates the kind of arid situationism that led psychologists on such a long and unnecessary detour until the "rediscovery" of the interactionist high road.

Second, the effort has identified a major direction of development between adolescence and young adulthood for these cohorts: an overall developmental trend toward increasing conventionality. No claim can be made that such a trend is general beyond the particular cohorts studied, of course, or beyond the particular time in history over which

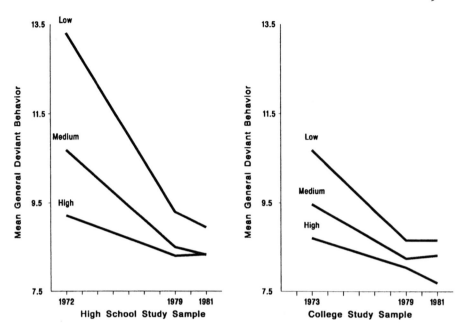

Figure 7.17. Adolescent conventionality (High, Medium, and Low groups in 1972/1973) and subsequent development of General Deviant Behavior.

the data were collected. Nevertheless, it is a direction of change that is consonant with the developmental or age-graded move away from the school context and with the assumption of work and family roles in young adulthood. Research appraisals with other cohorts, in other contexts, at other times in history, are obviously called for.

Third, the evidence suggests, at least in the domain of conventionality, that there is a tendency toward convergence and homogenization with development into young adulthood. The antecedent individual differences in psychosocial conventionality that can be specified in adolescence/youth are associated with differential developmental change that reduces that antecedent variation. Not only, then, does there appear to be an overall developmental increase in the conventionality mean, but also there appears to be a developmental decrease in the variance around that mean.

Finally, the findings strengthen the Problem-Behavior Theory perspective by bringing into view the theoretical consonance of the developmental changes in personality and the perceived environment, on the one hand, and in behavior, on the other. That consonance, based as it is on descriptive data, provides only indirect support for the theory. For more direct and compelling support of its developmental usefulness, it is necessary to examine its *predictive* capability over a significant segment of the life trajectory. That is the topic of the chapter that follows.

Note

1   Component measures of the Year IV (1972/73) Total Conventionality Index were Social Criticism, Religiosity, Attitudinal Intolerance of Deviance, Sex-Role Attitudes (available in College Study only), Friends Models for Drug Use, Friends' Approval of Drugs, Friends Models for Religiosity, and Friends' Strictness.

In Wave V (1979) and Wave VI (1981), all of these measures with the exception of Friends' Strictness were available, and Friends Controls was selected as a replacement for the latter. With this one exception, the component measures of the 1979 and 1981 Total Conventionality indexes are the same as those of the Year IV Total Conventionality Index.

References

Backteman, G., & Magnusson, D. (1981). Longitudinal stability of personality characteristics. *Journal of Personality, 49,* 147–160.

Costa, P. T., Jr., & McCrae, R. R. (1988). Personality in adulthood: A six-year longitudinal study of self-reports and spouse ratings on the NEO Personality Inventory. *Journal of Personality and Social Psychology, 54,* 853–863.

Dannefer, D. (1984). Adult development and social theory: A paradigmatic reappraisal. *American Sociological Review, 49,* 100–116.

Dusek, J. B., & Flaherty, J. F. (1981). The development of the self concept during the adolescent years. *Monographs of the Society for Research in Child Development, 46* (4, Serial No. 191).

Hoge, D. R., & Ankney, T. L. (1982). Occupations and attitudes of former student activists 10 years later. *Journal of Youth and Adolescence, 11,* 355–371.

Jessor, R. (1983). The stability of change: Psychosocial development from adolescence to young adulthood. In D. Magnusson & V. Allen (Eds.), *Human development: An interactional perspective* (pp. 321–341). New York: Academic Press.

Jessor, R., Donovan, J. E., & Widmer, K. (1980). *Psychosocial factors in adolescent alcohol and drug use: The 1978 national sample study and the 1974–78 panel study* (pp. 1–167). Boulder: Institute of Behavioral Science, University of Colorado.

Jessor, R., & Jessor, S. L. (1977). *Problem behavior and psychosocial development: A longitudinal study of youth.* New York: Academic Press.

Levinson, D. J. (1986). A conception of adult development. *American Psychologist, 41,* 3–13.

Magnusson, D. (1988). *Individual development from an interactional perspective: A longitudinal study.* Hillsdale, NJ: Erlbaum.

Montada, L., & Schmitt, M. (1982). Issues in applied developmental psychology: A life-span perspective. *Life-Span Development and Behavior, 4,* 1–32.

Mortimer, J. T., Finch, M. D., & Kumka, D. (1982). Persistence and change in development: The multi-dimensional self-concept. *Life-Span Development and Behavior, 4,* 263–313.

Nassi, A. J. (1981). Survivors of the sixties: Comparative psychosocial and political development of former Berkeley student activists. *American Psychologist, 36,* 753–761.

Ramos, M. R. (1980). The hippies: Where are they now? In F. R. Scarpitti & S. K. Datesman (Eds.), *Drugs and the youth culture* (pp. 223–247). Beverly Hills, CA: Sage.

Schuerger, J. M., Tait, E., & Tavernelli, M. (1982). Temporal stability of personality by questionnaire. *Journal of Personality and Social Psychology, 43,* 176–182.

Stein, J. A., Newcomb, M. D., & Bentler, P. M. (1986). Stability and change in personality: A longitudinal study from early adolescence to young adulthood. *Journal of Research in Personality, 20,* 276–291.

Wohlwill, J. F. (1973). *The study of behavioral development.* New York: Academic Press.

8

Linking proneness to problem behavior in adolescence with involvement in problem behavior in young adulthood

A key objective of this longitudinal research effort has been to explore the linkage between problem-behavior proneness in adolescence/youth and involvement in problem behavior later on in young adulthood. Are the values, attitudes, behaviors, and peer group associations of adolescence/youth influential in shaping later patterns of behavior despite the major changes in life circumstances that inevitably occur? Or does the transition from one life stage to the next entail such discontinuity that little predictability of later problem behavior involvement is possible?

Longitudinal research findings remain somewhat equivocal about the linkage between adolescent characteristics and later, young adult problem behavior. Newcomb and Bentler (1988) found that variation in social conformity in late adolescence is a significant predictor of later drug use, drug–crime involvement, and other criminal activities in young adulthood. Magnusson (1988) has shown a relationship between early adolescent aggressiveness and motor restlessness and later young adult criminality. On the other hand, Temple and Fillmore (1985–86) report little predictability between measures of academic self-concept, family support, and positive and negative peer networks assessed at age 18, and drinking to the point of drunkenness at age 31 (but for another interpretation, see Windle, 1988).

In this chapter, we examine the predictability of young adult problem behavior from psychosocial proneness for problem behavior measured in adolescence/youth. The focal concern is whether those participants in our study who were at greater psychosocial risk (personality risk, perceived environment risk, and behavioral risk) for

problem behavior in adolescence/youth are the ones most likely to
be involved in problem behavior later on as young adults.

The predictability of later-life involvement in problem behavior
from earlier psychosocial antecedents is, of course, of pragmatic import. Given that the magnitude of predictability is nontrivial, a logical
basis for early, salutary intervention would become available. Also
important is the theoretical import of establishing predictability over
time; the theory gains strength from the fact that the constructs it
includes are demonstrably relevant beyond a particular moment in
time or a particular phase of the life course. But the overriding significance of predictability lies in what it can reveal about the nature
and course of human development. If development is seen as the
outcome of the interaction of person and environment over time, then
the establishment of predictability between Time 1 and Time 2 implies some degree of stability and continuity of person and environment, or of both, over time, or else it must imply that there has been
consonance in their change over time. In short, the matter of predictability, often treated as an end in itself, is at bottom a developmental issue. To explore predictability is to explore development, to
try to establish how much change has taken place and where it is
located – in the person, in the environment, or in both. This chapter,
then, is the second one concerned with development, and it employs
analytic methods that ultimately suggest at least partial answers to
such developmental questions.

Predicting young adult involvement in problem behavior

In order to permit exploration of the linkage over time, we relied on
the summary measure of variation in *intensity of current involvement* in
five areas of young adult problem behavior. Those areas, as noted in
Chapter 5, include problem drinking, marijuana use, use of other
illicit drugs, general deviant behavior, and cigarette smoking. The
summary measure, the Multiple Problem Behavior Index, served as
the main "outcome" criterion in young adulthood in a systematic set
of over-time correlation analyses. These correlations are presented
in Table 8.1. What is most evident in the table is, with few exceptions,
a consistent and pervasive linkage between psychosocial proneness to

Table 8.1. *Pearson correlations of measures of psychosocial proneness in adolescence/youth (1972/1973) with the summary measure of problem behavior in young adulthood (1981), by group*

Measures of psychosocial proneness in adolescence/youth (1972/1973)	Multiple Problem Behavior Index (1981)			
	High School Study		College Study	
	Men (N = 160)	Women (N = 222)	Men (N = 84)	Women (N = 100)
Personality System measures				
Motivational-Instigation Structure				
Value on Academic Achievement	−.19**	−.24***	−.07	−.11
Value on Independence	.03	.09	.08	.04
Independence–Achievement Value Discrepancy	.19**	.27***	.11	.12
Expectation for Academic Achievement	−.11	−.25***	−.07	−.12
Expectation for Independence	.01	.04	.05	−.12
Personal Belief Structure				
Social Criticism	.20**	.12*	.32**	.36***
Alienation	.12	.04	.26**	.22*
Self-Esteem	.04	−.06	−.14	−.03
Internal–External Control	−.30***	−.04	−.29**	−.11
Personal Control Structure				
Intolerance of Deviance	−.27***	−.22***	−.19*	−.21*
Religiosity	−.29***	−.12*	−.22*	−.28**
Drinking Disjunctions	.19**	.09	.19*	.22*
Drug Disjunctions	.36***	.25***	.32***	.41***
Sex Disjunctions	.30***	.13*	.37***	.18*

(*continued on next page*)

Table 8.1 *(cont.)*

Measures of psychosocial proneness in adolescence/youth (1972/1973)	Multiple Problem Behavior Index (1981)			
	High School Study		College Study	
	Men (N = 160)	Women (N = 222)	Men (N = 84)	Women (N = 100)
Perceived Environment System measures				
Distal Structure				
Parent–Friends Compatibility	−.21**	−.07	−.40***	−.25**
Parent–Friends Influence	.16*	.17**	.22*	.21*
Proximal Structure				
Parent Approval Problem Behavior	.15*	.01	.11	.10
Friends' Approval Problem Behavior	.34***	.26***	.36***	.42***
Friends Models Problem Behavior	.26***	.26***	.37***	.31***
Behavior System measures				
Problem Behavior Structure				
Times Drunk in Past Year	.16*	.18*	.30**	.30***
Marijuana Involvement	.29***	.32***	.51***	.40***
Psychedelic Drug Use	.31***	.15*	.48***	.33***
General Deviant Behavior	.36***	.36***	.24*	.35***
Multiple Problem Behavior Index	.28***	.35***	.41***	.50***
Conventional Behavior Structure				
Church Attendance/ Past Year	−.13*	−.07	−.26**	−.25**
School Performance/ Past Year	−.29***	−.13*	−.10	−.06

Table 8.1 (*cont.*)

Measures of psychosocial proneness in adolescence/youth (1972/1973)	Multiple Problem Behavior Index (1981)			
	High School Study		College Study	
	Men ($N = 160$)	Women ($N = 222$)	Men ($N = 84$)	Women ($N = 100$)
Sociodemographic measures				
Father's Education	.08	−.00	.06	−.09
Mother's Education	.11	−.06	−.07	−.02
Father's Occupation	.13*	−.00	.10	−.09
Family's Socioeconomic Status	.11	−.01	.08	−.10

***$p \leq .001$ (one-tailed test); **$p \leq .01$; *$p \leq .05$.

problem behavior in adolescence/youth and later involvement in problem behavior in young adulthood. For all four gender-by-study groups, and in all three systems of Problem-Behavior Theory, various measures of psychosocial risk in adolescence/youth are significantly associated with the criterion measure of intensity of young adult involvement in problem behavior.

In the Personality System, the adolescence/youth measures of psychosocial risk that relate most consistently to young adult problem behavior are personal controls against problem behavior. Weaker personal controls against problem behavior involvement in adolescence/youth (less intolerance of deviance, less religiosity, and more importance on positive than on negative reasons for engaging in drinking, drug use, and sex) relate significantly to greater involvement in problem behavior in young adulthood for all four gender-by-study groups. Personal beliefs in adolescence/youth that involve criticism of American society and of its institutions and policies also relate consistently to later, young adult involvement in problem behavior. Greater alienation is a significant predictor for the College sample, and lower internal control is a significant predictor for the males in both samples. With regard to the motivational-instigation measures, lower value on achievement, greater value on independence than achievement, and lower expectations for achievement (females only) are significant in the High School sample; none of these correlations reaches significance for the College sample, however.

In the Perceived Environment System, greater adolescent/youth psychosocial proneness (less compatibility of interests and outlook between parents and friends, greater friends' than parents' influence on decision-making, and greater friends' approval of and models for involvement in problem behavior) relates consistently to greater involvement in problem behavior in young adulthood. And in the Behavior System, the findings are also very consistent; greater involvement in the different areas of problem behavior and lower involvement in conventional behavior in adolescence/youth are related to greater intensity of involvement in problem behavior in young adulthood.

In contrast to these theoretically based findings, it is of interest to note that the sociodemographic measures of family background that were assessed in adolescence/youth show essentially no relationship at all to variation in later involvement in problem behavior in young adulthood.

The pervasiveness of significant bivariate relationships in Table 8.1 over such a long time interval is impressive. What such relationships do not reveal, however, is the predictiveness of overall psychosocial proneness, that is, of the *combined* risk factors that characterized the participants in adolescence/youth. In order to assess the latter, a series of multiple regression analyses was carried out. These were designed to test the predictiveness of the Problem-Behavior Theory framework as a whole across the eight- or nine-year interval that separated the earlier adolescence/youth measures from the later young adult summary measure of problem behavior.

The same predictor sets were used that had been used *within* the adolescent/youth phase of the research (see Jessor & Jessor, 1977). The first predictor set represents *personality proneness* for problem behavior in adolescence/youth; it includes five measures: the Independence–Achievement Value Discrepancy, Expectation for Academic Achievement, Social Criticism, Self-Esteem, and Attitudinal Intolerance of Deviance. The second predictor set reflects *perceived environment proneness* for problem behavior in adolescent/youth; it includes four measures: Parent–Friends Compatibility, Parent vs. Friends Relative Influence, Parental Approval–Disapproval of Problem Behavior, and Friends Models for Problem Behavior. The third predictor set, the field pattern, represents *personality and perceived environment proneness, jointly,* for problem behavior in adolescence/youth; it includes six measures selected on theoretical rather than empirical grounds from the nine in the first two sets: Independence–Achievement Value Discrepancy, Expectation for Academic Achievement, Social Criticism, Attitudinal Intolerance of Deviance, Parent–Friends Compatibility, and Friends Models for Problem Behavior. The fourth predictor set represents *behavior system proneness* in adolescence/youth; it includes three behavior measures: two measures of conventional behavior, Church Attendance Frequency and School Performance, and a summary measure of adolescent involvement in problem behavior. The fifth and final predictor set reflects *overall psychosocial proneness,* or risk, for problem behavior in adolescence/youth; it includes 14 measures: the six measures from the field pattern, the two conventional behavior measures, the summary measure of adolescent problem behavior involvement, two additional measures of drug and sex disjunctions (positive minus negative reasons for involvement), and three measures of socioeconomic background (Father's Education, Mother's Education, and Father's Occupational Status). Each of these five different predictor sets includes measures that had been established as key theoretical variables in the earlier adolescent/youth phase of this research (see Jessor & Jessor, 1977, chap. 5).[1]

   The multiple correlations between these five sets of predictor measures, assessed in adolescence/youth (1972/73), and the Multiple Problem Behavior Index, assessed in young adulthood (1981), are presented in Table 8.2. As can be seen, overall psychosocial proneness in adolescence/youth yields significant levels of prediction – across the eight- or nine-year interval – of variation in young adult involvement in problem behavior. The set of 14 measures (Run V in Table 8.2) accounts for 18–27 percent of the variance in young adult problem behavior for the High School Study subsamples, and 35–44 percent of the variance for the College Study subsamples. This level of predictability is especially impressive in view of the fact that the eight- and nine-year intervals included the major developmental transition between late adolescence/youth and young adulthood, a transition that involves pervasive life changes and situational discontinuities for most young people.

As can also be seen in Table 8.2, young adult involvement in problem behavior is more predictable for the members of the College Study than it is for the members of the High School Study, and it is more predictable for the men than for the women within each study. The fact that the interval between the adolescent/youth and young adult data collections is a year shorter for the College Study participants than it is for the High School Study participants is the most obvious, but probably least important, reason for this difference between the study results. A more probable explanation is the likelihood of greater actual change in the life situations of the High School Study participants than in the life situations of the College Study participants. The younger group were living at home with their parents and attending high school when the adolescent data were collected, whereas they were living out on their own, most were working full-time, and many had their own families when the young adult data were collected. In contrast, the College Study youth were already away from home, either finishing up college or working, and they had already made progress toward emotional and financial independence from their parents when the earlier data were collected.

With respect to the gender difference in overall predictability, the lower predictability observed for the women in both studies may reflect the greater constraints placed on young women by the social roles and life situations they are involved in as young adults and, therefore, some restriction in the influence of individual difference variables assessed in adolescence/youth. Alternatively, of course, there may be gender-related differences in variation on the measures involved.

Beyond establishing that the linkage is substantial between earlier psychosocial proneness and later involvement in problem behavior, the results in Table 8.2 also make clear that all three of the systems of Problem-Behavior Theory contribute to the explanatory account. Psychosocial proneness in the Personality System (Run I) accounts for 11–16 percent of the variation in problem behavior involvement in young adulthood, with little difference by study or by gender. Psychosocial proneness in the Perceived Environment System in adolescence/youth (Run II) accounts for just about the same level of

Table 8.2. *Multiple correlations of psychosocial proneness in adolescence/youth (1972/1973) with the summary measure of problem behavior in young adulthood (1981)*

| Psychosocial proneness in adolescence/youth (1972/1973) | Multiple Problem Behavior Index (1981) | | | |
| | High School Study | | College Study | |
	Men ($N = 160$)	Women ($N = 222$)	Men ($N = 84$)	Women ($N = 100$)
Run I. Personality System proneness (5 measures)	.33**	.33***	.38*	.40**
Run II. Perceived Environment System proneness (4 measures)	.32**	.31***	.54***	.38**
Run III. Psychosocial proneness – Field Pattern (6 measures)	.36**	.38***	.59***	.42**
Run IV. Behavior System proneness (3 measures)	.36***	.37***	.43**	.50***
Run V. Overall psychosocial proneness (14 measures)	.52***	.42***	.66***	.59***

Note: Sets of predictor variables are the same as those used in the adolescent/youth phase of the study (Jessor & Jessor, 1977).
***$p \leq .001$ (by F-test); **$p \leq .01$; *$p \leq .05$.

variation (10–14%) for three of the four samples, and for somewhat more of the variation (29%) for the College Study men. The six psychosocial measures representing the Field Pattern (Run III) account for somewhat more of the variation in young adult problem behavior involvement than either the personality or the perceived environment predictor set alone.

Proneness in the Behavior System in adolescence/youth accounts for 13–14 percent of the variation in young adult problem behavior for the High School Study sample, and for 18–25 percent for the College Study sample. This level of predictability reflects in large part the contribution of the summary measure of problem behavior in adolescence/youth. Regressions utilizing only the two conventional behavior measures as predictors account for much less of the variation in young adult involvement in problem behavior (i.e., only 2–10%); this is, nevertheless, still a statistically significant contribution (Rs = .32, .15, .27, and .26, respectively, for the High School sample men and women and for the College sample men and women).

Given that the explanatory contribution of earlier involvement in problem behavior in adolescence/youth is substantial, additional regressions were performed deleting that variable from the overall psychosocial proneness set (Run V). This procedure permitted a determination of the extent to which this highly proximal behavior system measure may have inflated the overall levels of predictability shown for Run V in Table 8.2. Excluding this summary behavioral predictor measure had *no* impact on the multiple correlations for the two male samples, and relatively little impact for the High School Study women (a reduction from $R = .42$ to $R = .39$). Only for the College Study women was there a notable impact; the multiple correlation in this subsample was reduced from .59 to .51.

The independent predictive power of each of the antecedent proneness measures in each predictor set is indicated by the size of its standardized regression coefficient. Within the set of personality proneness measures (Run I), the two strongest antecedent predictors of young adult problem behavior involvement were the following for each subsample: for the High School Study men, Intolerance of Deviance and Social Criticism; for the High School Study women, Expectation for Academic Achievement and the Independence–Achievement Value Discrepancy; and for both the College Study men and women, Social Criticism and Intolerance of Deviance. Within the set of perceived environment proneness measures (Run II), the two strongest predictors were Friends Models for Problem Behavior and Parent–Friends Compatibility for the High School Study men, and, in reverse order, for the College Study men; for the High School and College Study women, the two strongest predictors were Friends Models for Problem Behavior and Parent–Friends Influence.

In regard to the field pattern (Run III), the two strongest predictors included one personality proneness measure and one perceived environment proneness variable in three of the four gender-by-study samples. For the High School Study men, the two strongest predictors of later problem behavior involvement were Friends Models for Problem Behavior and Intolerance of Deviance, whereas for the High School Study women, they were Friends Models for Problem Behavior and Expectations for Academic Achievement. For the College Study men, the two strongest antecedent predictors were Parent–Friends Compatibility and Friends Models for Problem Behavior, and they were Social Criticism and Friends Models for Problem Behavior for the College Study women.

Among the measures of behavior proneness (Run IV), problem behavior involvement in adolescence/youth was the strongest predictor of young adult involvement in problem behavior in three of the four samples. For the High School Study men, it was the second strongest, after School Performance.

When all 14 psychosocial proneness and sociodemographic measures were used in the regressions (Run V), the relative strengths of the predictors varied considerably across the four samples. For the High School Study men, the three strongest antecedent predictors of young adult problem behavior involvement were School Performance, the Drug Disjunctions measure, and Expectations for Academic Achievement. For the High School Study women, the three strongest predictors were adolescent Multiple Problem Behavior Involvement, Expectation for Academic Achievement, and Parent–Friends Compatibility. For the College Study men, the strongest predictors were Parent–Friends Compatibility, Friends Models for Problem Behavior, and the Sex Disjunctions measure. Lastly, for the College Study women, the three strongest antecedent predictors of young adult problem behavior involvement were adolescent Multiple Problem Behavior Involvement, Social Criticism, and Father's Occupational Status.

In summary, these multivariate analyses reveal a substantial relationship between the measures of Problem-Behavior Theory assessed in adolescence/youth and a summary measure of intensity of involvement in problem behavior eight or nine years later, in young adulthood. The relationship holds across all three explanatory systems of the theory – personality, perceived environment, and behavior – and for male and female participants in both the High School Study and the College Study. Despite the apparent developmental "return to conventionality" noted in Chapter 7, these findings demonstrate continuity in the explanatory relevance of the psychosocial framework. Even though the samples became less prone to problem behavior as they made the transition from adolescence/youth to young adulthood, those who were most prone to involvement in problem behavior as adolescents were the ones most likely to be involved in problem behavior as young adults.

Predicting young adult involvement in specific problem behaviors

Although the foregoing analyses have established the across-time predictability of involvement in the general class of problem behavior in young adulthood, they have revealed little about the predictability of the various component behaviors that comprise the summary criterion measure: problem drinking, marijuana use, other illicit drug use, general deviance, and smoking. Given the differential prevalence of these problem behaviors in young adulthood, they may well be differentially predictable from proneness to problem behavior in adolescence/youth.

In order to determine how psychosocial proneness or risk in adolescence/youth is linked to young adult involvement in the different problem behaviors, and in order to determine whether the various problem behaviors are indeed differentially predictable over this time interval, we carried out the same bivariate and multivariate analyses for each of the five component behaviors that had been done for the overall summary measure, the Multiple Problem Behavior Index.

Table 8.3 presents Pearson bivariate correlations between the psychosocial risk factors assessed in adolescence/youth and three young adult measures of problem behavior: Times Drunk in the Past Six Months; Frequency of Marijuana Use in the Past Month; and Intensity of Other Illicit Drug Use in the Past Six Months. For economy of presentation, the bivariate correlations with General Deviance and Cigarette Smoking are not included in the table but are discussed in the text instead. The multiple correlations between adolescent/youth psychosocial proneness and all five of the specific problem behaviors in young adulthood are presented in Table 8.4.[2] In general, these multiple correlations are smaller in magnitude than those for the summary Multiple Problem Behavior Index.

With respect to the *Frequency of Drunkenness* measure in young adulthood, nearly all of the adolescent/youth risk factors relate as expected. Many of the across-time correlations are smaller than they were for the overall summary measure, but their patterning is very similar. The most consistent adolescent/youth predictors of young adult drunkenness are from the same structures of the psychosocial framework that related most consistently with the summary measure of young adult involvement in the larger class of problem behavior: measures of personal controls, of environmental support for problem behavior, and of prior involvement in problem behavior in adolescence/youth. The weaker the personal controls against problem behavior, the greater the perceived approval and models for problem behavior, and the greater the reported involvement in other kinds of problem behaviors in adolescence/youth, the greater the frequency of reported drunkenness in the preceding six months among the young adults.

Multiple correlations of the 14 measures of problem-behavior proneness in adolescence/youth account for substantial percentages of the variance in young adult drunkenness. The results for Run V can be seen in Table 8.4. Between 16 and 21 percent of the variance is accounted for in the High School Study samples, and between 29 and 36 percent of the variance is accounted for in the College Study samples. For the most part, the antecedent psychosocial risk factors in all three theoretical systems relate significantly to frequency of drunkenness in young adulthood.

With respect to the measure of *Marijuana Use* in young adulthood, the correlations in Table 8.3 show that the most consistent antecedent risk factors in adolescence/youth are, again, lower personal controls, perceptions of greater social support for involvement in problem behavior, and greater actual involvement in other areas of problem behavior. The major difference between these results and those for the drunkenness measure is that fewer of the personal control measures in adolescence/youth relate significantly to variation in young

Table 8.3. *Pearson correlations of measures of psychosocial proneness in adolescence/youth (1972/1973) with measures of specific problem and conventional behaviors in young adulthood (1981), by group*

	Times Drunk/Past Six Months (1981)				Frequency Marijuana Use/Past Month (1981)			
Measures of psycho-social proneness in	High School Study		College Study		High School Study		College Study	
adolescence/youth (1972/73)	Men (N=148)	Women (N=191)	Men (N=82)	Women (N=93)	Men (N=162)	Women (N=222)	Men (N=84)	Women (N=100)
Personality System measures								
Motivational-Instigation Structure								
Value on Academic Achievement	−.17*	−.18**	−.20*	−.02	−.07	−.12*	−.01	−.02
Value on Independence	−.05	−.06	−.11	−.17+	−.01	.17**	−.00	.11
Independence– Achievement Value Discrepancy	.12+	.14*	.13	−.07	.06	.20***	.00	.08
Expectation for Academic Achievement	−.11+	−.19**	−.15+	−.08	−.08	−.10+	.03	−.06
Expectation for Independence	−.05	.04	−.08	−.15+	−.07	−.01	.07	.04
Personal Belief Structure								
Social Criticism	.13+	.14*	.23*	.28**	.23**	.01	.14	.13
Alienation	.22**	.08	.12	.09	.05	−.02	.21*	.03
Self-Esteem	−.06	−.03	−.14+	.07	.07	−.04	−.13	−.02
Internal–External Control	−.20**	−.01	−.15+	−.10	−.19**	−.03	−.33***	−.02
Personal Control Structure								
Intolerance of Deviance	−.23**	−.21**	−.29**	−.12	−.17*	−.06	−.14	−.16+
Religiosity	−.16*	−.16*	−.33***	−.14+	−.23**	−.05	−.10	−.21*
Drinking Disjunctions	.17*	.05	.20*	.22*	.10+	.00	.12	.04
Drug Disjunctions	.35***	.20**	.13	.29**	.34***	.15*	.32***	.17*
Sex Disjunctions	.20**	.08	.19+	.25*	.20**	.02	.37***	.10

Table 8.3 (*cont.*)

Intensity of Other Illicit Drug Use/Past 6 Months (1981)				Church Attendance/Past Year (1981)			
High School Study		College Study		High School Study		College Study	
Men (N = 160)	Women (N = 221)	Men (N = 84)	Women (N = 100)	Men (N = 161)	Women (N = 222)	Men (N = 84)	Women (N = 100)
−.09	−.19**	−.02	−.11	.16*	.22***	−.10	.07
.03	.10+	.02	.13	−.13*	−.11*	.06	−.22*
.11+	.23***	.03	.17*	−.24***	−.27***	.14	−.19*
−.03	−.19**	.03	−.09	−.07	.20***	−.09	−.06
.05	.01	.02	−.05	−.14*	−.17**	.18*	−.16+
.21**	.11*	.24*	.30**	−.24***	−.14*	−.14	−.26**
.09	.09+	.10	.25**	−.02	−.13*	−.15+	−.19*
.06	−.13*	−.00	−.16+	−.13+	.05	.15+	.08
−.23**	−.09+	−.27**	−.07	.10	.16**	.11	.08
−.18*	−.15*	.01	−.11	.10+	.21***	.22*	.22*
−.28***	−.12*	−.12	−.30***	.46***	.30***	.34***	.52***
.16*	.06	.10	.04	.05	−.03	−.08	−.18*
.25***	.23***	.31***	.37***	−.18*	−.22***	−.16+	−.25**
.26***	.08	.19+	.02	−.15*	−.23***	−.39***	−.13

(*continued on next page*)

Table 8.3 (*cont.*)

Measures of psycho-social proneness in adolescence/youth (1972/73)	Times Drunk/Past Six Months (1981)				Frequency Marijuana Use/Past Month (1981)			
	High School Study		College Study		High School Study		College Study	
	Men (N=148)	Women (N=191)	Men (N=82)	Women (N=93)	Men (N=162)	Women (N=222)	Men (N=84)	Women (N=100)
Perceived Environment System Measures								
Distal Structure								
Parent–Friends Compatibility	−.20**	−.03	−.32**	−.05	−.17*	.06	−.29**	−.24**
Parent–Friends Influence	.16*	.13*	.04	.03	.16*	.22***	.18+	.11
Proximal Structure								
Parent Approval Problem Behavior	.04	.14*	.18+	.16+	.21**	−.04	−.01	.14+
Friends' Approval Problem Behavior	.31***	.24***	.28**	.30**	.31***	.16**	.26**	.28**
Friends Models Problem Behavior	.24**	.23***	.35***	.20*	.16*	.12*	.15+	.22*
Behavior System measures								
Problem Behavior Structure								
Times Drunk in Past Year	.09	.03	.60***	.15+	.11	.24***	.07	.47***
Marijuana Involvement	.20**	.22***	.32**	.19*	.28***	.24***	.37***	.32***
Psychedelic Drug Use	.21**	.09	.31**	.19*	.31***	.18**	.34***	.15+
General Deviant Behavior	.23***	.22***	.22*	.24**	.25***	.24***	.12	.13
Multiple Problem Behavior Index	.13+	.21**	.27**	.42***	.21**	.23***	.26**	.20*
Conventional Behavior Structure								
Church Attendance/ Past Year	−.13+	−.08	−.13	−.12	−.04	.01	−.21*	−.15+
School Performance/ Past Year	−.20**	−.03	.01	−.01	−.19**	−.06	.02	.07

Table 8.3 (*cont.*)

Intensity of Other Illicit Drug Use/Past 6 Months (1981)				Church Attendance/Past Year (1981)			
High School Study		College Study		High School Study		College Study	
Men (N=160)	Women (N=221)	Men (N=84)	Women (N=100)	Men (N=161)	Women (N=222)	Men (N=84)	Women (N=100)
−.17*	.02	−.28**	−.31***	.10+	.16**	.11	.20*
.19*	.10+	.03	.21*	−.26***	−.18**	.02	−.19*
.06	.05	.17+	−.01	−.20**	−.19**	−.18+	−.14+
.25***	.20**	.26**	.26**	−.24***	−.27***	−.04	−.28**
.26***	.13*	.28**	.30***	−.24***	−.14*	−.13	−.30***
.05	.12+	.21*	.13	.07	.02	−.13	−.11
.26***	.28***	.44***	.34***	−.14*	−.17**	−.30**	−.25**
.28***	.16**	.28**	.50***	−.06	−.09+	−.25**	−.32***
.25***	.27***	.12	.20*	−.03	−.16**	−.05	−.12
.19**	.23***	.35***	.31***	−.11+	−.22***	−.18*	−.38***
−.15*	−.03	−.14+	−.17*	.43***	.34***	.43***	.39***
−.20**	−.12*	−.08	−.03	.04	.01	.07	.02

(*continued on next page*)

Table 8.3 (*cont.*)

Measures of psycho-social proneness in adolescence/youth (1972/73)	Times Drunk/Past Six Months (1981)				Frequency Marijuana Use/Past Month (1981)			
	High School Study		College Study		High School Study		College Study	
	Men (N=148)	Women (N=191)	Men (N=82)	Women (N=93)	Men (N=162)	Women (N=222)	Men (N=84)	Women (N=100)
Sociodemographic measures								
Father's Education	.10	.03	.16+	−.08	.11+	−.06	.00	−.11
Mother's Education	.14*	−.11+	−.06	−.00	.17*	−.04	−.03	−.18*
Father's Occupation	.14*	.09	.17+	−.01	.18*	−.12	.02	−.09
Father's Hollingshead SES	.13+	.09	.19*	−.04	.15*	−.10	.01	−.11

***$p \leq .001$ (one-tail test); **$p \leq .01$; *$p \leq .05$; +$p \leq .10$.

adult marijuana use. At the multivariate level, the multiple correlations predicting young adult marijuana use show much the same patterning in Table 8.4 as those predicting young adult drunkenness. Multiple correlations based on the 14 adolescent/youth measures of problem-behavior proneness account for 21 and 12 percent of the variance for the High School Study men and women, respectively, and 29 and 14 percent of the variance in young adult marijuana use for the College Study men and women, respectively. For the overall predictor set, three of the four multiple correlations are statistically significant, and the *R*s are larger for men than for women in both samples. For the smaller sets of adolescent/youth psychosocial predictors, the majority of the multiple correlations with young adult marijuana use are also significant for both High School Study samples, but not for the College Study samples, even though the magnitude of the multiple correlations is similar. This difference is largely due to the smaller sample sizes in the College Study.

The third specific criterion measure is *Other Illicit Drug Use* in young adulthood. For this measure, too, there is a similar level of relationship with the antecedent measures of problem-behavior proneness in adolescence/youth. Across the interval between adolescence/youth and young adulthood the pattern of bivariate rela-

Table 8.3 (*cont.*)

Intensity of Other Illicit Drug Use/Past 6 Months (1981)				Church Attendance/Past Year (1981)			
High School Study		College Study		High School Study		College Study	
Men	Women	Men	Women	Men	Women	Men	Women
(*N* = 160)	(*N* = 221)	(*N* = 84)	(*N* = 100)	(*N* = 161)	(*N* = 222)	(*N* = 84)	(*N* = 100)
.12 +	.10 +	− .07	− .07	.00	.08	− .12	− .06
.10 +	.00	.04	.08	.01	.07	− .06	− .01
.21**	.09 +	.11	− .12	− .14*	.03	− .13	− .05
.18*	.10 +	.03	− .11	− .09	.05	− .14	− .00

tionships in Table 8.3 is similar to that for young adult drunkenness and for marijuana use, and it need not be detailed here. Multiple correlations between the adolescent/youth measures of psychosocial risk and the measure of intensity of other illicit drug use in young adulthood are, as shown in Table 8.4, all statistically significant; they account for 14 and 20 percent of the variance for the High School Study samples, and for 28 and 32 percent of the variance for the College Study samples. With the exception of the personality proneness measures, all of the less inclusive sets of psychosocial predictor measures account for significant portions of the variance in young adult use of illicit drugs other than marijuana.

The predictability of *General Deviant Behavior* in young adulthood is somewhat lower than was just seen with respect to the other three specific problem behaviors, particularly for the College Study samples. Although delinquent-type behavior in young adulthood is associated with the personal control measures in adolescence/youth, it has only a slight relationship to environmental support for problem behavior, or to alcohol and drug use in adolescence/youth. And, as may be seen in Table 8.4, overall psychosocial proneness or risk in adolescence/youth (Run V) accounts for only 7–23 percent of the variance in young adult involvement in general deviance. This reduced level

Table 8.4. *Multiple correlations of psychosocial proneness in adolescence/youth (1972/1973) with measures of specific problem and conventional behaviors in young adulthood (1981)*

Psychosocial proneness in adolescence/youth (1972/1973)	Times Drunk/Past 6 Months (1981)				Marijuana Use/Past Month (1981)				Other Illicit Drug Use/Past 6 Months (1981)			
	High School Study		College Study		High School Study		College Study		High School Study		College Study	
	Men	Women	Men	Women	Men	Women	Men	Women	Men	Women	Men	Women
Run I. Personality System proneness (5 measures)	.26+	.28**	.39*	.39**	.29*	.22+	.22	.19	.26+	.27**	.25	.32+
Run II. Perceived Environment System proneness (4 measures)	.29**	.28**	.50***	.23	.30**	.31***	.33+	.32*	.30**	.19+	.42**	.39**
Run III. Psychosocial proneness – Field Pattern (6 measures)	.31*	.34***	.53***	.36*	.29*	.27*	.38+	.30	.32**	.31**	.45**	.41**
Run IV. Behavior System proneness (3 measures)	.24*	.21*	.16	.37**	.22+	.20*	.26	.19	.26**	.24**	.35*	.32*
Run V. Overall psychosocial proneness (14 measures)	.46**	.40**	.60**	.54**	.46**	.35*	.54*	.38	.45**	.37**	.57**	.53**

Note: Sets of predictor variables are the same as those used in the adolescent/youth phase of the study (Jessor & Jessor, 1977).
***$p \leq .001$ (by F-test); **$p \leq .01$; *$p \leq .05$; +$p \leq .10$.

of predictability may well be due to the restricted variation in involvement in general deviant behaviors in the young adult samples noted in Chapter 5.

The final specific problem behavior is *Cigarette Smoking* in young adulthood. This behavior has the weakest relationship of all to problem-behavior proneness assessed in adolescence/youth. The strongest adolescent/youth antecedents of young adult smoking are friends models for problem behavior, involvement with marijuana, and less involvement in the conforming behaviors of church attendance and school performance. Taken together, the adolescent/youth measures

Table 8.4 (*cont.*)

General Deviance/Past Year (1981)				Cigarette Smoking Involvement (1981)				Church Attendance/Past Year (1981)			
High School Study		College Study		High School Study		College Study		High School Study		College Study	
Men	Women	Men	Women	Men	Women	Men	Women	Men	Women	Men	Women
.26*	.25*	.27	.40**	.31**	.21+	.20	.24	.35**	.31**	.33+	.39**
.20	.17	.35*	.28+	.20	.30***	.25	.10	.35***	.28**	.24	.35*
.26+	.24*	.30	.34+	.30*	.29**	.29	.24	.38***	.31**	.36+	.42**
.21+	.18+	.14	.35**	.37***	.29***	.26	.25+	.43***	.36***	.43**	.46***
.40*	.27	.46	.48*	.43**	.35*	.44	.41	.55***	.44***	.56*	.57**

of psychosocial risk account for only 12–19 percent of the variance in young adult cigarette smoking, and none of the multiple correlations for the College Study reaches statistical significance. A possible reason for this may be that cigarette smoking has only marginal status as a young adult problem behavior. A second possible reason may be that there is progressive, physical dependence on cigarette smoking with use; to that extent, its level in young adulthood may become relatively independent from psychosocial proneness in adolescence/ youth (see Bachman, 1987).

Given this variety of specific young adult problem behaviors, it is difficult to characterize the relative predictive power of each of the antecedent proneness measures in each of the five predictor sets for each of the criterion problem behaviors in young adulthood. What can be said, however, is that in the regression equations accounting for variation in young adult drunkenness, marijuana use, and other illicit drug use, the patterning of the relative importance of the antecedent predictor measures is similar to that described earlier in this chapter for the prediction of the summary measure of involvement in problem behavior in young adulthood.

In summary, these analyses have shown that personality, perceived environment, and behavior attributes reflecting psychosocial proneness for problem behavior in adolescence/youth are indeed associated with later involvement in a variety of different, specific problem behaviors in young adulthood. The problem behaviors of drunkenness, marijuana use, and other illicit drug use are more predictable than are delinquent-type behavior or cigarette smoking in young adulthood. The results again make apparent that adolescent/youth socioeconomic background variables play a generally nonsignificant role in accounting for variation in these specific problem behaviors in young adulthood. With the exception of the positive relation of family socioeconomic status to the substance use measures for the High School Study men, there are no consistent relations of the demographic antecedents with these young adult problem behavior data. Most importantly, however, the analyses of specific behaviors make clear that the results presented earlier for the summary measure of young adult involvement in problem behavior are not an artifact of using such a composite score. Rather, the results based on the summary measure reflect, and probably more reliably so, the same relationships that antecedent problem-behavior proneness has to a variety of different problem behaviors in young adulthood.

Predicting young adult involvement in conventional behavior

If the psychosocial proneness measures in adolescence/youth do indeed represent risk factors for problem behavior in later life, they should also relate to conventional behaviors in adulthood – but in the opposite direction. To pursue this demonstration, we correlated the array of adolescent/youth measures of psychosocial proneness with a measure of conventional behavior in young adulthood, the Frequency of Church Attendance in the Past Year. These correlations are also shown in Table 8.3 so they can be compared more easily to the correlations for the specific problem behaviors.

The bivariate correlations in Table 8.3 show that the measure of church attendance in young adulthood does relate as expected, and consistently so: The *lower* the psychosocial proneness in adolescence/ youth, the *more frequent* the church attendance in young adulthood. Wherever personality, perceived environment, or behavior proneness measures assessed in adolescence/youth relate positively to problem behavior in young adulthood, they relate *negatively* to young adult church attendance; and the converse is also true.

Given such evidence at the bivariate level, it is reasonable to expect that the psychosocial measures of problem-behavior proneness in adolescence/youth, taken together, might account for a significant portion of the variance in young adult church attendance frequency. The multiple correlations in Table 8.4 indicate that this is in fact the case. When the set of 14 adolescent/youth predictors representing overall psychosocial proneness for problem behavior (Run V) is used, 30–32 percent of the variance in young adult church attendance is accounted for in three of the gender-by-study groups, and 19 percent is accounted for in the fourth group (the High School women). The personality predictors (Run I) and perceived environment predictors (Run II) account for statistically significant portions of the variance for three of the four subsamples (the College Study men excepted). This predictability of young adult church attendance is of special interest because the theoretically most proximal antecedent measure, Religiosity, was not even included in the sets of risk factors that were examined. Its inclusion would clearly have enhanced the predictability of later church attendance since its across-time bivariate correlations, shown in Table 8.3, range from .30 to .52.

These results demonstrate that the psychosocial risk factors of Problem-Behavior Theory assessed in adolescence/youth account nearly as well for variation in *conventional* behavior in young adulthood – in this case, church attendance – as they do for variation in problem behavior in young adulthood.

Predicting young adult educational and occupational attainment

If, as shown thus far, psychosocial proneness to problem behavior, assessed in adolescence/youth, is predictive of actual involvement in problem behavior in young adulthood, a further question arises: Is that same psychosocial proneness predictive of *other* outcome domains in young adulthood, especially those that may be compromised by earlier involvement in problem behavior? Stated somewhat differently, is the demonstrated predictiveness of the antecedent psychosocial proneness measures *specific to* later problem behavior, or is it more general in its reach? Since this is a question that does not follow necessarily from the logic of Problem-Behavior Theory, our inquiry here should be seen as exploratory in nature.

The two young adult outcome domains selected for examination are those of educational attainment and occupational attainment. These are both domains in which attainment may be seen as resulting from long-term, sustained striving within the conventional opportunity structure of American society, and in which actual attainment status may be dependent upon conventionality of orientation and action. Greater psychosocial proneness for problem behavior in adolescence/ youth may well compromise later educational and occupational attainment, either indirectly by influencing greater involvement in problem behavior, or directly through lower young adult commitments to achieving conventional goals. It seems reasonable, therefore, to explore the possibility that greater psychosocial proneness to problem behavior in adolescence/youth might be associated with lower levels of educational and occupational attainment by young adulthood.

Educational attainment in young adulthood was measured by a series of questions in the 1979 and 1981 Young Adult Questionnaires. In 1979, respondents were asked an array of questions about their education: whether they had graduated from high school, whether they had attended college, how many years they had attended college, whether they graduated, whether they attended graduate or professional school and for how long, whether they completed graduate or professional school and with what degree, and whether they had had other kinds of vocational or technical training. In 1981, they were asked whether they had pursued any further formal education since they had taken the 1979 questionnaire. If so, they were asked to report what type of school they had attended (e.g., vocational-technical school, junior college, etc.), and, if they had completed a course of study, they were asked to indicate the diploma, certificate, or degree(s) they had earned. All of this information was then used to construct a seven-category measure indicating the highest level of education completed by 1981 (from some high school to receipt of a doctoral degree) similar to the education component in the standard Hollingshead Index.

Occupational attainment was assessed by two questions similar to those used by the U.S. Census. In 1981, respondents were asked to report, in an open-ended format, "what kind of work" they do, and to describe what they "actually do at work" and their "responsibilities on the job." This information was used to classify each of the young adults on a scale of occupational prestige (ranging from 0.0 to 100.0) using Siegel's (1971) updated version of the National Opinion Research Center's scoring system. This measure is widely used in the sociological literature on occupational attainment (see Hauser & Featherman, 1977). The correlation between the measures of educational attainment and of occupational attainment in young adulthood is positive and substantial in the various subsamples: .51 and .50 for the High School Study men and women, respectively, and .52 and .39 for the College Study men and women.

In order to examine the possibility that it is, in fact, involvement in problem behavior *in young adulthood* that could serve to mediate the relationship of psychosocial proneness in adolescence/youth to attainment in young adulthood, we correlated the young adult summary measure of problem behavior involvement with the measures of educational and of occupational attainment. The summary measure of problem behavior in young adulthood does not correlate significantly with either educational attainment or occupational attainment in any of the four gender-by-study subsamples. For educational attainment, the bivariate correlations are .11 and −.11 for the High School Study men and women, and .21 and −.17 for the College Study men and women, respectively. For occupational attainment, the bivariate correlations are −.03 and .08 for the High School Study men and women, and .15 and .14 for the College Study men and women, respectively. The absence of association between the summary measure of young adult problem behavior involvement and the measures of young adult educational and occupational attainment suggests quite strongly that any relationship found between antecedent psychosocial proneness to problem behavior and young adult educational and occupational attainment is unlikely to be mediated by problem behavior involvement in young adulthood.

A more direct linkage between psychosocial proneness in adolescence/youth and educational and occupational attainment in young adulthood was then explored. The array of antecedent psychosocial proneness measures was correlated with the two measures of status attainment in young adulthood. These across-time, bivariate correlations are presented in Table 8.5. Because these analyses are exploratory, two-tailed tests of significance are employed. Multiple regression analyses, using the same predictor sets employed earlier in this chapter, were also carried out; those results are presented in Table 8.6.

Predicting educational attainment in young adulthood

With respect to educational attainment, there are several significant across-time correlations that are consistent for the different gender-by-study samples. Among the Personality System variables assessed in adolescence/youth, the most consistent correlates are those that are theoretically most proximal to later educational attainment. Value on academic achievement and the independence–achievement value discrepancy both correlate in the expected direction with young adult educational attainment; they are statistically significant for three of the four samples (excepting the College Study men). Expectation for academic achievement correlates positively, as expected, and significantly for all four samples. Among the other measures of personality system antecedents, alienation correlates negatively with young adult educational attainment, but only for the two male samples, and internal control also correlates positively for the two male samples. None of the personal control measures assessed in adolescence/youth correlates with young adult educational attainment; these were the personality measures, it will be recalled, that correlated most consistently with young adult involvement in problem behavior.

Among the adolescent/youth measures of psychosocial proneness

Table 8.5. *Pearson correlations of measures of psychosocial proneness in adolescence/youth (1972/1973) with measures of Educational and Occupational Attainment in young adulthood (1981), by group*

Measures of psychosocial proneness in adolescence/ youth (1972/1973)	Educational Attainment (1981)				Occupational Attainment (1981)[a]			
	High School Study		College Study		High School Study		College Study	
	Men (N = 162)	Women (N = 222)	Men (N = 84)	Women (N = 100)	Men (N = 162)	Women (N = 222)	Men (N = 84)	Women (N = 100)
Personality System measures								
Motivational-Instigation Structure								
Value on Academic Achievement	.24**	.18**	.11	.19+	.07	.02	.06	-.01
Value on Independence	-.06	-.13*	-.08	-.05	-.00	.05	-.09	-.02
Independence–Achievement Value Discrepancy	-.26***	-.24***	-.15	-.21*	-.07	.01	-.11	-.00
Expectation for Academic Achievement	.37***	.31***	.40***	.33***	.24**	.07	.03	-.02
Expectation for Independence	.02	-.21**	-.04	-.08	-.00	.01	-.12	-.09

(continued on next page)

Table 8.5 (cont.)

Measures of psychosocial proneness in adolescence/youth (1972/1973)	Educational Attainment (1981)				Occupational Attainment (1981)[a]			
	High School Study		College Study		High School Study		College Study	
	Men (N = 162)	Women (N = 222)	Men (N = 84)	Women (N = 100)	Men (N = 162)	Women (N = 222)	Men (N = 84)	Women (N = 100)
Personal Belief Structure								
Social Criticism	-.16*	.07	-.04	.01	-.02	-.02	-.13	.11
Alienation	-.28***	-.08	-.24*	-.04	-.08	-.06	.10	.12
Self-Esteem	.16*	.12+	.21+	.07	.21*	.05	-.01	.01
Internal–External Control	.24**	.07	.27*	.08	.11	.08	.08	.02
Personal Control Structure								
Intolerance of Deviance	.03	.05	-.05	-.13	.08	.03	.22*	-.05
Religiosity	.11	-.06	-.03	-.03	.01	-.04	.10	-.17+

Drinking Disjunctions	.02	−.12+	−.12	.08	−.03	.02	−.09	−.04
Drug Disjunctions	−.06	−.05	−.03	.06	−.04	−.03	−.06	.11
Sex Disjunctions	−.04	−.07	−.06	.16	.14	−.07	−.16	.07
Perceived Environment System measures								
Distal Structure								
Parent–Friends Compatibility	.27***	.15*	.07	.01	.12	.06	.12	.06
Parent–Friends Influence	−.16+	.01	.15	−.08	.16+	−.06	−.21+	.02
Proximal Structure								
Parent Approval Problem Behavior	.10	.14*	−.10	.20*	.09	.00	−.25*	−.06
Friends' Approval Problem Behavior	−.00	−.08	−.05	.12	.06	−.05	−.13	−.03
Friends Models Problem Behavior	−.07	−.18**	−.05	.11	.07	−.10	−.07	.00

(continued on next page)

Table 8.5 (*cont.*)

Measures of psychosocial proneness in adolescence/youth (1972/1973)	Educational Attainment (1981)				Occupational Attainment (1981)[a]			
	High School Study		College Study		High School Study		College Study	
	Men (N = 162)	Women (N = 222)	Men (N = 84)	Women (N = 100)	Men (N = 162)	Women (N = 222)	Men (N = 84)	Women (N = 100)
Behavior System measures								
Problem Behavior Structure								
Times Drunk in Past Year	.01	−.01	.01	−.06	.05	−.03	−.24*	.04
Marijuana Involvement	−.06	−.07	−.09	.10	−.08	.00	−.12	.00
Psychedelic Drug Use	−.05	−.07	−.04	.10	−.01	−.02	−.28*	.13
General Deviant Behavior	−.20**	−.19**	−.26*	.10	−.06	.05	.04	−.11
Multiple Problem Behavior Index	−.13+	−.25***	−.16	.11	.00	−.07	−.02	.11

Conventional Behavior								
Structure								
Church Attendance/								
Past Year	.08	.07	.02	.00	.02	$-.12+$	.05	.14
School Performance/								
Past Year	.39***	.33***	.29*	.37**	.26**	.11	$-.01$	$-.18$
Sociodemographic measures								
Father's Education	.31***	.39***	$.20+$	.34***	.00	.19**	$-.07$	$-.04$
Mother's Education	.32***	.26***	.12	.15	$-.12$	.05	$-.10$	.07
Father's Occupation	.28***	.30***	.14	.35**	$-.03$	.11	$-.07$	$-.10$
Family Socioeconomic								
Status	.31***	.36***	$.19+$	.40***	$-.01$	.16*	$-.08$	$-.09$

^{a}These are partial correlations controlling for educational attainment in young adulthood.
***$p \leq .001$ (two-tailed test); **$p \leq .01$; *$p \leq .05$; +$p \leq .10$.

in the Perceived Environment System, only two of the five variables show any consistent relation to later educational attainment. Perceptions of greater compatibility of interests and outlook between parents and friends in adolescence/youth are associated with higher educational attainment for the two High School Study samples, but not for the two College Study samples. And, contrary to what we might have expected on theoretical grounds, perceptions of *greater* parental approval for involvement in problem behavior in adolescence/youth are associated, for the two female samples only, with *higher* educational attainment by 1981.

Among the behavior system measures of proneness in adolescence/youth, there are again only two that relate to young adult educational attainment. Involvement in general deviant behavior correlates negatively and significantly with later educational attainment for three of the four samples (not for the College Study women). Involvement in multiple problem behaviors in adolescence/youth also correlates negatively, but not strongly, for the High School Study men and women. The strongest antecedent correlate of young adult educational attainment, as might well be expected, is school performance assessed in adolescence/youth; the higher the grade-point average for the past year in school in 1972/73, the higher the level of education attained by young adulthood (see also Willits, 1988).

The family socioeconomic background measures assessed in adolescence/youth also bear consistent relationships to young adult educational attainment. In sharp contrast to their lack of association when the criterion was young adult problem behavior, Father's Education, Father's Occupational Status, and Family Socioeconomic Status all correlate positively and significantly with educational attainment level in young adulthood in three of the four samples (for all except the College Study men). In addition, Mother's Education correlates significantly for the two High School Study samples.

In general, the across-time, bivariate correlations with young adult educational attainment are far less pervasive and much less consistent than were the across-time correlations with young adult problem behavior. Further, the measures that do relate are different ones. Most notably, there is a lack of relationship of the personal control measures, of the measures of perceived social support for involvement in problem behavior, and of the measures of actual involvement in problem behavior to educational attainment; on the other hand, there are now substantial relations of earlier academic performance and of the family background measures.

The multiple regression analyses in Table 8.6 indicate that the 14 measures of psychosocial proneness (Run V) account for 35 percent and 28 percent of the variance in educational attainment for the High School Study men and women, respectively, and for 21 percent and 36 percent of the variance for the College Study men and women, respectively. Even though different measures are doing the "work," this overall level of predictability is comparable to that found for the earlier regressions predicting variation in the summary measure of young adult problem behavior involvement.

As may also be seen in Table 8.6, proneness measures from all three systems of Problem-Behavior Theory account for statistically significant portions of the variance in young adult educational attainment in three of the four gender-by-study samples. For the College Study men, the observed predictability derives mainly from Expectation for Academic Achievement, Alienation, and School Performance rather than being more broadly based on the larger framework of predictor measures. Part of the reason for the low level of relationship and predictability for the College Study men may well be their restricted variance in educational attainment, since most of them are college graduates.

Predicting occupational attainment in young adulthood

We examined the linkage between psychosocial proneness in adolescence/youth and later occupational attainment while holding educational attainment constant statistically. The reason for this is the assumption that occupational attainment is mediated by educational attainment, and not vice versa. Partial correlations were used to remove the influence of educational attainment from the across-time correlations between antecedent proneness and later occupational attainment, and multiple partial correlations were used to hold educational attainment constant while assessing the multivariate linkage.

The partial correlations in Table 8.5 show essentially no relationship between the measures of psychosocial proneness assessed in adolescence/youth and later occupational attainment. Only a few of

Table 8.6. *Multiple correlations of psychosocial proneness in adolescence/youth (1972/1973) with measures of Educational and Occupational Attainment in young adulthood (1981)*

Psychosocial Proneness in Adolescence/Youth (1972/1973)	Educational Attainment (1981)				Occupational Attainment (1981)[a]			
	High School Study		College Study		High School Study		College Study	
	Men (N = 162)	Women (N = 222)	Men (N = 84)	Women (N = 100)	Men (N = 162)	Women (N = 222)	Men (N = 84)	Women (N = 100)
Run I. Personality System proneness (5 measures)	.42***	.35***	.43**	.41**	.28*	.10	.26	.13
Run II. Perceived Environment System proneness (4 measures)	.29**	.27**	.23	.22	.25*	.11	.35*	.11

Run III. Psychosocial proneness – Field Pattern (6 measures)	.46***	.37***	.41*	.41**	.29*	.14	.28	.17
Run IV. Behavior System proneness (3 measures)	.39***	.39***	.32+	.39**	.28**	.19+	.05	.29*
Run V. Overall psychosocial proneness (14 measures)	.59***	.53***	.46	.60**	.42*	.29	.32	.37

Note: Sets of predictor variables are the same as those used in the adolescent/youth phase of the study (Jessor & Jessor, 1977).

[a]These are multiple partial correlations in which educational attainment in young adulthood has been controlled for.

***$p \leq .001$ (by F-test); **$p \leq .01$; *$p \leq .05$; +$p \leq .10$.

the partial correlations are statistically significant, and none is significant for more than one subsample for any given measure of antecedent proneness for problem behavior. Despite the nonsignificant bivariate results, multiple regressions were run. At the multivariate level, antecedent psychosocial proneness provides a significant account of variation in later occupational attainment for only one of the four gender-by-study groups, the High School Study men. Overall, then, occupational attainment is not predictable from antecedent psychosocial proneness to problem behavior in these largely middle-class samples when educational attainment is held constant.

These exploratory analyses suggest that the psychosocial framework of Problem-Behavior Theory has some predictiveness for an area of young adult life not directly related to problem behavior, namely, educational attainment. Holding values and expectations during adolescence/youth that reflect less attachment to and involvement in the conventional institution of school may well compromise later educational attainment, especially for those in high school.

Linking latent-variable measures of problem behavior proneness in adolescence/youth and in young adulthood

Another way of examining the linkage between problem-behavior proneness in adolescence/youth and problem behavior involvement in young adulthood utilizes structural equation modeling. These procedures were employed in order to circumvent two limitations of the preceding analyses. First, none of the earlier analyses has taken account of the unreliability of the independent-variable measures of antecedent problem behavior proneness or of the dependent-variable measure of young adult problem behavior involvement. The linkages between adolescence/youth and young adulthood that have been presented may all be attenuated by the fact that none of the measures examined is a perfectly reliable indicator of the underlying "true score" on that variable. It is likely that even stronger linkages would be obtained between psychosocial proneness or risk in adolescence/youth and young adult involvement in problem behavior if the across-time correlations were corrected for unreliability (disattenuated). Second, the across-time multiple regression analyses do not reveal the structure or the causal pathways through which psychosocial prone-ness in adolescence/youth influences young adult problem behavior involvement. Although those analyses do establish an across-time linkage between these two sets of variables, one that is both significant and theoretically coherent, they do not reveal the pathways of influence over time.

Through the application of structural equation modeling tech-niques (Jöreskog & Sörbom, 1979), however, it is possible to estab-lish relationships between latent variables representing true scores on psychosocial proneness and problem-behavior involvement at both life stages, and to determine the structural pathways by which problem-behavior proneness in adolescence/youth influences prob-lem behavior in young adulthood.

A two-stage procedure was used for the structural equation mod-eling analyses. In the first stage, latent-variable measures of person-ality system proneness, perceived environment system proneness, and behavior system proneness were developed for both the adolescent/ youth data and the young adult data. This measurement model was then tested separately for the High School Study sample and for the College Study sample. The second stage involved derivation of a fully saturated structural model for each sample, in which each of the latent-variable measures of proneness for problem behavior in ado-lescence/youth was linked to each of the young adult latent-variable measures of proneness for problem behavior.

Development of the latent-variable measures of proneness

Because of the number and diversity of theoretical variables reflecting proneness for problem behavior in each system at each of the two life stages, it was necessary in the interest of parsimony to select only the most proximal variables as indicators for the structural equation modeling. For the assessment of personality system proneness in the adolescent/youth data, three measures were selected from the Per-sonal Control Structure: Attitudinal Intolerance of Deviance, Reli-giosity, and the measure of Drug Disjunctions. Perceived environment system proneness was assessed by two measures from the Proximal Structure: Friends' Approval of Problem Behavior and Friends Models for Problem Behavior. Behavior system proneness measures in adolescence/youth were: Times Drunk in the Past Year, Frequency of Marijuana Use in the Past Six Months, and General Deviant Behavior in the Past Year. All of these measures were available in the Year IV (1972) data for the High School Study sample and in the Year IV (1973) data for the College Study sample.

The three latent-variable measures of proneness for problem behavior in young adulthood were composed of much the same sets of measures. The only difference was the substitution of the measure of Moral Attitude for the adolescent/youth measure of Drug Disjunctions in the assessment of personality system proneness in young adulthood. Despite the availability in the young adult data of measures of cigarette smoking and of use of illicit drugs other than marijuana, behavior system proneness was assessed by the same behaviors as in the adolescent/youth data in order to maintain the comparability of the latent variable over time. Precisely because it is a *latent-variable* construct, it is more appropriate to refer to it as behavior system proneness for problem behavior than to treat it simply as a measure of multiple problem behavior involvement in young adulthood.

The LISREL VI structural equation program (Jöreskog & Sörbom, 1984) was used to evaluate the adequacy of this measurement model in which 16 observed measures reflect six latent variables. The overall fit of the measurement model was satisfactory for both the High School Study and College Study samples. In the High School Study sample, the goodness-of-fit index (GFI) was .95,[3] the adjusted goodness-of-fit index (AGFI) was .92, and root mean square residual (RMR) was .04. Although the chi-square measure of fit was still significant (138.6, $df = 82$, $p = .000$), it was only 1.7 times the degrees of freedom, indicating an adequate degree of fit to the data. In the College Study sample, a similar level of fit was obtained: The GFI was .95, the AGFI was .91, the RMR was .04, and the chi-square was nonsignificant ($p = .31$).

Table 8.7 presents the standardized factor loadings of each of the observed measures on their respective latent variables. Every one of the observed variable measures loads significantly on the appropriate latent variable in both the adolescent/youth data and the young adult data for both samples. With only a couple of exceptions, these loadings are also substantial in magnitude.

The estimated correlations among the latent-variable measures of proneness for problem behavior in the three systems – within ado-

Table 8.7. *Standardized factor loadings of observed variables on latent variables of Personality, Perceived Environment, and Behavior System proneness, in adolescence/youth (1972/1973) and young adulthood (1981), by study*

Latent variables/Observed variables	High School Study sample ($N = 355$)[a]	College Study sample ($N = 179$)[a]
Adolescent/Youth Data (1972/1973)		
Personality System proneness		
Intolerance of Deviance	.65	.43
Religiosity	.43	.45
Drug Disjunctions	−.69	−.69
Perceived Environment System proneness		
Friends' Approval Problem Behavior	.80	.83
Friends Models Problem Behavior	.78	.69
Behavior System proneness		
Times Drunk/Past Year	.63	.57
Frequency of Marijuana Use/Past 6 Months	.66	.76
General Deviant Behavior/Past Year	.69	.46
Young Adult Data (1981)		
Personality System proneness		
Intolerance of Deviance	.54	.29
Moral Attitude	.93	.82
Religiosity	.59	.54
Perceived Environment System proneness		
Friends' Approval Problem Behavior	.69	.61
Friends Models Problem Behavior	.79	.85

(continued on next page)

Table 8.7 (*cont.*)

Latent variables/Observed variables	High School Study sample ($N = 355$)[a]	College Study sample ($N = 179$)[a]
Behavior System proneness		
Times Drunk/Past 6 Months	.71	.62
Frequency of Marijuana Use/Past Month	.64	.58
General Deviant Behavior/Past Year	.46	.50

Note: All factor loadings are significant (i.e., greater than twice their standard errors) and in the expected direction.
[a]N values are reduced because of the listwise deletion procedure used in the analyses.

lescence/youth, within young adulthood, and, especially, between adolescence/youth and young adulthood – are of particular interest. Table 8.8 presents these correlations for the High School Study and College Study samples.

A high level of correlation may be seen in Table 8.8 among these latent-variable measures of proneness for problem behavior. Within the adolescent/youth data, personality, perceived environment, and behavior system proneness are strongly related in both the High School and College Study samples. Personality system proneness correlates .84 and .77 with perceived environment system proneness, and .83 and .82 with behavior system proneness for the High School Study and College Study samples, respectively. Perceived environment system proneness correlates .89 and .85, respectively, with behavior system proneness in the two samples. These correlations of the latent or true-score measures of personality and perceived environment system proneness with behavior system proneness are considerably larger in magnitude than the multiple correlations reported for these adolescent/youth data by Jessor and Jessor (1977; see Table 7.2).

Within the young adult data, the correlations among the latent-

Table 8.8. *Correlations among latent-variable measures of Personality, Perceived Environment, and Behavior System proneness in adolescence/youth (1972/1973) and young adulthood (1981), by study*

	Proneness in 1972/1973			Proneness in 1981		
	Personality	Environment	Behavior	Personality	Environment	Behavior
Proneness in 1972			*High School Study*			
Personality System	1.00					
Perceived Environment System	.84	1.00				
Behavior System	.83	.89	1.00			
Proneness in 1981						
Personality System	.56	.37	.35	1.00		
Perceived Environment System	.58	.50	.54	.70	1.00	
Behavior System	.56	.41	.56	.66	.88	1.00
			College Study			
Proneness in 1973						
Personality System	1.00					
Perceived Environment System	.77	1.00				
Behavior System	.82	.85	1.00			

(continued on next page)

Table 8.8 (cont.)

	Proneness in 1972/1973			Proneness in 1981		
	Personality	Environment	Behavior	Personality	Environment	Behavior
Proneness in 1981						
Personality System	.65	.33	.43	1.00		
Perceived Environment System	.66	.64	.73	.56	1.00	
Behavior System	.75	.55	.69	.54	.80	1.00

Note: All of these correlations are statistically significant ($p < .05$). For ease of presentation, minus signs have been dropped from all correlations between Personality System proneness and proneness in the other two systems.

variable measures of proneness are also high. Personality system proneness in young adulthood correlates .70 and .56 with perceived environment system proneness and .66 and .54 with behavior system proneness for the High School Study and College Study samples, respectively. Perceived environment system proneness correlates .88 and .80 with behavior system proneness for the two samples of young adults. These levels of correlation are only slightly lower than those seen for the adolescence/youth data, but, again, as expected, are larger than the multiple correlations between the young adult personality and perceived environment measures and problem behavior reported in Table 6.3 in Chapter 6.

There are also substantial relationships between adolescence/youth and young adulthood on these latent-variable true score measures of proneness for problem behavior. As may be seen in Table 8.8, proneness within each theoretical system is highly stable over the eight- to nine-year interval encompassed by the research. For the High School Study sample, personality system proneness correlates .56 between adolescence/youth and young adulthood, perceived environment system proneness correlates .50 over time, and behavior system proneness correlates .56 between the two life stages. For the College Study sample, the across-time correlations (stabilities) are even stronger: .65 for personality system proneness, .64 for perceived environment system proneness, and .69 for behavior system proneness.

Of greatest relevance for this chapter, however, are the disattenuated correlations between the latent-variable measures of psychosocial proneness in adolescence/youth and the latent-variable measure of behavior system proneness in young adulthood. According to Table 8.8, personality system proneness and perceived environment system proneness in adolescence/youth correlate .56 and .41, respectively, with behavior system proneness in young adulthood for the High School Study sample. For the College Study sample, the respective correlations with young adult behavior system proneness are .75 and .55 for personality system proneness and perceived environment system proneness in adolescence/youth. These true-score correlations demonstrate that there is a substantial relationship between psychosocial proneness for problem behavior in adolescence/ youth and behavior system proneness in young adulthood, a rela-

tionship that is considerably greater than that revealed in the preceding multiple regression analyses.

These correlational findings, now based on the latent-variable
measures, are important for several reasons: They indicate the coherence of problem proneness across all three explanatory systems,
both within adolescence/youth and within young adulthood. They
also reveal the continuity of problem-behavior proneness between
adolescence/youth and young adulthood. Further, they highlight the
substantial magnitude of the predictive relationship between personality system and perceived environment system proneness measured
in adolescence/youth and variation in behavior system proneness,
eight or nine years later, in young adulthood.

Structural relations over time

Correlations between latent-variable measures of psychosocial proneness in adolescence/youth and behavior system proneness in young
adulthood do not, however, establish the pathways by which proneness
in adolescence/youth influences later problem-behavior involvement.
That can be accomplished only by examination of a structural model
relating adolescent/youth proneness to the young adult measure of
behavior system proneness. Our interest in describing the across-time
linkages (rather than in testing an explicit hypothesis about these
linkages) led us to examine a fully saturated structural model in which
all possible across-time paths were included. Whereas the relations
between the adolescent/youth latent-variable measures of proneness
and the young adult measures of proneness presented in Table 8.8
were correlation coefficients, the coefficients of interest here are
regression coefficients reflecting the independent contribution over
time of each latent variable measure of proneness from adolescence/
youth. Figure 8.1 presents the standardized regression coefficients
for the structural model in the High School Study sample.

As may be seen in the figure, there are nine paths (denoted by
single-headed arrows) that directly link proneness in adolescence/
youth with proneness in young adulthood. Of these nine direct paths,
four have significant path coefficients (i.e., regression coefficients
twice the size of their standard errors). Personality system proneness
in adolescence/youth has a direct, significant influence on later, young

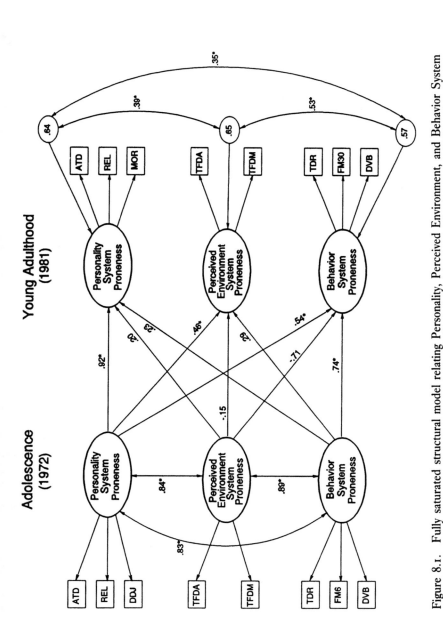

Figure 8.1. Fully saturated structural model relating Personality, Perceived Environment, and Behavior System proneness in adolescence/youth and in young adulthood, High School Study sample. Acronyms: ATD = Intolerance of Deviance; REL = Religiosity; DDJ = Drug Disjunctions; MOR = Moral Attitude; TFDA = Friends' Approval of Problem Behavior; TFDM = Friends Models for Problem Behavior; TDR = Times Drunk; FM6 = Frequency of Marijuana Use in Past 6 Months; FM3o = Frequency of Marijuana Use in Past Month; DVB = General Deviant Behavior.

adult personality system proneness (beta = .92), on later perceived environment system proneness (beta = .46), and on later behavior system proneness (beta = .54). It is important to emphasize that the effect of personality system proneness in adolescence/youth on later behavior system proneness is significant even when earlier problem behavior involvement is controlled. Perceived environment system proneness in adolescence has no significant ($p < .05$) direct influence on young adult problem behavior proneness in any of the three theoretical systems, although its relation to later behavior system proneness almost reaches significance ($p < .10$). Behavior system proneness in adolescence has a significant direct impact only on young adult behavior system proneness (beta = .74). With respect to young adult behavior system proneness, then, only personality system proneness and behavior system proneness in adolescence have significant direct influences.

There are, however, a variety of alternate *indirect* paths linking psychosocial proneness in adolescence with young adult behavior system proneness. Personality system proneness in adolescence displays indirect linkages through both adolescent perceived environment proneness and adolescent behavior system proneness. Perceived environment system proneness in adolescence, similarly, has indirect linkages to young adult behavior system proneness through its synchronous correlations with personality system and behavior system proneness in adolescence.

Figure 8.2 presents the results for the saturated structural model in the College Study sample. In these data, the only significant direct path linking problem behavior proneness in adolescence/youth with proneness in young adulthood is that between personality system proneness in the two life stages (beta = .96). Several other direct paths have regression coefficients that are not sufficiently greater in size than their standard errors to reach significance at the .05 level; these include the path between adolescent personality system proneness and behavior system proneness in young adulthood (beta = .63, $p < .10$), the path between behavior system proneness in adolescence and perceived environment system proneness in young adulthood (beta = .54, $p = .13$), and the path between behavior system proneness at both times (beta = .44, $p = .24$). The lack of significance of these paths is due to their large standard errors which themselves

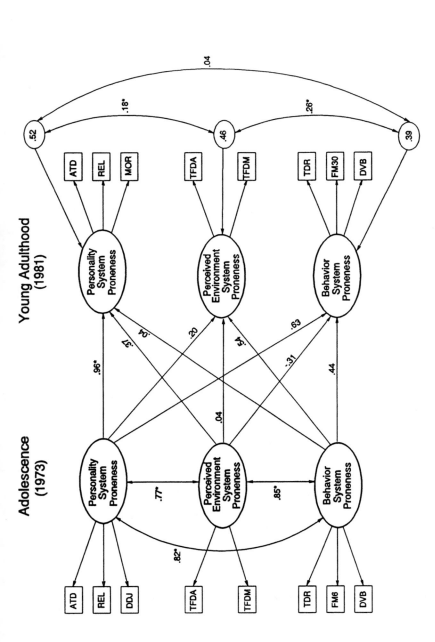

Figure 8.2. Fully saturated structural model relating Personality, Perceived Environment, and Behavior System proneness in adolescence/youth and in young adulthood, College Study sample. Acronyms: ATD = Intolerance of Deviance; REL = Religiosity; DDJ = Drug Disjunctions; MOR = Moral Attitude; TFDA = Friends' Approval of Problem Behavior; TFDM = Friends Models for Problem Behavior; TDR = Times Drunk; FM6 = Frequency of Marijuana Use in Past 6 Months; FM3o = Frequency of Marijuana Use in Past Month; DVB = General Deviant Behavior.

reflect the high degree of multicollinearity among the latent-variable measures of proneness in this sample (see Table 8.8).

Despite the instability of the estimates of the path coefficients for the College Study sample, these results are quite consonant with those found for the High School sample. Both studies demonstrate the importance of the continuity over time of personality system proneness for the account of young adult behavior system proneness. They both also show that perceived environment system proneness has little direct influence over time on later, young adult behavior system proneness, and that most of its across-time influence is due to its synchronous relations with personality system and behavior system proneness. Neither of these findings is even suggested by the multiple regression analyses presented earlier in the chapter, and they reflect the unique contribution of structural equation modeling to an *understanding* of the linkage between the two life stages.

Summary

The analyses presented in this chapter have revealed pervasive and coherent linkages between a systematic set of antecedent measures of psychosocial proneness for problem behavior in adolescence/youth and a variety of measures of later problem behavior and conventional behavior in young adulthood. Proneness measures in each of the explanatory systems of the psychosocial framework were related to young adult problem and conventional behavior. The most consistent across-time predictors were the earlier measures of personal controls, of social support and models for problem behavior, and of earlier involvement in problem behaviors.

Antecedent psychosocial proneness related significantly not only to the summary measure of intensity of involvement in problem behavior in young adulthood, but also to the component measures of problem behaviors, including drunkenness, marijuana use, other illicit drug use, and – to a lesser degree – general deviant behavior, and cigarette smoking. According to the multiple regression analyses, psychosocial proneness in adolescence/youth accounted for about a third of the variance in the summary measure of involvement in problem behavior in young adulthood, and for about 20–25 percent of the variance in the measures of specific young adult problem behaviors. For the most part, psychosocial proneness in adolescence/youth predicted better for the men than for the women in each study, and better for College Study participants than for High School Study participants.

Further validity for the theoretical framework was established by correlations across time between the antecedent proneness measures and conventional behavior – church attendance – in young adulthood. As theoretically expected, these correlations had the opposite sign to those for the problem behavior criterion measures.

One strength of this research is its inclusion of *nonbehavioral* measures as antecedent predictors of young adult problem behavior. In the regression analyses linking antecedent proneness to young adult problem behavior, both the personality proneness measures (Run I) and the perceived environment proneness measures (Run II) accounted for significant portions of the variance. Personality proneness in adolescence/youth was linked most consistently with the summary measure of problem behavior involvement, with drunkenness, and with general deviant behavior in young adulthood. Perceived environment proneness in adolescence/youth was linked most consistently with the summary measure and with drunkenness, marijuana use, and other illicit drug use. Based on the regression coefficients, the most consistent personality proneness predictor of later problem behavior was social criticism in adolescence/youth, whereas the most consistent perceived environment proneness predictor was friends models for problem behavior in adolescence/youth.

The interactionist perspective of Problem-Behavior Theory is supported by the fact that, in the great majority of cases, the multivariate field pattern (Run III), composed of only six theoretically selected personality and perceived environment measures, accounted for more of the variation in young adult problem behavior than either the personality proneness set (five measures) or the perceived environment proneness set (four measures) alone. There is, then, an increment in the predictability of young adult problem behavior when antecedent personality proneness measures *and* antecedent perceived environment proneness measures are included in the regression equation. The relatively small size of this increment may be due to the substantial correlation between proneness in the personality system and proneness in the perceived environment system, as seen in Table 8.8.

The relation of psychosocial proneness in adolescence/youth to a *non*problem behavior criterion – educational attainment – in young adulthood is based almost entirely on the proneness measures that are most proximal to education – for example, expectations for academic achievement and also the measure of school performance, rather than on those that are proximal to problem behavior. In regard to occupational attainment, once educational attainment has been controlled for, there are almost no proneness antecedents in either study that show significant relations.

The magnitude of the variance in young adult problem behavior that is accounted for by antecedent psychosocial proneness is substantial, especially considering the length of the eight- or nine-year hiatus between the earlier predictor data and the later criterion data. These findings provide new support for the developmental relevance of Problem-Behavior Theory. Not only does the framework account for substantial portions of the cross-sectional variation in involvement in problem behavior, both within adolescence/youth and now within young adulthood, but the present findings show it to account also for developmental variation *between* adolescence/youth and young adulthood.

The linkage between antecedent psychosocial proneness and young adult involvement in problem behavior has emerged from several different kinds of analyses in this chapter. It was apparent in the significant bivariate correlations between the adolescent/youth measures of personality, perceived environment, and behavior system proneness and the various young adult measures of problem behavior involvement. It was also apparent in the results of the multiple regression analyses showing across-time predictability of young adult problem behavior involvement from sets of psychosocial proneness measures in adolescence/youth. And it was especially clear in the analyses that utilized LISREL methodology.

These latter analyses, employing structural equation modeling, clarify a number of points left unresolved by the regression analyses. First, they show a substantial correlation between the latent-variable measures of proneness in the personality and in the perceived environment systems in the adolescent/youth data; this helps explain why combining these two systems does not account for a much greater percentage of the variance in young adult problem behavior than that accounted for by each system separately. Second, the results of the structural modeling show that antecedent perceived environment proneness does not have a direct influence on variation in young adult problem behavior; instead, its influence is mediated through its synchronous relations with adolescent personality or behavior system proneness, and depends upon their stability between adolescence/ youth and young adulthood. The structural modeling results also demonstrate that, even when the stability over time of problem behavior involvement is included in the model, adolescent personality system proneness *still* has a significant direct relation with variation in young adult problem behavior.

Third, the direct path relating adolescent personality proneness to young adult environmental proneness suggests that personality proneness may influence the *selection* of young adult social environments in a way relevant to proneness for problem behavior (see also Bachman, O'Malley & Johnston, 1984; Newcomb & Bentler, 1985). Finally, the analyses show that proneness in adolescence/youth accounts for as much as 43 percent of the variance in the behavior system latent variable in young adulthood, for the High School Study, and 61 percent of the variance for the College Study.

Structural models were also established for the separate genders in the High School Study despite the marginally adequate size of the two subsamples. They replicate the major findings of the combined-gender analyses that were presented. For both the males and the females, the path between personality system proneness at the two life stages was the strongest path over time, and perceived environment system proneness had little direct influence on problem behavior proneness in young adulthood. The small Ns in the College Study precluded similar analyses by gender.

Although the predictive findings in this chapter are theoretically important, it is also important to note that a large amount of the variance in young adult problem behavior is still to be accounted for. Possible reasons why the level of predictability over time is not still greater need mention. First, in the interval from 1972/73 to 1981, there had been a great deal of situational or environmental change – in life situations, in marital status, in work, in education, in life events, in behavioral involvements – that is simply not measured in the predictive framework (see Hammer & Vaglum, 1990a, 1990b; Kandel

& Yamaguchi, 1987; Power & Estaugh, 1990a, 1990b; Yamaguchi & Kandel, 1985). Second, even within the adolescent/youth phase of the research, psychosocial proneness or risk was able to account for only about 50 percent of the variance in involvement in problem behavior, and this, of course, places a ceiling on the level of pre- dictability that proneness measures could be expected to achieve across an extended time period – here, between adolescence/youth and young adulthood.

The fairly substantial predictability established in this chapter has significance for the understanding of development into young adult- hood. The findings make clear what was previously suggested in Chapter 7, namely that there is considerable continuity and stability over time – and even over a major life transition – in person, perceived environment, and behavior attributes. It is this degree of continuity that underlies and accounts for, at least in part, the empirically ob- served predictability. Further, the evidence of the greater stability/ continuity of person attributes is compelling; it is, indeed, stability of personality system proneness that carries the main predictive weight, both directly and indirectly, in the latent-variable models. Attention to personality in understanding psychosocial development beyond ad- olescence would seem to be essential.

Notes

1   The five sets of predictor variables reflecting adolescent proneness for problem behavior differ slightly from the predictor sets described in Chapter 6 that assess young adult proneness for problem behavior. In the predictor set representing personality proneness in adolescence/ youth, the Independence–Achievement Value Discrepancy was included rather than just Value on Achievement; Self-Esteem was included instead of Alienation; and Religiosity was not included. In the predictor set representing perceived environment proneness in adolescence/youth, measures assessing relative orientation toward parents versus peers, and both parental and peer supports for problem behavior involvement were included, whereas in young adulthood, the predictors focus largely on peer influences on behavior. The strategy used to construct the set of predictors representing psychosocial proneness for problem behavior also differed between adolescence/youth and young adulthood. In the ado- lescent/youth data analyses, six measures were selected to reflect both

personality and perceived environment proneness, whereas in the young adult analyses, all ten measures figuring in the personality and perceived environment proneness sets were included in the set reflecting their joint influence. Lastly, in regard to behavior system proneness, Church Attendance in the Past Year and School Performance were relied upon in adolescence/youth, whereas only Church Attendance was available in the young adult data.

2   In multiple correlations predicting specific problem behaviors in young adulthood, the summary measure of adolescent involvement in problem behavior was not used as a predictor in the *behavior system proneness* set or in the *overall psychosocial proneness* set. Instead, a modified summary measure was used for each specific problem behavior that did not include a component representing adolescent involvement *in that specific area of problem behavior*. For example, problem drinking involvement was not included in the summary measure of adolescent problem behavior when drunkenness in young adulthood was the criterion behavior being predicted.

3   Seven correlated residual variances were added to the High School Study model: Three linked the same measures assessed at the two time points (Intolerance of Deviance, Religiosity, Friends' Approval of Problem Behavior), two linked Intolerance of Deviance and General Deviant Behavior *within* each time point (reflecting common behavioral referents), and two linked variables sharing drug-use context (Frequency of Marijuana Use and Drug Functions in 1972; Friends Models for Problem Behavior and Frequency of Marijuana Use in 1981). A total of 15 correlated residual variances were added to the College Study model; eight were similar to those described in the High School Study model. Seven of the correlated residual variances had to be added to reduce the very high level of correlations among the latent variables so that estimates of path coefficients could be derived for the saturated structural model.

References

Bachman, J.G. (1987). Changes in deviant behavior during late adolescence and early adulthood. Presented at the IXth Biennial Meetings of the International Society for the Study of Behavioral Development, Tokyo, Japan.

Bachman, J.G., O'Malley, P.M., & Johnston, L.D. (1984). Drug use among young adults: The impacts of role status and social environment. *Journal of Personality and Social Psychology, 47*, 629–645.

Hammer, T., & Vaglum, P. (1990a). Initiation, continuation or discontinuation of cannabis use in the general population. *British Journal of Addiction, 85,* 899–909.

Hammer, T., & Vaglum, P. (1990b). Use of alcohol and drugs in the transitional phase from adolescence to young adulthood. *Journal of Adolescence, 13,* 129–142.

Hauser, R. M., & Featherman, D. L. (1977). *The process of stratification: Trends and analyses.* New York: Academic Press.

Jessor, R., & Jessor, S. L. (1977). *Problem behavior and psychosocial development: A longitudinal study of youth.* New York: Academic Press.

Jöreskog, K. G., & Sörbom, D. (1979). *Advances in factor analysis and structural equation models.* Cambridge, MA: Abt Books.

Jöreskog, K. G., & Sörbom, D. (1984). *LISREL VI: Analysis of linear structural relationships by maximum likelihood, instrumental variables, and least squares methods.* Mooresville, IN: Scientific Software.

Kandel, D. B., & Yamaguchi, K. (1987). Job mobility and drug use: An event history analysis. *American Journal of Sociology, 92,* 836–878.

Magnusson, D. (1988). *Individual development from an interactional perspective: A longitudinal study.* Hillsdale, NJ: Lawrence Erlbaum Associates.

Newcomb, M. D., & Bentler, P. M. (1985). The impact of high school substance use on choice of young adult living environment and career direction. *Journal of Drug Education, 15,* 253–261.

Newcomb, M. D., & Bentler, P. M. (1988). *Consequences of adolescent drug use: Impact on the lives of young adults.* Newbury Park, CA: Sage Publications.

Power, C., & Estaugh, V. (1990a). Employment and drinking in early adulthood: A longitudinal perspective. *British Journal of Addiction, 85,* 487–494.

Power, C., & Estaugh, V. (1990b). The role of family formation and dissolution in shaping drinking behavior in early adulthood. *British Journal of Addiction, 85,* 521–530.

Siegel, P. M. (1971). Prestige in the American occupational structure. Doctoral dissertation, Department of Sociology, University of Chicago.

Temple, M. T., & Fillmore, K. M. (1985-6). The variability of drinking patterns and problems among young men, age 16–31: A longitudinal study. *The International Journal of the Addictions, 20* (11 & 12), 1595–1620.

Willits, F. K. (1988). Adolescent behavior and adult success and well-being: A 37-year panel study. *Youth & Society, 20* (1), 68–87.

Windle, M. (1988). Are these adolescent to early adulthood drinking patterns so discontinuous? A response to Temple and Fillmore. *The International Journal of the Addictions, 23*(9), 907–912.

Yamaguchi, K., & Kandel, D. B. (1985). On the resolution of role incompatibility: A life event history analysis of family roles and marijuana use. *American Journal of Sociology, 90,* 1284–1325.

9

Involvement in problem behavior in adolescence/youth and outcomes in young adulthood

In this chapter, the last in the triad concerned with development, we take up another important question, one not addressed by the other two: Does involvement in problem behavior in adolescence/youth constrain subsequent development? Does it, in some way, result in lesser attainment, or in more limited success, or, perhaps, in less satisfaction in young adult life? In short, is there evidence that problem behavior among the adolescents and youth in our samples mortgages their future as young adults?

Although not clearly defined as such in the literature, this issue is inherently a developmental one. Development is considered to be the outcome of the interaction of person and environment over time. Whatever the person attribute specified and assessed in adolescence – for example, high value on achievement, or low self-esteem, or, as in our focus here, involvement in problem behavior – its implications for and potential impact on later life are realized only in interaction with the concrete situations, contexts, and environments of ongoing experience. The fact that the latter are rarely measured in the usual longitudinal design does not in any way controvert the *logic* of their intrinsic contribution to whatever outcome is specified in later life. To argue otherwise is again to commit, in yet another way, the "ontogenetic fallacy" (Dannefer, 1984) noted in Chapter 7, that is, to attach the causal vector to the person attribute at Time 1, and then to explore the apparent unfolding of its consequences over time. Yet those "consequences" are, logically, outcomes of person–environment interactions rather than mere "unfoldings."

The adoption of an interactionist interpretation of development has substantial relevance for how linkages between person attributes at

Time 1, here adolescent problem behavior, and outcomes at Time 2, say lower status attainment, are framed. A characterization of that outcome as a "consequence" of the person attribute at Time 1 has to be taken as elliptical, a shorthand for a considerably longer and more qualified statement of the following sort: "Problem behavior in adolescence, for this kind of person, experiencing this kind of social context, over this time in history, tends to eventuate in lower status attainment." The longer statement makes it clear that the outcome is a "consequence" of the *interaction* of person attribute and environment over time rather than of the attribute itself. It also acknowledges that there might well be very different outcomes of the same attribute, depending on the stage of the life course, the time in history, the particular cultural and social context, and the relevant aspects of the larger social setting. In an effort to promote an interactionist perspective on development, we have chosen to avoid the word "consequence" in favor of the more neutral and less causal-sounding term, "outcome."

In considering outcomes in later life of earlier involvement in problem behavior (or of earlier involvement in certain specific behaviors – e.g., frequent drunkenness, illicit drug use, or general deviance/delinquency), we intend to explore two rather different domains. The first outcome domain is that of problem behavior itself: Is greater involvement in problem behavior in later life one of the likely outcomes of greater involvement in problem behavior in adolescence/youth? We have already seen a partial answer to this question in both Chapter 7, in the stability data, and in Chapter 8, in the significant path coefficients linking the behavior system proneness latent variable for adolescence/youth with that for young adulthood. We address this domain again, in other ways, in this chapter.

The second major outcome domain has to do with facets of later life *other than* problem behavior. Here the key question is whether earlier involvement in problem behavior reverberates developmentally throughout later life and has implications for other kinds of young adult outcomes such as physical and mental health, marriage and partnering, childbearing and parenting, work and income, friendships, or educational attainment. In brief, for youth growing up in contemporary American society in the 1970s and early 1980s, is young adult life, *in general,* compromised by earlier involvement in problem behavior?

Distinguishing between these two outcome domains is important because the findings that have been generated about them in the literature are, indeed, quite disparate. Data from a large, nationally representative, longitudinal study of British youth, followed from age 16 to age 23, nicely illustrate the point. With regard to the problem behavior domain, particularly heavy alcohol consumption, the study's main finding was that "those who drank most heavily and more frequently at 16 were the most likely to drink heavily at 23" (Ghodsian & Power, 1987, p. 179). Thus, there is support for the outcome of greater problem behavior in young adulthood, reflecting its stability and continuity over time. On the other hand, with regard to other young adult life areas – now it was employment history – the main finding of the study was quite different: "Teenage drinking was found to be generally unrelated to early adult experience of either obtaining or remaining in employment" (Power & Estaugh, 1990, p. 493). Thus, there is no support, in the very same research, for a "spillover" into outcomes other than problem behavior in young adulthood. This latter finding is consonant with at least some of the results reported from an elaborate American inquiry that utilized latent-variable techniques over time to explore young adult outcomes of adolescent illicit drug use (Newcomb & Bentler, 1988). They reported, on the one hand, that "one of the primary consequences of teenage drug use is young adult drug use" (p. 86), and, on the other, that they found "very little support for teenage drug use creating an amotivational syndrome in young adulthood" (p. 229). In that same monograph, they examined a large number of other life areas and reported some other similar findings. In an earlier report focused on the health status of young adults and their utilization of health services, for example, the same investigators (Newcomb & Bentler, 1987) were unable, with one minor exception, to find any direct effects of involvement in general drug use four years earlier. Much the same findings were arrived at by Kandel, Davies, Karus, and Yamaguchi (1986) in a young adult follow-up of adolescent drug involvement. These authors stated that "adolescent use retains no direct unique effect *once use between adolescence and young adulthood is taken into account* (p. 753, italics added).

Exploring the linkage between earlier involvement in problem behavior and later life outcomes is a problematic endeavor. Beyond the
usual issues that attenuate such linkages – for example, unreliability
of measurement – there is the further issue of controlling for spuriousness in whatever linkage is established, that is, controlling for
the possibility that the linkage is due to one or more "third variables."
In earlier research on the effects of youthful use of marijuana on
young adult outcomes, Halikas, Weller, Morse, and Hoffman (1983)
concluded that "being a regular marijuana user does not have a
consistently deleterious effect on outcome variables *when earlier history, especially childhood misbehavior and school behavior problems, and
associated use of other illicit drugs are taken into account*" (p. 235, italics
added). It is possible, in short, that it is the same factors that led to
marijuana use at Time 1, rather than the marijuana use itself, that
influenced the later outcomes in young adulthood. Recognition of this
possibility is evident also in all of the Newcomb and Bentler (1988)
analyses; those investigators consistently enter the factor of adolescent
Social Conformity as a control when examining the young adult outcomes of adolescent drug use.

Both the Halikas and the Newcomb and Bentler research were
concerned with controlling for potentially influential factors other than
drug use at Time 1, when linking earlier drug use to later life outcomes. Welcome as that effort is, it does not include another kind of
control, one that needs to be instituted at Time 2. A linkage between
adolescent problem behavior and, say, occupational attainment in
young adulthood might well be due to a *Time 2* "third variable,"
namely, problem behavior in young adulthood, because problem behavior
in young adulthood could well have an influence on occupational attainment cross-sectionally. It is already clear that there is substantial
stability and consistency in problem behavior across this Time 1–
Time 2 developmental period. Control for spuriousness at Time 2
would seem as important, therefore, as instituting such control at
Time 1. On the basis of our earlier experience with analyses of both
sets of controls (Donovan & Jessor, 1985), we have emphasized the
latter approach in this chapter.

This chapter, then, serves to complement the developmental analyses in the two that preceded it. Chapter 7 provided a description
of developmental changes in a variety of conceptual attributes of

Problem-Behavior Theory and a description of the consonance among those changes. Chapter 8 took on a predictive task, seeking to establish that earlier psychosocial proneness could forecast variation in later problem behavior involvement. In the present chapter, we explore whether involvement in problem behavior in adolescence/youth entails outcomes in young adult life that bear the imprint of that earlier involvement.

Outcomes of group differences in involvement in problem behavior in adolescence/youth

Given the limitations of any single analytic procedure, we rely in this chapter on three different methods and on the convergence of their findings. The first approach was to establish groups that differed in the number of problem behaviors they were involved in in Year IV (1972 or 1973), when they were adolescents in high school or youth in college, and then to examine whether there were systematic group differences in outcomes in young adulthood, when they were in their late twenties (High School Study) or had reached the age of thirty (College Study). Three groups were established in each study-by-gender subsample, depending on their involvement in problem drinking, heavier marijuana use, and general deviant behavior (defined according to the criteria described in Chapter 5). Group I had *no* problem behavior involvement in adolescence/youth, Group II had *one* problem behavior involvement, and Group III was involved in *two or three* of the problem behaviors in Year IV (1972/73). One-way analysis of variance and contingency analyses were then used, in both the High School Study and the College Study and for males and females separately, to examine a large and diverse set of continuous and discrete young adult "outcome" measures. A representative selection of the larger set of continuous measures is presented in Table 9.1.

With respect to the domain of problem behavior in young adulthood, the data in Table 9.1 are quite clear and consistent: Greater earlier involvement in problem behavior is indeed linked to greater involvement in problem behavior later on in young adulthood. This conclusion holds for both the High School Study and the College Study, and for both genders in each study. It also holds for an overall

Table 9.1. *Mean differences on selected young adult (1981) measures for the three adolescent/youth (1972/1973) problem behavior involvement groups*

Young adult outcome measures (1981)	High School males (1972)				High School females (1972)			
	Group I (N=80)	Group II (N=41)	Group III (N=39)	F-ratio	Group I (N=136)	Group II (N=62)	Group III (N=22)	F-ratio
Problem Behavior								
Multiple Problem Behavior Index	238.8[a]	255.2[ab]	263.0[b]	7.7***	240.7[a]	257.4[b]	282.9[c]	22.7***
Times Drunk/Past 6 Months	1.6	2.0	2.6	2.3	0.8[a]	1.3[ab]	1.8[b]	4.2*
Neg. Consequences of Drinking	9.9[a]	11.6[b]	11.6[b]	5.4**	9.2[a]	9.8[a]	11.5[b]	4.6**
Marijuana User Status	2.9[a]	3.7[ab]	4.3[b]	6.8**	2.4[a]	3.5[b]	4.6[c]	18.9***
Frequency Marijuana Use/Past Month	8.9	9.0	16.4	2.2	3.9[a]	6.8[a]	15.0[b]	6.3**
Other Drugs Currently Used	0.6	0.8	1.1	2.2	0.2[a]	0.7[b]	1.4[c]	16.1***
Smoking Status	2.5[a]	4.2[b]	4.4[b]	16.7***	3.0[a]	4.1[b]	5.4[c]	13.7***
Number Cigarettes Smoked Daily	3.1	3.8	3.6	0.8	3.6	3.3	4.1	1.5
General Deviant Behavior	1.4	2.0	2.0	2.9+	1.5[a]	2.0[b]	2.4[b]	5.9**
Work and Education								
Job Prestige	49.3	45.6	47.3	0.9	41.7	37.8	43.1	1.9
Personal Annual Income	4.8	4.3	4.3	1.4	3.2	3.2	3.1	0.0
Satisfaction with Work	43.6	44.0	40.5	2.2	41.4	41.2	40.6	0.1
Educational Attainment	3.8	3.6	3.5	0.7	3.7[a]	3.3[b]	3.2[ab]	3.6*
Friends								
Number Close Friends	2.8	2.8	2.9	0.2	2.6	2.6	2.2	1.5
Friends' Support	7.1	7.6	6.9	2.2	7.9	8.0	7.8	0.1
Friendship Satisfaction	29.9	30.8	29.7	0.9	31.5	31.2	29.5	1.3
Family								
Relationship Satisfaction Index	13.1	12.2	12.6	0.5	13.6[a]	12.1[b]	11.2[b]	4.2*
Mental Health								
Self-Esteem	63.5	62.8	66.5	0.3	66.9	71.0	60.1	1.8
Negative Life Experiences	1.4	1.7	1.4	1.0	1.4[a]	1.7[ab]	2.3[b]	5.6**
Alienation	16.7	16.8	16.6	0.0	16.6[a]	17.5[ab]	19.1[b]	4.3*

Note: Group I: Involvement in 0 problem behaviors; Group II: Involvement in 1 problem behavior; Group III: Involvement in 2 or 3 problem behaviors. Superscripts refer to the Scheffé Multiple Range Test: Groups that share a superscript have means on that measure that are not significantly different. (The experiment-wise alpha was set at .10.) Scheffé tests were calculated only where the F-ratio was significant.

$p < .10$ (by F-test); $*p < .05$; $**p < .01$; $***p < .001$.

Table 9.1 (*cont.*)

College males (1973)				College females (1973)			
Group I (N=24)	Group II (N=32)	Group III (N=28)	F-ratio	Group I (N=54)	Group II (N=33)	Group III (N=13)	F-ratio
232.1^a	245.8^a	270.2^b	14.7***	237.5^a	259.4^b	277.9^b	14.2***
0.9^a	1.6^a	2.7^b	6.4**	0.3^a	0.9^a	1.8^b	7.7***
9.5^a	10.4^{ab}	11.5^b	3.4*	8.7^a	9.6^{ab}	10.8^b	3.4*
2.6^a	3.9^b	4.6^b	8.6***	2.3^a	3.9^b	4.6^b	19.6***
0.9^a	4.4^{ab}	9.0^b	4.7*	0.8	2.6	3.1	2.0
0.1^a	0.7^a	1.3^b	9.4***	0.2^a	0.6^{ab}	1.1^b	5.6**
3.1	2.9	3.9	1.6	2.9	3.7	3.9	2.4+
4.7^a	4.2^{ab}	2.6^b	4.1*	3.7	2.7	4.5	1.6
1.0	1.4	1.9	2.2	0.9^a	1.8^b	2.5^b	8.8***
55.3	51.3	47.5	1.8	47.4	43.8	52.1	1.2
5.7	5.7	5.1	0.8	4.1	3.5	4.7	1.4
44.0	44.0	42.1	0.5	43.2	42.5	43.0	0.1
4.9	4.7	4.5	0.7	4.5	4.6	4.9	0.6
2.4	2.8	2.9	2.5+	3.0	3.0	3.4	0.8
7.0	7.5	7.4	1.1	8.3^{ab}	8.0^a	9.1^b	2.6+
29.8	31.6	29.4	2.5+	32.7	30.6	31.0	2.0
13.1	13.1	12.5	0.1	12.7	12.1	11.3	0.7
60.3	72.8	61.1	2.3	72.3^a	61.8^b	71.5^{ab}	2.6+
1.2	1.0	1.5	1.2	1.3	1.4	1.9	1.8
15.3^a	16.0^a	18.0^b	4.7*	16.3	17.0	17.5	0.8

summary measure of involvement in problem behavior, the Multiple Problem Behavior Index, as well as for a variety of specific problem behaviors. Where the F-ratios are significant, the Scheffé test indicates that the location of the significant difference is for the most part between Group I and the other two groups; for the High School Study women, however, there are significant differences among all three groups on a number of the problem behavior measures. This analysis makes clear that involvement in problem behavior in adolescence/youth *is* associated with significantly greater involvement in problem behavior in young adulthood.

Contingency analyses of a variety of discrete measures of young adult problem behavior outcomes (not tabled) provide further support: Those who were more involved in problem behavior in adolescence/youth are significantly more likely, as young adults, to drive after use of alcohol and after use of marijuana (High School women only), to be classified as heavier marijuana users in young adulthood, and to drink alcohol at work (College Study men and women) and to use marijuana at work (High School Study men and women only).

It is when we turn our attention, in Table 9.1, to young adult life areas *other than problem behavior*, that the picture is sharply and consistently different. With only a very few exceptions, there are no significant differences in young adult outcomes associated with differential involvement in problem behavior in adolescence/youth. In regard to the exceptions, they tend not to be consistent across the four subsamples, and in two cases are in a direction opposite to that expected. Only on the mental health measure of Alienation is there some consistency and significance for at least two subsamples, High School Study women and College Study men. With regard to the other measures of outcomes in the young adult life-areas of work, education, friends, and family, the three adolescent/youth problem behavior involvement groups have all had quite similar experiences and accomplishments as young adults.

The contingency analyses (not tabled) are again consistent with this generalization. Across a wide array of diverse young adult indicators – marital status, divorce experience, status as parents, abortion experience (except for College females), number of jobs held, self-reported health, frequency of illness, visits to a physician in the past year, past and present experience with psychotherapy or counseling, or participation in voting in the 1980 election – there are no significant chi-squares associated with differential involvement in problem behavior in adolescence/youth.

The analyses, thus far, have examined young adult outcomes in relation to degree of involvement in problem behavior in adolescence/youth rather than in one or another of the *specific* problem behaviors. Most of the work of other investigators has employed the latter strategy, focusing particularly on earlier involvement in illicit drug use (e.g., Kandel, 1984; Newcomb & Bentler, 1988) or in alcohol abuse (e.g., Andersson & Magnusson, 1988). Indeed, our own first inquiry on this general topic was concerned with examining young adult outcomes associated with differential involvement in the specific problem behavior of heavier marijuana use in adolescence/youth. In those early analyses, done under special contract with the National Institute on Drug Abuse, we established three groups based on their differential degree of involvement with marijuana in adolescence/youth (Year IV, 1972/73): (1) a *No–Low Use Group* that had no, or very little, experience with marijuana, that is, used only once or twice in the past six months; (2) an *Occasional Use Group* that used marijuana less than twice a week but at least three or more times in the past six months; and (3) a *Heavier Use Group* that used marijuana at least 20 times in the past six months and also used it twice a week or more when it was available.

On the basis of these criteria, the mean frequency of use of marijuana in the past six months, for the High School Study men, was actually 77.9 times for the Heavier Use Group, 8.7 times for the Occasional Use Group, and 0.2 times for the No–Low Use Group. For the High School Study women, the mean frequencies of use for the respective groups were 65.9, 9.5, and 0.2. For the College Study men and women, respectively, the means were 64.4, 9.7, and 0.4; and 58.2, 10.5, and 0.3. Thus, the mean scores for the four Heavier Use Groups, ranging between 58 and 78 times over the previous six months, translate into a pattern of use of between two and three times a week on average. Although this is not necessarily an indication of extreme use, it does imply regular use, especially for the senior high school age youths, and it represents a level of involvement with marijuana that is very substantially higher than that of the other two groups.

Findings from those earlier analyses linking adolescent/youth marijuana involvement with young adult outcomes were, with only minor exceptions, entirely consonant with the findings just reported for adolescent/youth problem behavior involvement (see Donovan & Jessor, 1985). Heavier use of marijuana in adolescence/youth was associated with greater continuity of use of marijuana and with a higher likelihood of heavier marijuana use in young adulthood. It was also associated with greater involvement in other problem behaviors in young adulthood, including other illicit drug use, problem drinking, and general deviant behavior.

But when we turned to other areas of outcomes in young adult life, the picture was, again, very different. Across a wide spectrum of young adult outcomes, in a variety of different life areas, there were almost no associations with variation in adolescent/youth marijuana use that were significant. This included the areas of work, education, family, friendships, and mental health. A few exceptions should be noted: Heavier Marijuana Use in adolescence/youth was associated with more negative life events (High School and College women only), greater alienation (High School women and College men only), less likelihood of being married or of being a parent (College men only), greater abortion experience (College women only), and greater frequency of visits to a physician in the past year (High School women only). These exceptions were few, however, and they tended not to be consistent across the four subsamples. In general, the specific marijuana involvement findings parallel closely the general problem behavior involvement findings presented earlier. A similar conclusion was reached in follow-up analyses of specific problem drinking involvement in adolescence (see Jessor, 1985). Overall, these findings can be summarized by saying that there are consistent outcomes in relation to greater young adult involvement in problem behavior, and there is little evidence for compromising "spillover" into the other areas of young adult life that were measured.

Multiple regression analyses of young adult outcomes, with controls in young adulthood

The second analytic approach to the issue of whether involvement in problem behavior in adolescence/youth has implications for later young adult life employed hierarchical multiple regression. In this approach, it was possible to use the full range of variation on the antecedent problem behavior measures (rather than establishing discrete groups based on the number of their problem behavior involvements), and to institute a control for the Time 2 variable of *young adult* involvement in problem behavior. (In our earlier analyses of differential involvement in marijuana use for the National Institute on Drug Abuse [Donovan & Jessor, 1985], controls were instituted first at Time 1, then at Time 2, and finally at *both* Times 1 and 2, and the pattern of findings described in the preceding section remained essentially unchanged. Given the established stability of problem behavior involvement over time, it seemed most critical for present purposes to control for problem behavior involvement at Time 2, that is, in young adulthood, when examining young adult outcomes other than problem behavior.)

The analyses in this section are concerned with pursuing further those outcomes in young adulthood *other than* involvement in problem behavior. Measures of a variety of young adult outcomes were regressed on three measures of problem behavior in adolescence/youth: Frequency of Drunkenness in the Past Year, Frequency of Marijuana Use in the Past Six Months, and Involvement in Deviant Behavior (e.g., lying, stealing, aggression) in the Past Year. The three antecedent measures were all continuous and were based on the Year IV (1972/73) data. In order to control for the effect of problem-behavior involvement in young adulthood, the Year VI (1981) Multiple Problem Behavior Index score was entered as the first step in each of the hierarchical regressions.

Hierarchical regressions were carried out for seven different outcome measures drawn from a diversity of young adult life areas including status attainment, overall life satisfaction, health, self-esteem and alienation, and political participation. Regressions were done separately for men and women in both the High School Study and the College Study. Table 9.2 presents the findings for one of the four subsamples, the High School Study women.

As can be seen in Table 9.2, young adult involvement in problem behavior – that is, the 1981 Multiple Problem Behavior Index entered in Step 1 – correlates significantly with three out of seven of the young adult outcome measures: Education, General Health, and

Table 9.2. *Hierarchical multiple regressions of selected outcome measures in young adulthood (1981) on adolescent/youth (1972/1973) measures of involvement in three problem behaviors, with multiple problem behavior in 1981 as control, High School Study females (*N = 222*)*

Young adult (1981) outcome measures	(1) R Step 1	(2) R Step 2	(3) R^2 Step 2	(4) R^2 change Step 1 − Step 2
Job Prestige	.05	.13	.017	.014
Education	.14*	.22*	.047*	.027
Political Participation	.11	.26**	.070**	.059**
General Health	.14*	.21*	.046*	.026
Overall Life Satisfaction	.02	.02	.002	.002
Self-Esteem	.003	.13	.016	.016
Alienation	.20**	.25**	.061**	.021

Note: In Step 1, only the 1981 Multiple Problem Behavior Index was entered. In Step 2, the 1972/73 measures of Frequency of Drunkenness, Frequency of Marijuana Use, and Deviant Behavior were entered.
**$p \leq .01$ (by *F*-test); *$p \leq .05$.

Alienation. Although these cross-sectional correlations are small and account for no more than 4 percent of the variance in any of the outcome measures, they nevertheless support the decision to control for young adult problem-behavior involvement as a possible Time 2 "third variable."

The main concern in these hierarchical regressions is, of course, with whether there are significant multiple correlations at Step 2, and, if so, whether they represent a significant increment in variance accounted for over that accounted for in Step 1. The multiple correlations in column 2 indicate that now four of the young adult outcome measures are significantly predicted at Step 2, Political Participation joining the three that already had significant multiple *R*s at Step 1. Although the four multiple *R*s are significant, it is important to emphasize that the amount of variance accounted for at Step 2 reaches only 7 percent at best.

The key point, however, is what is evident in column 4 of Table 9.2, the column showing the *change in R^2* between Step 1 and Step 2. As can be seen, that change is *non*significant for six out of seven of the young adult outcome measures. What this means is that, when young adult problem behavior is controlled, variation in problem behavior involvement in adolescence/youth has no relation to variation in young adult outcomes having to do with occupational prestige, educational attainment, general health status, overall life satisfaction, self-esteem, or alienation. Only for the measure of young adult political participation is there a significant linkage, and that linkage, as was already noted, is small in magnitude.

These findings from the hierarchical regressions for the High School Study women are quite representative of those for the other three subsamples. For High School Study men, the increment in R^2 between Step 1 and Step 2 is significant for three of the young adult outcome measures – Overall Life Satisfaction, Self-Esteem, and Alienation – but, again, the amount of variance accounted for in these cases remains small, less than 12 percent. For the College Study men, the increment in R^2 is significant for only one of the seven young adult outcome measures (Political Participation), and for the College Study women, none of the R^2 increments is significant.

Across the four subsamples, the seven young adult outcome measures yield a total of 28 separate tests for a significant increment in R^2 between Step 1 and Step 2. Only five of those 28 tests were significant, and they refer to four different outcome measures, no outcome emerging consistently in the different subsamples. Even where the R^2 change was significant, only a very small portion of variance was accounted for. The interpretation of these hierarchical regressions is, therefore, quite clear. There is almost no support for a relationship between variation in involvement in problem behavior in adolescence/youth and variation in life outcomes later on in young adulthood. This conclusion gains strength from the number and the diversity of the young adult outcome criteria examined, from the control instituted for young adult problem behavior involvement, and from the consonance between the regression findings and those from the analyses of variance presented in the preceding section of this chapter.

Structural modeling of young adult outcomes of involvement in problem behavior in adolescence/youth

The focal concern of this chapter – whether there is a linkage between earlier involvement in problem behavior and later outcomes in young adulthood – was addressed in yet a third way. In this third approach, the relations between the measures in the two life stages – adolescence/youth and young adulthood – were expressed in structural models, and the LISREL VI program (Jöreskog & Sörbom, 1984) was used for their analyses.

For the adolescent/youth life stage, a latent variable of behavior system proneness in 1972/73 was constituted based upon the same three observed measures we used in the two preceding sections of this chapter and also in Chapter 8: Frequency of Drunkenness, Frequency of Marijuana Use, and Deviant Behavior. For the later life stage, the behavior system proneness latent-variable measure was based on measures of involvement in all five areas of problem behavior: problem drinking, marijuana involvement, involvement with other illicit drugs, deviant behavior, and cigarette smoking. Four different latent variables were constituted to represent diverse areas of outcome in young adulthood (1981). The latent variable of Overall Life Satisfaction was established on the basis of four observed measures: Satisfaction with Family Life, Satisfaction with Work Life, Satisfaction with Friendships, and Satisfaction with Sex Life. The latent variable of Status Attainment was established using two observed measures: Educational Attainment and Occupational Prestige Rating. The latent variable of Mental Health refers to four observed measures: Self-Esteem, Alienation, Depression, and Therapy Experience. And the fourth latent variable, Physical Health, is based on two observed measures: Visits to a Physician and Subjective Rating of Health.

Two parallel sets of structural models were tested for each of the four young adult outcome latent variables in each gender in the High School Study, and for the College Study with genders combined (due to small *N*s). The parallel structural models differed only in that one set included the latent variable for behavior system proneness *in young adulthood* (1981), whereas in the other set, that latent variable and,

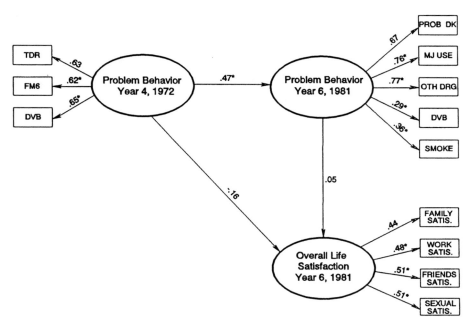

Figure 9.1.   Structural model for the latent variable of Overall Life Sat-
isfaction in young adulthood (Year 6, 1981), High School Study. Acronyms:
TDR = Times Drunk; FM6 = Frequency of Marijuana Use; DVB =
General Deviant Behavior; PROB DK = Problem Drinking; MJ USE =
Marijuana Involvement; OTH DRG = Highest Intensity of Other Illicit
Drug Use; SMOKE = Involvement with Smoking; FAMILY SATIS. =
Famiy Satisfaction; WORK SATIS. = Work Satisfaction; FRIENDS
SATIS. = Friendship Satisfaction; SEXUAL SATIS. = Sexual Rela-
tionship Satisfaction.

hence, that indirect pathway between Time 1 antecedents and Time
2 outcomes, were omitted.

The structural models for the young adult latent outcome variable
of Overall Life Satisfaction for the High School Study and for the
College Study, with genders combined, are shown in Figures 9.1 and
9.2, respectively. The models in Figures 9.1 and 9.2 fit the data well,
as indicated by the nonsignificant chi-square in each case. The chi-
square for the High School Study model was 59.5 ($p = .12$) with
48 degrees of freedom; for the College Study model, the chi-square

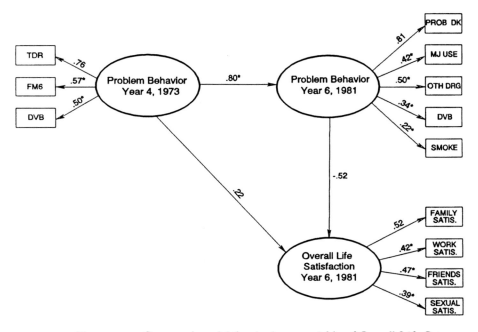

Figure 9.2.   Structural model for the latent variable of Overall Life Satisfaction in young adulthood (Year 6, 1981), College Study. Acronyms: TDR = Times Drunk; FM6 = Frequency of Marijuana Use; DVB = General Deviant Behavior; PROB DK = Problem Drinking; MJ USE = Marijuana Involvement; OTH DRG = Highest Intensity of Other Illicit Drug Use; SMOKE = Involvement with Smoking; FAMILY SATIS. = Family Satisfaction; WORK SATIS. = Work Satisfaction; FRIENDS SATIS. = Friendship Satisfaction; SEXUAL SATIS. = Sexual Relationship Satisfaction.

was 45.8 (p = .52) with 47 degrees of freedom. The other measures of fit are also excellent. The High School Study model (Figure 9.1) has a GFI of .97, an AGFI of .95, and a root mean square residual (RMR) of .05. The respective fit indexes for the College Study model (Figure 9.2) are .96, .93, and .05. (The model for the High School Study includes only three residual correlations, while the model for the College Study includes four residual correlations among the indicator measures.)

What is clear, and consistently so in both models, is that the regression coefficient for the direct path from adolescent/youth involvement in problem behavior to Overall Life Satisfaction in young adulthood is nonsignificant. In the parallel set of structural models (not shown) in which the 1981 latent variable of problem behavior proneness is omitted, that same path coefficient remains nonsignificant for both the High School and College Study models. When separate structural models for the two genders in the High School Study are tested, the findings are essentially the same as for the genders combined model. These findings, then, are entirely consonant with those presented in the preceding two sections of this chapter: There is no direct effect of earlier problem behavior involvement on this particular young adult outcome, the latent variable of Overall Life Satisfaction, in either study. Indeed, the two models indicate that there is no indirect effect either.

It was possible, with only two exceptions, to fit structural models for the three other latent variables in both the High School Study and the College Study, and for both genders in the former study as well. In all cases, the path coefficient between earlier problem behavior involvement and later young adult outcome was nonsignificant. For the combined gender analyses in the High School Study and the College Study, respectively, these nonsignificant regression coefficients were .07 and − .24 for Status Attainment; − .10 and .08 for Mental Health; and − .04 and .59 for Physical Health. The findings from this analytic approach are consistent, then, across four rather diverse domains of young adult life outcomes. The structural modeling evidence is fully convergent with that presented in the two earlier sections of this chapter. Beyond providing an additional perspective on the same central issue, the use of structural modeling has the unique advantage of eliminating measurement error from the relationships examined.

Summary

Three different analytic approaches were used in this chapter to converge upon a single, developmental issue, namely, whether involvement in problem behavior in adolescence/youth had long-range, compromising implications for young adulthood in our samples. Two important conclusions can be drawn from those analyses. First, it is clear that there is a consistent linkage between earlier adolescent/ youth involvement in problem behavior and later young adult involvement in problem behavior. There is stability and continuity over time in this domain, and greater involvement in problem behavior in adolescence/youth is significantly associated with greater involvement in young adulthood. The findings in support of this conclusion emerge from the analysis of variance of antecedent group differences in problem behavior involvement in relation to a variety of measures of young adult problem behaviors. The consistency of the findings across the High School and the College studies, and across both genders, is noteworthy; they are also fully consonant with related findings presented in Chapters 7 and 8. Over time, then, there is evidence for developmental continuity in problem behavior involvement.

The significance of these findings needs emphasis. Early involvement in problem behavior is not self-limiting but, instead, carries on into young adulthood and constitutes an important source of risk in that life stage. The risk is certainly for the increased morbidity and mortality associated with at least some of the problem behaviors, for example, the risk from drinking and driving.

The second conclusion from the analyses in this chapter is equally clear, namely, that earlier involvement in problem behavior is not associated in these samples with differential outcomes in *other* domains of young adult life. The evidence for this conclusion derives from the analyses of variance, the hierarchical multiple regressions, and the structural modeling, all of these methods yielding convergent findings. Problem behavior involvement in adolescence/youth appears not to have "spilled over" into other areas of young adult life, or to have compromised attainment and satisfaction, or to have mortgaged the futures of the young people in this research.

Although this conclusion is the appropriate one, given the consistency of the evidence, its reach needs to be qualified in several important respects. First, our research involved normal rather than clinical samples, and the extent of their adolescent/youth involvement in problem behavior – even at its greatest – has to be seen as moderate for the most part. Second, our samples were largely middle class in socioeconomic status, and the openness of the opportunity structure for them and their access to "second chances" have to be seen as far greater than might be the case for disadvantaged youth who had been involved in problem behavior. Third, it may well be that, even for samples such as ours, there can still be compromising outcomes in later life, but that more time is required for those outcomes to be manifested. Development *beyond* the third decade of life may need to be observed in order to identify their presence. If, as our data have shown, there is a linkage between early and later involvement in problem behavior, then it is certainly possible that the greater young adult involvement in problem behavior – drinking, drug use, general deviance – could ultimately interfere with work, or marriage, or friendships, and that longer-term follow-up into the fourth decade of life might make that apparent.

The robustness of the findings across a wide variety of young adult outcomes, their consistency across the four subsamples, and their consonance across different analytic methods are nevertheless compelling. From a developmental perspective, these findings are particularly interesting. They suggest that there is nothing inexorable about the course that psychosocial development must follow, that future options are not necessarily foreclosed by the past, and that there is resilience in growth and change – at least in social contexts that are not entirely malignant, and at a time in history when the social setting itself was relatively open and undergoing change. In short, the findings reinforce an interactionist perspective on psychosocial development between adolescence/youth and young adulthood.

References

Andersson, T., & Magnusson, D. (1988). Drinking habits and alcohol abuse among young men: A prospective longitudinal study. *Journal of Studies on Alcohol, 49*, 245–252.

Dannefer, D. (1984). Adult development and social theory: A paradigmatic reappraisal. *American Sociological Review, 49*, 100–116.

Donovan, J. E., & Jessor, R. (1985). *Young adult outcomes of heavier marijuana use in adolescence.* (Unpublished Research Report No. 12.) Boulder, CO: Institute of Behavioral Science.

Ghodsian, M., & Power, C. (1987). Alcohol consumption between the ages of 16 and 23 in Britain: A longitudinal study. *British Journal of Addiction, 82*, 175–180.

Halikas, J. A., Weller, R. A., Morse, C. L., & Hoffman, R. G. (1983).

Regular marijuana use and its effect on psychosocial variables: A longitudinal study. *Comprehensive Psychiatry, 24,* 229–235.

Jessor, R. (1985). Adolescent problem drinking: Psychosocial aspects and developmental outcomes. In L. H. Towle (Ed.), *Proceedings: NIAAA–WHO Collaborating Center Designation meeting.* (DHHS Publication No. ADM 85–1370; pp. 104–143). Rockville, MD: National Institute on Alcohol Abuse and Alcoholism.

Jörekog, K. G., & Sörbom, D. (1984). *LISREL VI: Analysis of linear structural relations by maximum likelihood, instrumental variables, and least square methods.* Mooresville, IN: Scientific Software.

Kandel, D. B. (1984). Marijuana users in young adulthood. *Archives of General Psychiatry, 41,* 200–209.

Kandel, D. B., Davies, M., Karus, D., & Yamaguchi, K. (1986). The consequences in young adulthood of adolescent drug use involvement. *Archives of General Psychiatry, 43,* 746–759.

Newcomb, M. D., & Bentler, P. M. (1987). The impact of late adolescent substance use on young adult health status and utilization of health services: A structural equation model over four years. *Social Science and Medicine, 24,* 71–82.

Newcomb, M. D., & Bentler, P. M. (1988). *Consequences of adolescent drug use: Impact on the lives of young adults.* Newbury Park, CA: Sage.

Power, C., & Estaugh, V. (1990). Employment and drinking in early adulthood: A longitudinal perspective. *British Journal of Addiction, 85,* 487–494.

Part IV

Conclusions

10

Problem behavior and young adulthood: Continuities in change

The primary aim of renewing and extending our longitudinal study of youth was to add to knowledge about psychosocial development beyond adolescence and, at the same time, to explore a portion of the life course – young adulthood – that was still largely uncharted. The research findings in the preceding chapters represent what we have been able to accomplish in pursuing that aim. Their significance, and the conclusions they support, are elaborated in this final chapter.

The approach that was taken was guided by a conceptual framework – Problem-Behavior Theory – that had proved useful earlier in achieving an understanding of problem behavior and psychosocial development in adolescence and youth. Whether its explanatory reach would include young adulthood as well was yet to be determined. Nevertheless, the domains of inquiry that were engaged – personality, the perceived environment, the social environment, behavior – and the key concepts that were measured – values, expectations, social and self attitudes, models for behavior – all derived from that theoretical perspective. The major theoretical formulation about the likelihood of occurrence of problem behavior was also retained: Psychosocial proneness to problem behavior in young adulthood was considered to be a resultant, reflecting the balance of instigations and controls in the various explanatory systems. And the theoretical position about psychosocial development as the outcome of person–environment interactions over time continued to shape the study and interpretation of developmental change.

Although the focus of the research was on a particular area of behavior – problem behavior – and on the utility of a particular theoretical formulation, the enterprise as a whole was also concerned with broader issues in behavioral science. Among those issues were how best to represent persons in research on social behavior, that is, what individual differences to measure; how to capture the environment as a source of variance in behavior, and the importance of distinguishing proximal from distal environments; the logic of person–environment interaction in both behavior and development; the organization and patterning of systems of social behavior; and the plasticity of development reflecting the contingencies of context and setting. In short, the pursuit of understanding about problem behavior was animated by the opportunity it provided to illuminate fundamental issues that transcend what might otherwise be a limited empirical focus.

The stability of change

With regard to one of those fundamental issues – the nature of psychosocial development – the weight of the evidence is quite clear: Despite substantial change between adolescence/youth and young adulthood, the developmental process is characterized by stability and continuity across those segments of the life course. This conclusion gains even greater significance, given that the two life stages tend to be markedly different in their social organization, their predominating roles, their life tasks, and their social norms, and that moving developmentally from the earlier to the later one entails major transitions for most young people, not only in daily activities and responsibilities but in social and self-definitions as well.

Stability and consistency of individual differences were apparent in all three of the major explanatory systems – personality, the perceived environment, and behavior – when examined directly by the stability coefficients that were presented in Tables 7.1 and 7.2. Somewhat stronger for the College Study than the High School Study, and considerably stronger across the two-year interval within young adulthood than across the eight-/nine-year interval between adolescence/youth and young adulthood, the magnitude of the coefficients provides compelling support, overall, for a continuity perspective on psychosocial development. Of special interest is the somewhat greater stability of the personality system attributes compared with those in the other two explanatory systems. Consonant with the reports of others (Mortimer, Finch, & Kumka, 1982; Stein, Newcomb, & Bentler, 1986), the evident stability of personality attributes over this time period is one more refutation of the sterile controversy a decade ago about the very "existence" of personality and its enduringness.

Further support for developmental continuity was evident, at the system level, in the latent-variable analyses in Chapter 8. Examining latent-variable measures of personality system proneness, perceived environment system proneness, and behavior system proneness between adolescence/youth and young adulthood, we found over-time correlations to be in the mid-.50s for the High School Study and in the mid- 60s for the College Study. Given the eight- or nine-year time interval and the major life changes involved, these are magnitudes that are, indeed, impressive.

In reviewing a large variety of studies of the development of personality *in* adulthood, their own included, McCrae and Costa (1990) report clear consensus on the repeated demonstrations of stability and consistency. And in a research effort more relevant to our own, on the development of attitudes, aspirations, self-concepts, and behaviors among young men between adolescence and adulthood, Bachman, O'Malley, and Johnston (1978) conclude: "The dominant picture that emerges from this research is not change but stability" (p. 221). Thus, our stability findings are in agreement with the work of others. Although important developmental change does occur, as we discuss in the next section, the research makes apparent that there is considerable stability and continuity in that change. It would be safe to conclude from our findings that the adolescent is parent of the young adult.

The direction of developmental change: Toward an increase in psychosocial conventionality

Within a developmental process characterized by stability, there is, of course, ample room for major change. Mean levels on the various attributes and characteristics being observed may increase or decrease with development, and all that stability implies is that the relative position of individuals in the distribution is conserved over the time interval: Those initially high on some characteristic – say, value on achievement – tend to remain high relative to the group; those initially low on some measure – say, on perceived friends models for deviance – tend to remain low relative to the group. Granted the evidence for stability, a major developmental question remains: Has there been significant psychosocial change between adolescence/youth and young adulthood, and, if so, what is its general nature?

As with the evidence on stability and consistency, the answer that emerges from the data is, again, quite clear. For our cohorts, psychosocial development beyond adolescence/youth was unmistakably in the direction of greater conventionality. This direction of change was apparent in all three explanatory systems; in each system, there was significant decline in problem behavior proneness, reflecting both a reduction in instigations and an increase in controls. The psychosocial "growth curves" plotted in Chapter 7 illustrate change on some of the key theoretical variables: an increase in value on achievement, a decline in social criticism and alienation, an increase in attitudinal intolerance of deviance, and a decline in friends models for drug use (in the College Study only). This general direction of change – toward greater conventionality – between adolescence/youth and young adulthood not only was significant but in several instances also represented a complete reversal of the direction of developmental change *within* adolescence/youth, namely, toward *greater* problem behavior proneness or *un*conventionality.

The same direction of change toward conventionality was evident in the Behavior System as well, as indicated by the significant decline in self-reported general deviant behavior and declines in the proportion of problem drinkers and heavier marijuana users. The theoretical consonance of the decline in problem behavior with the parallel declines in problem behavior proneness in both the Personality System and the Perceived Environment System strengthens conviction about the developmental inference being drawn, that is, that there is an overall trend toward a reduction in problem behavior proneness and an increase in conventionality with development into young adulthood. Theoretical consonance was demonstrated in yet another way in Chapter 7. It was demonstrated there that those who showed a decrease in overall problem behavior between adolescence/ youth and young adulthood showed an increase in psychosocial conventionality over that same time interval; those who showed an increase in problem behavior showed a decrease in conventionality; and those whose involvement in problem behavior did not change, did not change in conventionality either. These findings, at the group level, buttress the overall findings about the theoretical consonance of the developmental changes toward greater conventionality.

Although it is important to be able, empirically, to identify a major direction of developmental change associated with the passage into and through young adulthood, it would be mistaken to assume that all adolescents develop in the same way. Indeed, a particularly interesting contribution of this inquiry has been the demonstration of large individual differences in psychosocial development beyond adolescence. Partitioning the cohorts into groups that were High, Medium, or Low on conventionality (or problem behavior proneness) in adolescence/youth made it possible to reveal markedly different trajectories of development toward young adulthood for the three groups. Those who were initially high in conventionality showed little or no significant change between the two life stages on a number of key measures of problem behavior proneness; those, however, who were initially low in conventionality, that is, most unconventional, showed major change over time in the direction of greater conventionality; and those initially medium in conventionality fell in between, showing a medium amount of change toward conventionality. Where change occurred, then, it was toward increased conventionality for all three groups, but the amount of change and the rate of change yielded quite different developmental trajectories for the three groups. The similarity that all three groups show in level of conventionality by the time of reaching young adulthood belies the fact that *quite different paths were followed in getting there*. What is especially noteworthy in those findings is the evidence that the shift toward conventionality was most marked among those who were initially – in the early 1970s – the least conventional; by the early 1980s they had become much closer in conventionality to the other two groups, though still remaining less so as the stability findings would, of course, lead us to expect.

The developmental change toward a decline in problem behavior proneness or toward an increase in conventionality, while apparent in all three systems and on a variety of key theoretical attributes, was not without exception and qualification as discussed in Chapter 7. Nevertheless, it is a directional change that is compatible with what is well-established in the literature about the developmental course of involvement in problem behavior. According to Gove (1985), "Virtually all forms of deviance that involve substantial risk and/or physically demanding behavior occur mainly among young persons, and the rates of such deviance decline sharply by the late twenties and early thirties" (p. 115). And a leading scholar reviewing this field states: "All common forms of deviance (drug use, theft, drinking, sexual promiscuity, fighting) seem to drop off with age" (Robins, 1980, p. 37).

The term "maturing out" has been applied to the diminution or abandonment of involvement in problem behavior that seems to occur in the mid- to late twenties, but what it really refers to, that is, what the underlying determinants of that process are, has not been well understood. Most often, the term is assumed to implicate the assumption of adult roles and exposure to the informal social controls they entail. Our own data did not permit us to examine this process directly, unfortunately. However, a recent secondary analysis of the data from the classical longitudinal study of delinquency by the Gluecks (1950, 1968) has reported compelling support for such an interpretation: "We have shown that job stability and marital attachment in adulthood are significantly related to changes in adult crime – the stronger the adult ties to work and family, the less crime and deviance among both [former] delinquents and controls" (Sampson & Laub, 1990, p. 625). And they add that change in young adulthood "appears to be systematically structured by adult bonds to social institutions" (p. 625).

This emphasis on the assumption of social roles and on the effects of their associated informal social controls is entirely consistent with the age-related drop off in problem behavior, and the Sampson and Laub findings are a welcome contribution to an understanding of the process of "maturing out." What our own findings add to such understanding is new evidence about the changes in personality and perceived environment attributes that are also associated with "maturing out," that is, with a decline in involvement in problem behavior. Whether the psychosocial changes at the individual level that we have identified and summarized as an increase in conventionality may, in fact, mediate between the assumption of adult roles and exposure to informal social controls, on the one hand, and the decline in problem behavior involvement, on the other hand, is certainly worthy of a future research effort.

Beyond support for stability and continuity in psychosocial development, then, the findings from this longitudinal study provide substantial evidence for developmental change. The overall trajectory of change, theoretically in the direction of greater conventionality and less involvement in problem behavior, has to be seen, however, as a composite of trajectories reflecting individual differences in amount, in direction, and in rate of change.

The organization of problem behavior in young adulthood

The findings speak to another basic issue in behavioral science research, namely the degree to which there is organization, patterning, or structure in behavior in young adulthood. In the problem behavior field, the tradition has long been to specialize in one or another of its components – delinquency, drug use, drinking behavior, sexuality – and entire professional careers have been shaped by that tradition, as has also the organization of the research support bureaucracy in the various federal institutes. The alternative perspective places emphasis on the larger class to which, it can be argued, the various component behaviors all belong, namely, the category of normative transgression, or deviance, or, as we have referred to it throughout this book, problem behavior. The argument can be made that topographically different behaviors can serve the same purpose (e.g., the affirmation of peer group membership) and therefore can functionally substitute for one another. It can also be argued that the social ecology of problem behaviors is such that different problem behaviors – say, smoking and drinking, or drug use and crime, or alcohol use and aggression – are often learned together and expected to be performed together. Arguments such as these suggest that there should be organization or structure among the various problem behaviors and that they should show some degree of covariation. It was this kind of thinking that led to our formulation of behavior as a *system* in Problem-Behavior Theory, and to our including in the system a structure of interrelated problem behaviors and a structure of conforming behaviors (see Figure 2.1).

In our earlier work on adolescents, considerable attention was given to exploring the extent and degree of covariation that existed among the various measures of adolescent problem behavior. In light of the results of those explorations, it was proposed that problem behavior in adolescence might well constitute a *syndrome*. Since then, there has been substantial empirical support for that notion. Coming at the same basic issue from another perspective, Robins's conclusion from her review of longitudinal research on deviance is fully consonant with the connotations of the syndrome concept: "The best predictor of any later deviant act always seems to be earlier deviant behavior, and the specific *nature* of that earlier deviant behavior seems uniformly to be relatively unimportant" (1980, p. 36).

Having established earlier that the idea of covariation among problem behaviors and the syndrome concept were apposite to the adolescence/youth phase of this research, we undertook to examine the same issue in the young adult data. The key question was whether development beyond adolescence sustained the observed organization of problem behavior or, conceivably, resulted in its dissolution. The analyses that were concerned with answering this question were presented in Chapter 5.

The findings from the bivariate correlational analyses, the categorical cross-tabulations, and the maximum-likelihood factor analysis were all convergent in showing interrelatedness among the five different young adult problem behaviors – frequency of drunkenness, frequency of marijuana use, other illicit drug use, general deviant behavior, and cigarette smoking – and in showing also that a single underlying factor could account for the observed correlations among those behaviors. In this respect, the young adult findings were similar to those for adolescence/youth, and they provided support for the idea of a syndrome of problem behavior in young adulthood.

It was possible to examine the issue in yet another way by establishing, for the first time, latent variables for each of the different problem behaviors, and then applying structural equation modeling techniques to their interrelations. The results of that approach were seen in Figure 5.1 in which a single second-order latent variable of behavior system proneness can account for the correlations among the five latent-variable measures of problem behavior. This structural modeling approach adds particularly compelling support for the idea of covariation among problem behaviors in young adulthood.

It seems clear, then, at least for our cohorts, that there is, indeed, organization and structure among a variety of problem behaviors in young adulthood, just as there was in adolescence/youth. The importance of such knowledge lies in the impetus it provides for researchers to seek understanding of behavioral *repertoires*, rather than continuing to focus on single behaviors alone. It lies also in the challenge it poses for intervention efforts to transcend a preoccupation with separate problem behaviors as if they existed in isolation from one another.

Explaining young adult problem behavior

The explanatory reach of Problem-Behavior Theory as an account of variation in problem behavior in the later developmental stage of young adulthood – and in the historical era of the late 1970s and early 1980s – was not something that could simply be taken for granted. From a historical perspective alone, there had been major increases in the prevalence of certain problem behaviors – particularly illicit drug use and nonmarital sexual activity; normative orientations had been shifting toward greater acceptance, and social control responses were undergoing widespread modulation. From a developmental perspective, the constraints of age-graded norms and the idea of transition out of adolescence would no longer be apposite as explanatory formulations for problem behavior involvement. In addition, young adulthood entails exposure to very different institutional contexts – the family and work, for example, as contrasted with the school and peer group – and these settings provide different structures of opportunity, of norms, and of formal and informal controls. Whether a conceptual framework emphasizing personality and perceived environment variables that represented instigations to and controls against normative transgression among adolescents/youth in the early 1970s would retain its relevance for both a later developmental stage and a later historical era had to be treated, at the very least, as problematic. Efforts were made to enhance the age appropriateness of the item content of the measures, and to inquire about satisfactions and stress in the life areas of young adulthood, but the key variables remained those that had been relied on in the earlier phase of the longitudinal study.

The continuing relevance of the Problem-Behavior Theory framework for young adulthood is one of the major conclusions to be drawn from this follow-up study. The cross-sectional multivariate analyses, presented in Chapter 6, provide a substantial account of the variation in problem-behavior involvement in young adulthood, one that holds for both genders, in both studies, and in both years – 1979 and 1981 – of the follow-up. A summary appraisal of the overall findings can best be gained by considering the multiple regressions of the composite measure of involvement in problem behavior, the Multiple Problem Behavior Index, on the combined theoretical systems – personality, perceived environment, and behavior (see Table 6.3). The 11 key measures used in the Overall Psychosocial Proneness regressions yielded multiple correlations of .76, .75, .77, and .63 for the High School Study men and women and the College Study men and women, respectively. Thus, for the first three groups, over 50 percent of the variance in young adult problem behavior in 1981 is accounted for by the theoretical framework, and it is close to 40 percent for the fourth group. This magnitude of the account of variance is quite robust across the 1979, Year V data set, as well, and it also compares very closely with that obtained in the 1972/73, Year IV, adolescence/ youth data set, where the respective multiple correlations were .74, .77, .68, and .68.

When the theoretical framework is applied, separately, to the various component problem behaviors, the multiple correlations are similar for marijuana use, somewhat lower for frequency of drunkenness and for the use of other illicit drugs, somewhat lower still for general deviance, and lowest for cigarette smoking (on this latter measure, the multiple correlations fall short of statistical significance for the College Study men and women).

The young adult theoretical findings also parallel those from the adolescence/youth phase in the relative contribution made by the different explanatory systems. In general, the Perceived Environment System yields larger multiple correlations with the Multiple Problem Behavior Index (and with its various component behaviors) than does the Personality System. The reason for this, in the present data set, would seem to be the same one that applied in the 1972/73 data set: The key measures in the Perceived Environment System, especially Friends' Approval and Friends Models for Drug Use, are more proximal to problem behavior than are the measures in the Personality System. Where this is *not* the case – for example, for General Deviance – the Personality System includes the highly proximal (and parallel) measure of Attitudinal Intolerance of Deviance, and that is the reason why the Personality System now yields a larger multiple correlation than the Perceived Environment System (see Table 6.4). Another instance of such reversal of the contributions of the two systems occurs with regard to the conventional behavior of church attendance. The highly proximal measure of Religiosity is included in the Personality System, and that is what enables it to supervene the Perceived Environment System in amount of variance accounted for in Church Attendance. This general issue of the relative contribution of the two systems to explanation is important to clarify. Appropriate recognition of the role played by the proximal versus distal relation of a measure to a behavioral criterion can forestall inappropriate conclusions about whether it is personality or the environment that is more important in determining behavior. From an interactionist perspective, any such conclusion would be conceptually meaningless.

There is another issue, however, that *is* relevant to an interactionist perspective, and that pertains to the increase in the explanatory account that should occur when both the Personality System and the Perceived Environment System are considered *jointly*. In the multivariate, cross-sectional analyses of the Multiple Problem Behavior Index in Chapter 6, when personality proneness and perceived environment proneness are combined into psychosocial proneness, there is, indeed, a significant increment in variance explained (R^2) over the variance explained by either system alone. This is generally the case for the separate criterion behaviors as well. Findings such as these parallel those from the adolescence/youth phase of the research as well, and they contribute new empirical support for the logic of the interactionist position in behavioral science research.

Although the magnitude of the explanatory account in young adulthood is very nearly identical to that in adolescence/youth, the pattern of variables playing a key role is somewhat different. At the young adult stage, the motivational-instigation variables are relatively less important (Value on and Expectation for Achievement) or unimportant (Value on and Expectation for Independence) compared with the role they played in the earlier phase of the research. Internal–External Locus of Control and Self-Esteem are only weakly or inconsistently related to problem behavior, but this was also the case in the earlier phase. And, Alienation is more consistently related to problem behavior in young adulthood than it was in adolescence/youth. On the other hand, the similarity of the patterns is extensive; it includes the personal belief variable of Social Criticism, the personal control variables of Intolerance of Deviance and Religiosity, the proximal perceived environment variables of Friends' Approval of and Friends Models for Problem Behavior, and the Behavior System measure of conventional behavior, Church Attendance. The pattern of explanatory variables in young adulthood, representing all three of the theoretical systems, constitutes what we have been referring to as "psychosocial conventionality," and, in this regard, it is almost isomorphic with the conventionality pattern that emerged from the adolescence/youth phase of the research.

The applicability and relevance of the Problem-Behavior Theory framework for young adulthood suggest that there is a certain degree of developmental invariance in the explanation of problem behavior. In demonstrating explanatory invariance across the adolescent/youth and young adult life stages, the research extends the developmental generality of the theoretical framework. Kandel reached a similar conclusion for the specific behavior of marijuana use in her follow-up study of adolescents into young adulthood (to ages 24 and 25): "The social psychology of marijuana use is . . . much the same in young adulthood as in adolescence. . . . [M]arijuana involvement is associated with the same factors that had previously been reported for younger populations of junior high school, senior high school, and college students" (1984, p. 208). The evidence for developmental invariance in the explanatory account is complemented by evidence for a degree of historical invariance as well. In our own work over the years since the late 1960s, in both local and national samples (Donovan & Jessor, 1978; Jessor, Chase, & Donovan, 1980; Jessor, Donovan, & Widmer, 1980), very similar patterns of social and psychological variables have been found to be associated with adolescent problem behavior, and with remarkably similar magnitudes of association. And recently, in a new longitudinal study of over 2,000 urban middle school and high school adolescents, we have again found the same pattern; the multiple correlations of overall psychosocial proneness with the Multiple Problem Behavior Index in the new (1989) data are .70, .74, .70, .71, for middle school males and females and high school males and females, respectively. Such evidence for both developmental and historical invariance in the explanation of problem behavior strengthens conviction about the utility of the theoretical framework.

One of the adaptations that was made to the framework, both to extend it and to examine an alternative formulation about the determinants of problem behavior, was the addition of the concept of stress to the young adult phase of the research. The mapping and measurement of stress were admittedly limited, and that, in turn, sharply limits the conclusions that can be drawn. What was found, nevertheless, was that measures of stress related in a modest way to the Multiple Problem Behavior Index, and to one of its components, General Deviance, except for the College Study men in both instances. The amount of variance accounted for by the two stress measures taken together reached, at best, 11 percent for the Index and 18 percent for the measure of General Deviance. What was most persuasive theoretically, however, was that the addition of the stress measures to the measures of overall psychosocial proneness added no new source of variance and did not increase the R^2 associated with the latter (see Table 6.6). On the basis of these results, it seems clear that the concept of stress, at least as measured, does not extend the reach of the larger theoretical framework, nor does it capture a unique source of variance that is not already mapped by the larger framework.

As a theory of the middle range, an explanatory formulation limited to the social and psychological factors that account for involvement in normative transgression, Problem Behavior Theory – in addition to its established relevance for adolescence/youth – can now be considered apposite to the developmental stage of young adulthood.

The predictability of problem behavior in young adulthood

Conviction about the usefulness of the conceptual framework was strengthened by the results of the cross-sectional and the developmental analyses. Such conviction can be buttressed further, and in an especially compelling way, by a demonstration that the variables in the framework measured earlier, have *predictiveness*, over a significant time interval, for later involvement in problem behavior. The bivariate, multivariate, and structural equation modeling analyses in Chapter 8 were focused on just such a demonstration.

The results from the multiple regression analyses predicting variation in the 1981 Multiple Problem Behavior Index from overall psychosocial proneness measured in 1972/73 provide clear and consistent evidence of significant and – given the length of the time interval – substantial predictability. The multiple correlations for High School Study men and women and College Study men and women, respectively, are .52, .42, .66, and .59 (see Table 8.2). Problem behavior proneness in each of the theoretical systems – personality, perceived environment, and behavior – in adolescence/youth is significantly associated with later variation in actual involvement in problem behavior in young adulthood. The results for the various component problem behaviors are generally similar, although weaker for general deviant behavior and for cigarette smoking.

In order to assess the predictability of young adult involvement in problem behavior in a way that would take account of the unreliability of measurement at both time points, and that would illuminate the pathways by which the adolescent/youth precursors were linked to young adult problem behavior, we employed structural equation modeling with latent variables. These analyses reveal substantial correlations between the latent variable for personality system proneness and for perceived environment system proneness in adolescence/youth, on the one hand, and the latent variable for the Behavior System in young adulthood, on the other. For the High School Study, these respective latent-variable correlations are .56 and .41; for the College Study, they are .75 and .55.

More interesting, perhaps, than the magnitude of the over time correlations between these latent variables are the "causal" pathways in the structural diagrams for both the High School Study and the College Study (see Figures 8.1 and 8.2). The fact that is most salient in these figures is the key role of personality system proneness over the time interval. Personality system proneness in adolescence/youth has both direct and indirect linkages with the young adult behavior system latent variable in the High School Study, and a significant indirect path in the College Study. Neither the perceived environment system nor the behavior system latent variables in adolescence/youth show that extent of linkage over time. In providing a representation of "causal" structure, the structural model helps to illuminate what underlies the over-time correlations among the latent variables. The prime role of the Personality System, and of its stability, is noteworthy. The conventional wisdom in the field was cogently summarized by Robins as follows: "The best predictor of any later deviant act always seems to be earlier deviant behavior" (1980. p. 36). The present findings reopen that conclusion, and they raise an important question about the extent to which it may simply reflect the failure, in most investigations, to exhaust the causal contribution of other domains by more comprehensive and systematic measurement of *non*behavioral predictor variables.

That young adult involvement in problem behavior can be forecast by reliance on its theoretical precursors is another significant conclusion of this longitudinal study. The predictive findings not only strengthen the theory but also offer some potential for designing early intervention efforts on a more systematic basis than happens to be the usual practice.

Outcomes of adolescent involvement in problem behavior

Whether involvement in problem behavior in adolescence/youth creates a legacy for later life was another developmental issue that our longitudinal inquiry was able to address. The results of several types of analysis reported in Chapter 9 – analysis of variance, multiple regression, and structural equation modeling – were convergent in their support for two major conclusions. The first conclusion is that there is significant continuity in involvement in problem behavior across the two life stages for our cohorts; the greater the involvement in problem behavior in adolescence/youth, the greater the involvement in problem behavior in young adulthood. Our findings in this regard are entirely consistent with other research that has followed young people beyond adolescence.

The second conclusion, supported equally strongly by the analyses, is that involvement in problem behavior in adolescence/youth does *not* implicate variation in *other* outcomes in young adulthood – outcomes that range across status attainment, work, family, friendship, health, self-esteem, alienation, political participation, and overall life satisfaction. None of the results suggests that there is a "spillover" from the problem behavior area to these other life outcomes, or that adolescent involvement in problem behavior has compromised later development or has mortgaged the future for the youth in our research. This second conclusion will be somewhat more controversial with respect to the literature, and it warrants further attention. Some of the literature is quite compatible with this conclusion – for example, the reports by Power and Estaugh (1990) and by Newcomb and Bentler (1987, 1988) cited in Chapter 9. But Newcomb and Bentler (1988) do raise some differences in outcomes (they term them "consequences") in at least some areas of young adult life, such as marital and job instability, related to variation in earlier involvement in the specific behavior of drug use. Kandel and colleagues (1986), following up the later outcomes of earlier adolescent drug involvement, also report young adult variation in regard to work and marital stability (although the unique effects of adolescent drug use disappear when use *between* adolescence and young adulthood is controlled for). And in their secondary analysis of the Gluecks' delinquency data, Sampson and Laub (1990) state: "Childhood antisocial behaviors are also predictive of economic, family, educational, and employment problems up to eighteen years later," and they call attention to "the generality of the link between childhood delinquency and troublesome adult behavior" (p. 616).

Perhaps the most important fact to raise in attempting to reconcile discrepancies between our findings and those of others is that our research was based upon normal samples of youth drawn from school-based populations rather than from treatment centers or penal institutions. Thus, the seriousness of and committedness to problem behavior in adolescence/youth was likely to be less than that in samples of the latter sort. In the Gluecks' data, for example, the delinquent sample had a persistent record of adjudicated delinquency, with an average of 3.5 *convictions*, and had been committed to correctional school in Massachusetts (see also Farrington & West, 1990). The relevance of this issue of seriousness of involvement in problem behavior in adolescence is raised in another way by Newcomb and Bentler (1989) who, after stating that "all drug *abuse* is destructive and can have devastating consequences" (p. 247; italics added), go on to say that "infrequent, intermittent, or occasional use of drugs by a basically healthy teenager probably has few short-term and no long-term negative or adverse consequences" (pp. 247–248). Although the analyses we made of "heavier" marijuana use in adolescence yielded findings that were not different from those for problem behavior as a whole, and although "heavier" use in our study did mean regular use, that is, at least two or three times a week, still, even that level of involvement is simply not as serious or committed as, for example, a "daily use" criterion would connote.

The second most important fact to raise is that our research engaged youth who were largely middle-class in socioeconomic status and who had considerable access to opportunity. Their general well-being as young adults was apparent from the qualitative descriptions presented in Chapter 4. By contrast, Sampson and Laub describe the Gluecks' youth as boys who "grew up in high-risk environments characterized by poverty, social disorganization, and exposure to delinquency and antisocial conduct" (1990, p. 612). An interactionist position about development would consider that later-life outcomes of adolescent involvement in problem behavior would be contingent on the nature of the contexts in which later development takes place. Contexts of poverty and social disorganization are obviously less likely than middle-class contexts to provide resources for overcoming a history of problem behavior, or to make "second chances" available, that is, to be "forgiving" in the sense of maintaining open opportunity despite previous problem behavior involvement.

A third fact is age. The differential consequences of adolescent drug use that are described by Newcomb and Bentler (1988) refer to young adults with a mean age of just under 22 years (range, 21–23). This is, if anything, very young adulthood and, indeed, an age that we have characterized as "youth" rather than young adulthood. Such an early age of follow-up may yield differences that could well disappear with further development into young adulthood, that is, into the latter part of the third decade of life where our own follow-up took place. The issue of age is potentially important in another way, as we noted in Chapter 9. Although we found no differences in a wide variety of young adult life areas that were related to variation in earlier involvement in problem behavior, the possibility remains that differences will yet emerge with later development into adulthood and midlife. What makes that more than just a logical possibility is the fact that those who were more involved in problem behavior in adolescence/youth were also shown to be more involved in problem behavior in young adulthood. It is that greater young adult involvement that could, perhaps, reverberate into other life areas as development begins to traverse the fourth decade of life.

These issues and, of course, other kinds of sample differences may be relevant to the differences in findings that have emerged from the different studies. Nevertheless, it is important to emphasize that there is still considerable consonance between our findings and those of others, and that the present findings are coherent across different adolescent/youth problem behaviors and for a wide variety of young adult outcomes. For largely middle-class cohorts such as ours, growing beyond adolescence in the 1970s in the United States, early problem-behavior involvement does not seem to mortgage the future – at least through young adulthood.

The limits of inference

Whatever the compellingness and coherence of a set of findings, no inquiry – much less one that deals with complex human experience and behavior extended in time – can sustain inferences that are without some degree of ambiguity. That is to say, all scientific inference – even that drawn from exquisitely controlled laboratory experiments – is vulnerable to plausible alternative inferences being drawn from the same set of observations. The quest in every scientific investigation, and the very raison d'être of research design, is the reduction of ambiguity of inference (see Jessor, Graves, Hanson, & Jessor, 1968, chap. 4). In contemporary field studies, efforts to reduce the ambiguity of inference involve, increasingly, the collection of observations from different sources, with different methods, and in different contexts, in order to permit "triangulation" or convergence on the sought-after conclusions. This orientation to inquiry has been generalized under the rubric of "multiplism" in a seminal essay by Cook (1985) in which he argues for an approach to knowledge growth based upon a "critical multiplism." The latter entails multiple measures of a construct, multiple methods, multiple studies, multiple (i.e., rival) models and hypotheses, multiple analytic approaches, multiple populations, etc., along with an unremitting concern for eliminating bias (a chronic alternative inference) from knowledge generation.

The multiplist orientation is a useful frame of reference for considering the limitations, as well as the advantages, of our Young Adult Follow-Up Study. Its initial limitation was, of course, the sample drawn at the outset in 1969 for the High School Study and in 1970 for the College Study. Both samples had less than desirable initial participation rates. Although subsequent attrition was modest, and although retention beyond the adolescence/youth phase was quite remarkable, nevertheless, this constitutes a potential source of bias (i.e., an alternative inference) that needs to be acknowledged. We spent time in the earlier book (Jessor & Jessor, 1977) and now in Chapter 3 of this volume stressing the coherence and the robustness of our findings, as well as their replication in multiple studies by us and by others. Persuasive as those arguments may be, this limitation, unfortunately, remains.

A second limitation pertains to the racial/ethnic and socioeconomic homogeneity of the research samples. As we noted earlier, there is the possibility that particular findings might have been different had there been representation of other ethnic and social class groups in the samples whose lives we have followed. Clearly, multiple populations would have enhanced a claim for generality of inference. A third important limitation is the relative absence of participants who showed extreme involvement in problem behavior, an absence largely due to drawing normal samples from the schools and the university in a middle-class community. Although a substantial range of variation in problem behavior involvement did obtain, the distribution was doubtless truncated at its extreme tail.

The next limitation pertains to the key method employed in the research. The reliance on self-report throughout the research, in both its earlier and its later phases, means that multiple methods were not engaged, and this is the fourth important limitation. Whether or not the other methods would have been feasible in this inquiry is another question; the fact remains that the findings are tied to a single method rather than representing the convergence of multiple methods. Further, the reliance on a questionnaire as a single information source that included measures of all the variables of interest, can constitute what Cook refers to as a source of constant bias. Fortunately, on this issue, measurement was automatically made "heterogeneous" whenever we undertook time-extended analyses. In the descriptive analyses in Chapter 7, the predictive analyses in Chapter 8, and the outcome analyses in Chapter 9, the data being linked came from *different* questionnaires, questionnaires that were separated in time by as much as eight or nine years. In such instances, common method variance as a source of constant bias is no longer a reasonable alternative inference.

The fifth and final limitation has to do with the research design, itself, more particularly, with the long time interval between adolescence/youth and young adulthood in which no measurement was made. The result is that inferences drawn *across* that time period – for example, the information in the growth curves in Chapter 7 – can well be misleading in failing to represent changes in the trajectories that could possibly have occurred *within* that interval. All sorts of ups and downs rather than a smooth line may, in fact, have characterized the interim period between adolescence/youth and young adulthood. Multiple data points within the follow-up interval beyond adolescence would have been preferable, instead of just the two in 1979 and 1981. Happily, there was, at least, more than one!

Several positive features of the research enterprise balance these limitations. Most important, perhaps, has been our reliance on the same theoretical formulation that had proved useful in a variety of studies in a variety of contexts over a period of decades. This feature represents what might well be termed "cumulative multiplism." In addition, in the present study, there were multiple samples, multiple measures of the same construct, and multiple, even if sometimes redundant, analytic methods; in short, the general orientation of multiplism was, indeed, well represented in the Young Adult Follow-Up Study.

Further, the research findings were always examined separately in the four groups – the High School Study men and women and the College Study men and women. Neither gender differences nor study differences emerged as important or consistent in the analyses, and therefore, the generality of findings across the four subsamples became a criterion for conviction about a particular relationship. Although conservative, this approach constituted another implementation of the multiplist orientation.

Two additional points are worth noting. First, when personality concepts are employed in social research, they usually have their origin in psychopathology or clinical theory. Thus, the different formulation employed in this research made the concept of personality and its measurement heterogeneous. The present conceptualization is at the sociocognitive level, a concept of personality that includes values, and attitudes, and self-definitions that reflect social experience, on the one hand, and that can link logically to social behavior, on the other. The value of this kind of representation of the person, and the value of the particular variables that were assessed, are quite evident from the overall findings and, especially, from the key role that was played by the personality system in mediating the predictive relationships between adolescence/youth and young adulthood. The summary dimension of conventionality–unconventionality, a key aspect of the social personality concept, should certainly engage the interest of personality researchers in their future work on social behavior.

Second, the effectiveness of the theoretical formulation in accounting for *conforming* behavior warrants mention. The multivariate explanation of church attendance, for example, accounts for over 60 percent of its variance in young adulthood, and the prediction of young adult educational attainment was also successful, based largely on adolescent measures of expectation for academic achievement and of academic performance. Concern with conventional behavior makes the research criterion heterogeneous. To that extent, it is another basis for conviction about the usefulness of Problem-Behavior Theory.

A final word

We conclude this report with the sense of having added an increment to knowledge about young adulthood and about psychosocial development between adolescence and young adulthood. In our view, an increase in understanding of problem behavior beyond adolescence has also been achieved. The findings presented have a coherence and a consistency that, we believe, is compelling, and their theoretical relevance helps to amplify their significance.

The journey from the inception of this work, in 1969, has been a long one. As it comes to a close, we are reminded of the remarks of another scholar with the temerity to pursue complex longitudinal social research. He begins with the recognition that "research which tries to understand human experience within the time dimension is entering difficult and uncomfortable territory" (Edwards, 1989, p. 18). Nevertheless, such research is done, he goes on to tell us, "because of a belief that the years have more to teach about the human condition than can ever be learnt from one mere transient encounter with subject or sample." To this we would want to add only our own affirmation of assent.

References

Bachman, J. G., O'Malley, P. M., & Johnston, J. (1978). *Adolescence to adulthood: Change and stability in the lives of young men*. Ann Arbor: Institute for Social Research, University of Michigan.

Cook, T. D. (1985). Postpositivist critical multiplism. In R. L. Shotland & M. M. Mark (Eds.), *Social science and social policy* (pp. 21–62). Beverly Hills, CA: Sage.

Donovan, J. E., & Jessor, R. (1978). Adolescent problem drinking: Psychosocial correlates in a national sample study. *Journal of Studies on Alcohol, 39*, 1506–1524.

Edwards, G. (1989). As the years go rolling by: Drinking problems in the time dimension. *British Journal of Psychiatry, 154*, 18–26.

Farrington, D. P., & West, D. J. (1990). The Cambridge study in delinquent development: A long-term follow-up of 411 London males. In H. J. Kerner & G. Kaiser (Eds.), *Criminality: Personality, behavior and life history* (pp. 115–138). Berlin: Springer Verlag.

Glueck, S., & Glueck, E. (1950). *Unravelling juvenile delinquency*. New York: Commonwealth Fund.

Glueck, S., & Glueck, E. (1968). *Delinquents and nondelinquents in perspective*. Cambridge, MA: Harvard University Press.

Gove, W. R. (1985). The effect of age and gender on deviant behavior: A biopsychosocial perspective. In A. S. Rossi (Ed.), *Gender and the life course* (pp. 115–144). New York: Aldine.

Jessor, R., Chase, J. A., & Donovan, J. E. (1980). Psychosocial correlates of marijuana use and problem drinking in a national sample of adolescents. *American Journal of Public Health, 70,* 604–613.

Jessor, R., Donovan, J. E., & Widmer, K. (1980). *Psychosocial factors in adolescent alcohol and drug use: The 1978 National Study, and the 1974–78 Panel Study.* Final report to Research Triangle Institute. Boulder: Institute of Behavioral Science, University of Colorado.

Jessor, R., Graves, T. D., Hanson, R. C., & Jessor, S. L. (1968). *Society, personality, and deviant behavior: A study of a tri-ethnic community.* New York: Holt, Rinehart, & Winston.

Jessor, R., & Jessor, S. L. (1977). *Problem behavior and psychosocial development: A longitudinal study of youth.* New York: Academic Press.

Kandel, D. B. (1984). Marijuana users in young adulthood. *Archives of General Psychiatry, 41,* 200–209.

Kandel, D. B., Davies, M., Karus, D., & Yamaguchi, K. (1986). The consequences in young adulthood of adolescent drug involvement. *Archives of General Psychiatry, 43,* 746–754.

McCrae, R. R., & Costa, P. T., Jr. (1990). *Personality in adulthood.* New York: Guilford.

Mortimer, J. T., Finch, M. D., & Kumka, D. (1982). Persistence and change in development: The multi-dimensional self-concept. *Life-Span Development and Behavior, 4,* 263–313.

Newcomb, M. D., & Bentler, P. M. (1987). The impact of late adolescent substance use on young adult health status and utilization of health services: A structural equation model over four years. *Social Science and Medicine, 24,* 71–82.

Newcomb, M. D., & Bentler, P. M. (1988). *Consequences of adolescent drug use: Impact on the lives of young adults.* Newbury Park, CA: Sage.

Newcomb, M. D., & Bentler, P. M. (1989). Substance use and abuse among children and teenagers. *American Psychologist, 44,* 242–248.

Power, C., & Estaugh, V. (1990). Employment and drinking in early adulthood: A longitudinal perspective. *British Journal of Addiction, 85,* 487–494.

Robins, L. (1980). Alcoholism and labelling theory. In W. Gove (Ed.), *The labelling of deviance* (2nd ed., pp. 35–47). Beverly Hills, CA: Sage.

Sampson, R. J., & Laub, J. H. (1990). Crime and deviance over the life course: The salience of adult social bonds. *American Sociological Review, 55,* 609–627.

Stein, J. A., Newcomb, M. D., & Bentler, P. M. (1986). Stability and change in personality: A longitudinal study from early adolescence to young adulthood. *Journal of Research in Personality, 20,* 276–291.

Name index

Subject index

abortion: experience, 81–2, 83, 258, 260; moral attitudes toward, 73, 74, 96

achievement (goal), 26, 27, 28; recognition for, 51; *see also* value on achievement

adolescence: as life stage, 35; psychosocial development from, into young adulthood, 10–13, 168–81, 183, 184–92

adolescence/youth: conventionality in, 185–9, 186f, 188f, 189f, 190f, 191, 191f; correlations among personality, perceived environment, and behavior systems in, 233–4, 235–6t, 237; development within, 169, 170–6, 180; developmental linkages with young adulthood, 5–6, 11–13; direction of change in, 276; linking latent-variable measures of problem behavior proneness in, with young adulthood, 230–42, 233–4t, 235–6t, 239f, 241f; psychosocial proneness in, and later behavior, 242–6; stability of psychosocial attributes in, 168

adolescent/youth phase of the research, 39–42, 51, 65, 246, 280, 283; analytic strategy in, 139; generality of findings from, 52–4

adolescent/youth problem behavior: other studies of, using Problem-Behavior Theory, 18; outcomes of differences in levels of involvement in, 255–60, 256–7t; and outcomes in

young adulthood, 251–70, 287–9; as predictors of problem behavior in young adulthood, 200, 204, 205, 207–16, 240, 255–60, 264, 268, 269; Problem-Behavior Theory account of, 140–1, 143, 154–5; structural equation modeling of young adult outcomes of involvement in, 264–7, 265f, 266f

adolescent/youth proneness: relation to young adult proneness, 230–42

age of participants, 49; as factor in study results, 289–90

alcohol use/abuse, 4, 12, 17, 53–4, 69, 99–102; as coping mechanism, 95, 131; and drug use, 17; in leisure time, 87; and life satisfaction/ dissatisfaction, 95; moral attitudes toward, 73, 74, 96; and outcomes, 253, 259; at work, 86, 87; *see also* drunkenness; problem drinking

alienation, 27, 28, 56–7, 94, 130, 147, 148, 258, 260, 261, 262, 263, 264, 276, 284, 288; development of, 170, 172f, 174; and educational attainment, 220, 227; as predictor, 199; and problem behavior, 131

alpha index, 58; *see also* reliability of measures

attitudinal intolerance of deviance, 20, 27–8, 57, 130, 146, 147–8, 283; development of, 185, 187–8, 189f; as predictor, 200, 201, 204, 205; proneness measure, 231; stability of, 168

Printed in the United States
67214LVS00004B/178-225